P9-EDA-193

Pregnancy, Contraception, and Family Planning Services in Industrialized Countries

Pregnancy, Contraception, and Family Planning Services in Industrialized Countries

A STUDY OF
THE ALAN GUTTMACHER INSTITUTE

Elise F. Jones, Jacqueline Darroch Forrest,
Stanley K. Henshaw, Jane Silverman, and Aida Torres

Yale University Press
New Haven and London

The research for this report has been supported by
DHHS grant FPR 000046–01–0. The opinions expressed
herein are those of the authors and should not be con-
strued as representing the opinions or policies of any
agency of the United States government.

Set in Baskerville types by Keystone Typesetting, Inc.,
Orwigsburg, Pennsylvania.
Printed in the United States of America by Vail-Ballou Press,
Binghamton, New York.

Library of Congress Cataloging-in-Publication Data

Pregnancy, contraception, and family planning services
    in industrialized countries : a study of The Alan Gutt-
    macher Institute / Elise F. Jones . . . [et al.].
        p. cm.
Bibliography: p.
Includes index.
ISBN 0–300–04474–7 (alk. paper)

1. Birth control—Cross-cultural studies. 2. Fertility,
Human—Cross-cultural studies. 3. Birth control—
Government policy—Cross-cultural studies. I. Jones,
Elise F. II. Alan Guttmacher Institute.
HQ766.P679   1989
363.9'6—dc19   89–5475
                                                    CIP

10   9   8   7   6   5   4   3   2   1

Contents

Tables and Figures   vii

Acknowledgments   ix

Chapter 1.   Introduction   1

Chapter 2.   Fertility, Pregnancy, and Contraceptive Use   6

Chapter 3.   Institutional Factors   30

Chapter 4.   Background for the Country Reports   51

Chapter 5.   The United States   78

Chapter 6.   Ontario and Quebec   118

Chapter 7.   The Netherlands   151

Chapter 8.   Great Britain   181

Chapter 9.   Conclusions   217

Appendix A.   Data Sources   225

Appendix B.   Statistical Data   233

Appendix C.   Categorical Data and Codebook   245

Appendix D.   Country Survey Questionnaire   251

References   261

Index   271

Tables and Figures

TABLES

2.1	Total fertility, abortion, and pregnancy rates and abortion ratio	7
2.2	Total planned and unplanned pregnancy rates, total pregnancy rate, and ratio of total unplanned to total pregnancy rates	12
2.3	Characteristics of the fertility surveys	14
2.4	Distribution of countries by pattern of contraceptive use among women aged 15–44, according to quality of data	18
2.5	Level of contraceptive use	20
2.6	Total fertility rate by pattern of contraceptive use	23
2.7	Average total fertility, abortion, and pregnancy rates by use of effective methods of contraception	24
2.8	Average percentages of births unplanned and unwanted by use of effective methods of contraception	25
2.9	Average total unplanned, unwanted, and wanted fertility and unplanned and planned pregnancy rates, by use of effective methods of contraception	27
2.10	Average total fertility, abortion, and unplanned pregnancy rates, by use of sterilization	28
2.11	Average total fertility, abortion, and unplanned pregnancy rates, by use of the pill	29
3.1	Distribution of countries by law and policy variables	33
3.2	Distribution of countries by service delivery variables	36

3.3   Distribution of countries by information delivery
         variables   41
3.4   Sources of service and pattern of contraceptive use   45
3.5   Sources of service and level of contraceptive use   47
3.6   Service delivery characteristics and level of
         contraceptive use   48
3.7   Information delivery and use of effective methods of
         contraception   49
4.1   Outline of the country reports   55
4.2   Total fertility and pregnancy rates by planning status   65
4.3   Percentage of births unplanned or unwanted, by age
         and income   65
4.4   Percentage of births unplanned or unwanted, by age
         and education   66
4.5   Percentage of distribution of all women aged 15–44
         and selected age and marital status groups by
         current contraceptive use   69
4.6   Percentages of currently married women practicing
         contraception, by age and income   73
4.7   Percentages of currently married women practicing
         contraception, by age and education   74
7.1   Percentage distribution of women practicing
         contraception, by reasons for changing from
         previous method   170

FIGURES

1.1   Model for the analysis   3
2.1   Total fertility rate by total abortion rate   8
2.2   Total planned pregnancy rate by total unplanned
         pregnancy rate   13
4.1   Total fertility rates, 1975–84   56
4.2   Age-specific fertility rates, 1982   57
4.3   Total abortion rates, 1975–84   58
4.4   Age-specific abortion rates, 1982   59
4.5   Total pregnancy rates, 1975–84   60
4.6   Age-specific pregnancy rates, 1982   61
4.7   Proportions of all births occurring during the five
         years previous to the survey that were
         unplanned and unwanted   64
4.8   Percentage distribution of all women aged 15–44
         by current contraceptive use   70
4.9   Percentage distribution of women in selected age
         and marital status groups by current
         contraceptive use   71

Acknowledgments

The study below was conducted by a team of staff members of the Alan Guttmacher Institute (AGI), supported in part by a grant from the Office of Population Affairs of the U.S. Department of Health and Human Services. Elise F. Jones was coinvestigator and project coordinator. She is responsible for chapters 1 through 4 and chapter 9. Jacqueline Darroch Forrest was coinvestigator and wrote chapter 5. Chapter 6 was written by Stanley Henshaw, chapter 7 by Aida Torres, and chapter 8 by Jane Silverman. James Wheatley assisted the research throughout with patience and perseverance, and invaluable assistance was also provided by Nancy Dittes, Maura Fitzpatrick, and Henrieke Mayers, a Dutch-speaking consultant. At all stages of the study much constructive advice and criticism came from Jeannie Rosoff, Richard Lincoln, and Deirdre Wulf at AGI, and from Charles F. Westoff and Noreen Goldman of Princeton University.

The AGI is most grateful for the cooperation of many individuals and institutions in other countries, without which the study would not have been possible. The liaison persons for the case studies, Connie Clement in Ontario, Marthe Riopel Lefebvre in Quebec, Marianne C. Dersjant-Roorda in the Netherlands, and Zandria Pauncefort in the United Kingdom, provided expert guidance and contributed very generously of their time and effort.

A number of organizations and individuals helped in assembling the data from fertility surveys: Statistics Sweden gave permission to use a data tape from the 1981 Swedish Fertility Survey; the Central Bureau of Statistics in the Netherlands made available an abridged data tape from the 1982 Netherlands Fertility Survey; the United Nations Economic Commission for Europe provided access to its master file of data from surveys in Belgium, Denmark, Finland, France, Italy, Norway, Spain, and other countries; T. R. Balakrishnan at the University of Western Ontario and Mairé Ní Bhrolcháin at the Centre for Population Studies at the London School of Hygiene and Tropical Medicine ran special tabulations from surveys in Canada and the United Kingdom, respectively; Robert L. Cliquet of the Population and Family Study Center in Belgium, Haris Symeonidou of the Centre of Social Research in Greece, and Karen Dunnell of the Office of Population Censuses and Surveys in the United Kingdom provided unpublished tabulations from surveys in those countries. Finally, detailed tabulations of births and female populations for many countries were kindly made available by Gérard Calot of the Institut National d'Etudes Démographiques in Paris.

Pregnancy, Contraception, and Family Planning Services in
Industrialized Countries

1

Introduction

In recent years, social scientists and policy makers have become increasingly concerned about the prevalence of unintended pregnancy and childbearing in the United States. Unquestionably, a major factor determining the level of such pregnancy is the quantity and quality of contraceptive use, and contraceptive practice is influenced by access to means of fertility control and knowledge of the relevant methods and services. This study utilizes a comparative international approach to examine the relationships between fertility, pregnancy (especially unintended pregnancy), and contraceptive use and between contraceptive use and public policies and programs related to family planning. The U.S. experience is compared with that of a group of similarly advanced countries in order to identify ways in which the level of unintended pregnancy in the United States might be reduced.

The determinants and consequences of contraceptive use have been analyzed extensively both in the United States and elsewhere, but this book has two features that are unusual, especially in a comparative study. The first is that few attempts have been made to measure directly the overall extent of unintended conceptions. The second is the specific focus on the role of public policy, family planning services, and information as factors antecedent to unintended pregnancy. Much research has been done on contraceptive availability in relation to developing countries, where fertility control practices are only now becoming established, but little attention has been given to differences among developed countries, or to how such differences might affect contraceptive use.

A set of twenty Western countries has been selected as the most appropriate basis for comparison with the United States. These countries represent all of Western Europe and the four major European populations overseas:

Australia	Greece	Spain
Austria	Ireland	Sweden
Belgium	Italy	Switzerland
*Canada	*The Netherlands	*United Kingdom
Denmark	New Zealand	Great Britain
Finland	Norway	England and Wales
France	Portugal	*United States
Germany, Federal		
Republic of		

*Case-study countries

The study excludes not only developing countries but also the advanced countries of Eastern Europe and societies like Japan's that differ from the United States with respect to their social, economic, and demographic background considerably more than those chosen.[1]

The study focuses on the period from 1982 through 1986, although some of the data go back as far as 1975. A longer period of time was necessary to make the most of the information available on topics of central interest. Because relevant conditions were changing rapidly in many countries during this period, however, the results are blurred. Virtually all information used herein antedates the emergence of AIDS as an important public issue. Fundamental behavioral changes may now be taking place in many of the areas examined, but what they are—and how far they will go—remains to be seen. A recent study in the United States suggests that there has been no decline in sexual activity among the unmarried, although condom use has increased (Forrest and Fordyce 1988).

The analysis in this study has been conceptualized in terms of a simple model, shown schematically in figure 1.1. It utilizes four groups of variables. The first group includes national background characteristics that may have a bearing either on personal behavior or on public policies and programs involving family planning. Their effects are depicted in the figure as the a and b relationships, respectively. Examples of such characteristics would be religious composition and economic conditions. Because of the small number of countries surveyed, the background variables could not be treated systematically in the

---

1. The United Kingdom is shown with Great Britain and England and Wales as subheadings. Many data are available only for these smaller entities, and these have been substituted as necessary (see chapter 4).

analysis, but reference to their possible impact is made in the discussion.

The second group of variables represents institutional factors related to family planning and includes three subgroups: laws and policies, service delivery, and dissemination of information. These are considered the independent variables in the analysis. Laws and policies could have been taken as antecedent to service and information delivery, which often implements them, but many official demands, for example, the requirement of a pelvic exam before prescription of the pill, do no more than regulate activities and thus operate simultaneously with, not prior to, the provision of services and information. For the sake of simplicity, the three subgroups are treated in a parallel manner. The c relationships—how these independent variables directly affect contraceptive use—constitute a principal area of investigation.

The third group of variables refers to contraceptive use, and the

Figure 1.1. Model for the analysis

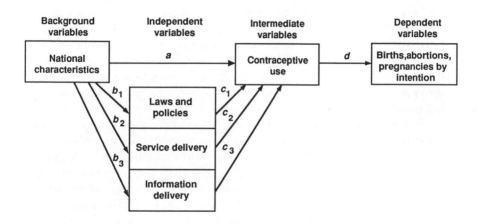

fourth consists of measures of fertility in general and unintended pregnancy in particular. These last are dependent variables which are assumed to be the results of contraceptive use via the d relationships, another major focus of the analysis. Contraceptive use plays an intermediate role. On the one hand, it is determined by public policies and programs related to family planning, and on the other hand, it determines fertility and pregnancy.

The work plan for this study was divided into two main parts: an analysis of the experience of all twenty countries, then case studies of the United States, Canada, the Netherlands, and the United Kingdom.[2] The main purpose of the first part was to assemble the widest possible range of objective data and to explore the kinds of generalizations to be drawn from them. Although twenty countries constitute too small a base of observation for statistical analysis, a variety of simple methods of comparison have been employed in an effort to gain useful insights. The case studies take advantage of more intensive and partly subjective information to elaborate on the findings and fill them out in greater detail. It should be emphasized that both parts of the study are based on aggregate comparisons. The nation rather than the individual is the unit of analysis.

All women of reproductive age, defined as 15 through 44 years, are included. In the course of this span, changes in contraceptive practice and service utilization occur, and these are associated with a typical pattern of shifting fertility intentions and behavior: from an initial period of postponing pregnancy, to spacing of births, and eventually to termination of childbearing. Two age subgroups have been singled out for special attention. The age group 20–29 years was selected to represent the earlier part of the cycle and the age group 35–44 years the later part.

In the United States, publicly subsidized family planning services are directed primarily toward low-income women. Because almost all other countries in the study have some form of national health program that includes family planning and provides for everyone regardless of income, very little basis for comparison exists in this respect. Many countries, nevertheless, recognize certain population groups as disadvantaged in one way or another and in need of special assistance with family planning. An effort has been made throughout this study to include materials from other countries that bear on this issue.

Chapters 2 and 3 present the overview analysis. Chapter 2 describes the dependent and the intermediate variables and gives the results for the relationships between them; chapter 3 describes the independent

2. The case study of Canada is largely restricted to the two provinces of Ontario and Quebec; that of the United Kingdom is limited to Great Britain (see chapter 4).

variables and gives the results for the relationship of the intermediate and independent variables. Chapter 4 introduces the case studies, and chapters 5–8 present reports for the United States, Ontario and Quebec, the Netherlands, and Great Britain, in that order. The final chapter summarizes the conclusions of the study and the implications for policy development in the United States.

Sources for the data used in the overview analysis are listed in appendix A, and a complete set of the statistical data is given in appendix B. Appendix C presents the categorical data used in the overview analysis, most of which were derived from a country-level survey conducted by the Alan Guttmacher Institute, together with a codebook. The questionnaire developed for the country survey is included as appendix D.

2

Fertility, Pregnancy, and Contraceptive Use

MEASURES AND LEVELS OF FERTILITY, ABORTION, AND PREGNANCY

The basic measures of fertility used in the overview analysis are the total fertility rate and the sums of the five-year age-specific fertility rates for the two age groups 20–29 and 35–44.[1] These rates are available for all twenty countries. They have been computed insofar as possible from age distributions of the female populations and births by age of mother, in order to ensure that data in the denominators of the fertility and abortion rates are the same. Where needed to augment the series for recent years, rates have been taken directly from other sources.

Total abortion rates and abortion rates for women 20–29 and 35–44 years old have been constructed in the same manner as the fertility rates. Abortion provides one approach to the assessment of unintended pregnancy.

Reasonably reliable data on abortions by age are available for nine countries (Canada, Denmark, Finland, the Netherlands, New Zealand, Norway, Sweden, Great Britain, and the United States), often covering several years between 1975 and 1984. Carefully considered estimates for at least one year, including details by age, have been found for two more countries (Belgium and France). For one country, Ireland, estimates by age understate the actual numbers, but possibly not by very much. For five other countries (Australia, the Federal Republic of Germany, Greece, Italy, and Switzerland), plausible estimates of the

---

1. The total fertility rate is computed as the sum of the fertility rates for five-year age groups of women from 15–19 years through 45–49 years. It represents the number of births a woman would have if she reproduced through her fertile years at the rates currently observed for women at successive ages.

6

Table 2.1 *Total fertility, abortion, and pregnancy rates and abortion ratio*

Country	Year of most recent abortion data	Total fertility rate	Total abortion rate	Total pregnancy rate	Abortion ratio[a]
Australia	1980	1.89	0.40	2.29	17.5
Belgium	1979	1.70	0.29	1.99	14.6
Canada	1982	1.68	0.36	2.04	17.6
Denmark	1982	1.42	0.58	2.00	29.0
Finland	1982	1.72	0.38	2.10	18.1
France	1982	1.92	0.63	2.55	24.7
F.R.G.	1983	1.33	0.31	1.64	18.9
Greece	1981	2.09	2.24	4.33	51.7
Ireland	1981	3.08	0.15	3.23	4.6
Italy	1983	1.53	0.80	2.33	34.3
Netherlands	1982	1.50	0.18	1.68	10.7
New Zealand	1982	1.92	0.26	2.18	11.9
Norway	1983	1.66	0.46	2.12	21.7
Sweden	1983	1.61	0.54	2.15	25.1
Switerland	1982	1.55	0.50	2.05	24.4
Great Britain	1982	1.76	0.34	2.10	16.2
United States	1983	1.80	0.76	2.56	29.7

[a]Total abortion rate as a percentage of the total pregnancy rate.

overall numbers of abortions for one or more years are available. Although these data can be used to calculate general abortion rates, such rates cannot be reliably combined with total fertility rates to form pregnancy rates. Comparison of the general abortion rates and the total abortion rates for the twelve countries that have age-specific data indicate that a close correspondence exists between the two measures, and the general abortion rates for these five countries may be converted to total abortion rates. Total abortion rates or estimates of these rates are thus available for seventeen countries, and measures for the two age subgroups are obtainable for twelve of them.

Total pregnancy rates and pregnancy rates for the two age subgroups have been computed as the simple sum of the corresponding fertility and abortion rates for all countries and years where both components are known. This procedure ignores involuntary fetal loss as well as discrepancies in age and time between conceptions leading to births and those leading to abortions among women of a given age in a given year, but neither of these considerations is likely to affect comparisons of pregnancy rates between countries appreciably.

Table 2.1 gives the total fertility rates, total abortion rates, total pregnancy rates, and abortion ratios of the seventeen countries with sufficient data.[2] The four measures appear as a graph in figure 2.1.

2. Abortion ratios are calculated here as the total abortion rate divided by the total pregnancy rate, then multiplied by 100, differing from the more conventionally computed ratio of the number of abortions to the number of births.

The reference year is that of the most recent abortion data, which varies from country to country. In the figure, the vertical axis represents the total fertility rate and the horizontal axis the total abortion rate. Thus, the total pregnancy rate for any given country can be read in terms of the diagonal on which it falls, linking that value of the total fertility rate with the same value of the total abortion rate. For example, Denmark, which has a total pregnancy rate of 2.0, falls on the broken line that has been drawn in. The abortion ratio, in turn, is indicated by the location of the country along this diagonal, with values increasing from zero at the upper left toward 100 at the lower right. Denmark has an abortion ratio of 29 and is located on its diagonal 29 percent of the way from the vertical axis toward the horizontal axis.

Figure 2.1. Total fertility rate by total abortion rate

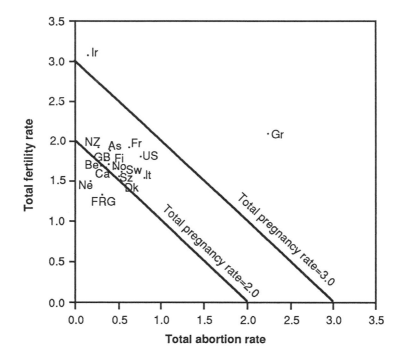

Greece and Ireland are the only countries where the pregnancy rate exceeds three pregnancies per woman. Moreover, even though Greece has a high birthrate, more than half of all pregnancies end in abortion. Abortion data for Greece are uncertain, and a rather small reduction in the estimated number of abortions would decrease the abortion ratio to below 50 percent; it is clear, however, that the number of abortions would have to have been grossly overestimated even to begin to close the gap between Greece and the other countries. Ireland is an almost equally anomalous case, with the highest birthrate by far and the lowest abortion rate. The number of abortions for Ireland is almost certainly underestimated, but just as for Greece, Ireland clearly represents an unusual situation, whatever the true level of abortion.

The total fertility, abortion, and pregnancy rates for the remaining fifteen countries cluster within a relatively narrow range. Fertility and abortion rates do not appear to be associated. Fertility rates range from 1.33 (Federal Republic of Germany) to 1.92 (New Zealand), with the U.S. rate (1.80) ranking twelfth in ascending order. The lowest total abortion rate is 0.18 (the Netherlands) and the highest 0.80 (Italy). The U.S. rate (0.76) is only slightly below the highest rate.

When fertility rates and abortion rates are added, the U.S. total pregnancy rate is highest, at 2.56. At the other extreme among these fifteen countries are the Federal Republic of Germany and the Netherlands, which have pregnancy rates of 1.64 and 1.68, respectively, almost one pregnancy per woman fewer than the United States. West Germany is another country whose abortion rate is estimated, but the actual abortion rate would have to be more than twice as high to bring the pregnancy rate up to the level of most countries.

Italy has the highest abortion ratio in this group of fifteen countries. Just over one-third of all pregnancies end in abortion. It is followed by the United States and Denmark (29.7 and 29.0 percent, respectively). With about one pregnancy in ten ending in abortion, the Netherlands has the lowest abortion ratio. Countries with relatively low abortion ratios include all of the English-speaking countries except the United States (Australia, Canada, New Zealand, and Great Britain). On the other hand, except for Finland, which is near the middle of the group, all the Scandinavian countries (Denmark, Norway, and Sweden) have abortion ratios on the high side.

MEASURES AND LEVELS OF UNPLANNED AND UNWANTED FERTILITY AND PREGNANCY

Unplanned and unwanted childbearing provide a second approach to assessing unintended pregnancy. Many of the fertility surveys containing information on contraceptive practice included questions about the planning status of each birth or pregnancy. These surveys are described in the introduction to the contraceptive-use data below. Ten of the twenty countries in the study (Belgium, Canada, Denmark, Finland, France, the Netherlands, Spain, Sweden, Great Britain, and the United States) have data on unplanned births—births that occurred sooner than desired or were not wanted at all. For all these countries except the Netherlands and Great Britain, it is also possible to distinguish unplanned births that were unwanted from those that came too soon. The questions used to determine planning status vary substantially, from survey to survey, however; in particular, the wording used in Great Britain was quite different from that of other countries (see chapter 4).

The data used to analyze the effects of contraceptive use take the form of the proportions of all births to women in a given category that were unplanned and unwanted. A given survey can yield data only on the planning status of previous births and of current pregnancies. However, the outcome of current contraceptive practice reported in the same survey is best observed shortly after the survey. In order to minimize this time disjuncture while still maintaining enough births for the various subgroups of women, original tabulations were produced that were limited to births occurring in the five years prior to the survey wherever this was feasible (Canada, Netherlands, Sweden, Great Britain, and the United States). In other countries, the proportions represent each respondent's lifetime experience, going back sometimes over two or even three decades. Poor time correspondence between the observation of contraceptive practice and the assessment of unplanned and unwanted fertility is a weak point in the analysis. As long as the data are used in the form of proportions, however, the only assumption is that the relative numbers of births by planning status from an earlier period remain applicable, not the absolute numbers of births, which have declined to a greater or lesser extent everywhere.

Acceptance of the distributions of past births by planning status as applicable to the outcome of current contraceptive practice opens up the possibility of combining this information with the total fertility rates and the total abortion rates to form a number of complex measures. Total unplanned, planned, unwanted, and wanted fertility rates can be computed as the product of the total fertility rate and the respective proportions of births by planning status.[3] If it is assumed that all abortions represent unplanned pregnancies, the total unplanned pregnancy rate can be computed as the sum of the total unplanned fertility rate and the total abortion rate. Because miscar-

3. These are rough calculations. Ideally, the multiplication should be carried out separately for each five-year age group and the results summed.

riages are excluded from this analysis, the total planned fertility rate is the same as the total planned pregnancy rate, which is the term used henceforth. Unfortunately, because it is usually not known whether pregnancies that lead to abortion are only mistimed or actually unwanted, total unwanted and wanted pregnancy rates cannot be estimated.

Two additional approximations were made in bringing together the data on births by planning status and the fertility and abortion rates. First, the surveys from which the planning status information was taken varied with respect to coverage of women by marital status. In order to achieve maximum comparability among the surveys, the tabulations of births used here employ a common base of currently married women.[4] All women, regardless of marital status, are represented in the fertility and abortion rates. The practical effect of this discrepancy should be small, however, since earlier nonmarital births would be included in the retrospective experience of women married at the time of the survey, and in most of the countries studied the great majority of births occurs after marriage.

Second, for several of the surveys, the age-specific tabulations of births by planning status that were available to the project covered ten year age groups: 15–24, 25–34, and 35–44 years. Because of this, results for the age group 25–34 were used for all countries in calculating the rates for women aged 20–29. This would matter only if the relationship of the distribution of births by planning status for women aged 25–34 to that for women aged 20–29 differed significantly among countries.

The fertility and abortion data used to compute the measures described above refer whenever possible to the calendar year following the survey. Data from the year before or after the target year sometimes had to be substituted, and in two cases substitutions involving data more than one year removed from the desired sequence were made. These were Belgium, where the abortion estimate is for 1979, and Canada, where it is for 1982.

Table 2.2 shows the total planned pregnancy rate, the total unplanned pregnancy rate, the total pregnancy rate, and the ratio of the unplanned to the total pregnancy rates for the ten countries for which data are available on births by planning status.[5] For Spain, only the planned pregnancy rate can be calculated because of the absence of

4. Where possible, the currently married category is defined to include all women currently in union, but it is sometimes restricted to currently married respondents still in their first marriage.

5. The total pregnancy rate for a given country may differ from that shown in table 2.1 since the time reference is not necessarily the same.

Table 2.2 *Total planned and unplanned pregnancy rates, total pregnancy rate, and ratio of total unplanned to total pregnancy rates*

Country	Year following fertility survey	Total planned pregnancy rate	Total unplanned pregnancy rate	Total pregnancy rate	Ratio of total unplanned pregnancy rate to total pregnancy rate
Belgium[a]	1977	1.17	0.83	2.00	41.5
Canada[b]	1985	1.24	0.79	2.03	38.9
Denmark	1976	1.32	1.18	2.50	47.2
Finland	1978	1.03	1.06	2.09	50.7
France	1979	1.18	1.35	2.53	53.4
Netherlands	1983	1.37	0.28	1.65	17.0
Spain	1978	2.35	u^c	u	u
Sweden	1982	1.39	0.80	2.19	36.5
Great Britain	1977	1.35	0.63	1.98	31.8
United States	1983	1.25	1.31	2.56	51.2

[a]Abortion estimate is for 1979.
[b]Abortion estimate is for 1982.
[c]Indicates data not available.

abortion data. In figure 2.2, the decomposition of the total pregnancy rate into the total planned pregnancy rate (vertical axis) and the total unplanned pregnancy rate (horizontal axis) is plotted analogously to the total fertility and total abortion rates in figure 2.1.

Except for Spain, the range in the planned pregnancy rates barely exeeds one-third of a birth per woman. Spain constitutes another outlying case, with a total planned pregnancy rate that was still as high as 2.35 in 1978. Among the other nine countries, the lowest rate by a clear margin is 1.03 (Finland) and the highest 1.39 (Sweden). The United States and Canada fall in the middle of the group with rates of 1.25 and 1.24, respectively. The unplanned pregnancy rates vary considerably more than the planned rates; there is a difference of just over one pregnancy per woman between the highest unplanned pregnancy rates (1.35 in France, 1.31 in the United States) and the lowest (0.28 in the Netherlands). There is a slight negative association between the planned and unplanned pregnancy rates, due presumably to the fact that an unplanned pregnancy leading to a birth that is wanted, but at a later time, preempts a later planned one.

Again, the United States has marginally the highest pregnancy rate among the nine countries. Even though the Netherlands has one of the higher planned pregnancy rates, its overall rate is the lowest in the group because its unplanned pregnancy rate is so low; only 17 percent of pregnancies are unplanned in the Netherlands. In contrast, more than 50 percent of all pregnancies are unplanned in Finland, France, and the United States.

MEASURES AND LEVELS OF CONTRACEPTIVE USE

Most of the data on contraceptive practice utilized here are taken from scientifically conducted fertility surveys carried out between 1975 and 1985 in sixteen of the twenty countries. Basic characteristics of the surveys are given in table 2.3. In three countries (Belgium, Spain, and Great Britain), two surveys taken during this period have been drawn upon, and the more recent data have been used as far as possible, but much of the detailed information is available only for the earlier year. All of the surveys were national except those in Belgium, which represent only the Flemish population. In addition, although the Greek survey covered the whole country, the available results were limited to the population of Greater Athens.

Figure 2.2. Total planned pregnancy rate by total unplanned pregnancy rate

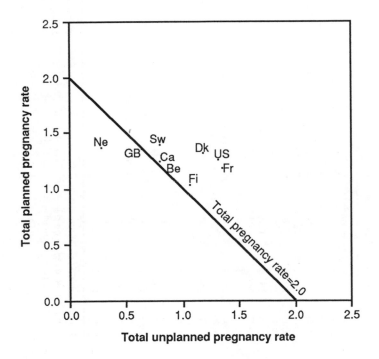

Table 2.3 *Characteristics of the fertility surveys*

Country	Year	Age limits	Marital[a] status	Special limitations	Source of tabulations
Austria	1981	—[b]	CM1	Marriage cohorts of 1974 and 1977	Published report
Belgium	1976	16–44	CM1	Flemish population	Special tabulations from ECE
	1982	20–44	T	Flemish population	Unpublished tabulations
Canada	1984	18–44	T		Special tabulations
Denmark	1975	18–44	CM		Special tabulations from ECE
Finland	1977	18–44	CM1		Special tabulations from ECE
France	1978	20–44	T		Published report, special tabulations from ECE
Greece	1983	15–44	CM	Results available for Greater Athens area only	Unpublished tabulations
Italy	1979	18–44	CM1		Special tabulations from ECE
Netherlands	1982	18–37	T		Data tape
Norway	1977	18–44	EM		Published report, special tabulations from ECE
Portugal	1980	15–49	T		Published report
Spain	1977	15–44	CM1		Special tabulations from ECE
	1985	18–49	T		Published report
Sweden	1981	15–44	T		Data tape
Switerland	1980	—[c]	CM1	Marriage cohorts of 1970–79	Published report
Great Britain	1976	16–49	T		Published report, special tabulations
	1983	18–44	T		Unpublished tabulations
United States	1982	15–44	T		Data tape

[a]CM = currently married; CM1 = currently married in first marriage; EM = ever married; T = all marital statuses.
[b]No age limits; sample restricted to marriage durations 4 and 8 years.
[c]No age limits; sample restricted to marriage durations 0–10 years.

The sample characteristics given in the table with respect to age and marital status refer specifically to the data in the overall tabulations used here. The samples on which these tabulations are based are often narrower than those of the original surveys. In particular, the special tabulations from the U.N. Economic Commission for Europe (ECE) come from the master file prepared for the comparative study conducted there in connection with the World Fertility Survey (WFS). This file was restricted to women between the ages of fifteen and forty-four currently in their first marriage. For France and Norway, overall tabulations based on broadly defined samples were available from published reports, but detailed tabulations by age and other characteristics had to be taken from the narrower ECE file. The Austrian and Swiss surveys were limited by design to recently married women. Data from these two surveys have, therefore, been used only in tabulations for the younger age group. The restriction of much of the data to married women, along with lower age limits that were typically well above fifteen years, effectively precluded the inclusion of teenagers in the examination of contraceptive behavior among younger women. The 1982 Dutch survey, with an upper age limit of thirty-seven years, is the only one that is seriously deficient at the older end of the age distribution.

Gross differences with respect to such characteristics as age and marital status are fairly easy to identify, but many less obvious sources of noncomparability among the surveys may affect the results profoundly. Although the ECE coordinated the preparation of a model questionnaire for the developed countries that participated in the WFS, the surveys carried out in connection with the WFS, as well as those that were not part of that program, were all financed, designed, and conducted by government bodies or other institutions in the individual countries. Under these circumstances, national motivations and traditions naturally tended to dominate, rather than concern for international comparability.

For example, basic terms are defined in various ways. Marital status may represent the situation de facto or de jure. In the former case, cohabiting women may or may not be included in the currently married category, and in the latter case, separated women may or may not be identified. Where options were available, this study has included cohabiting women and excluded separated women from the currently married category.

Another fundamental issue is the time reference for "current" contraceptive use. In the majority of countries, this is rather vaguely given as the time of the survey, but in some countries a period was specified, such as the four weeks prior to the interview (Denmark, Norway, and Sweden). In Italy, the question concerned the method used longest or most often since the last pregnancy or, if there had been no pregnancy, since marriage, which would not necessarily even be the most recent method used.

Probably the most difficult problem of definition relates to exposure to the risk of conception. Contraceptive use is most appropriately measured in relation to women or couples who are at risk of an unintended pregnancy. Women who are pregnant or desire to become so, couples who are physically incapable of conception, and women whose husbands are temporarily absent should be omitted from the base of the calculation. The countries differed widely in the questions asked and the information gathered to identify such cases. Even when countries try to address the issue of infecundity, many women simply do not know whether they and their partners are capable of conceiving a child, especially in societies where use of contraception is extensive. For these reasons, contraceptive use is measured here based on all women of reproductive age, including those not actually at risk of becoming pregnant. The implied assumption is that the proportions of women who are not at risk are much the same across countries, or at least that those differences are minor compared to the differences in the proportions using contraceptives.

Another important source of noncomparability involves survey procedures. The sample for the 1977 survey in Spain was selected two years before the fieldwork, so that the respondents were two years older and had been married two years longer than the data indicate (Berent, Jones, and Siddiqui 1982, 10). Interviews for the Canadian survey were conducted by telephone rather than face-to-face as elsewhere. These are two examples of the many technical differences that affect results, almost always in ways that are hard to detect and evaluate.

Beyond the survey data, there is much information of other kinds about contraceptive practice in the countries covered here. Such sources have been consulted mainly for two purposes, first to assess contraceptive use in the four countries that have had no national survey (Australia, the Federal Republic of Germany, Ireland, and New Zealand). Studies of contraceptive practice have been made in each of them, usually by putting together data from more limited surveys and sometimes from other kinds of information. The second purpose was to supplement and evaluate the results of the surveys and special studies. IMS International, based in London, collects data on sales of oral contraceptives, providing a basis for independent estimates of the percentages of women using this method across a number of years in most of the countries in this study. Evert Ketting and his colleagues have used sales data for the pill and IUD and medical data on sterilization operations to develop estimates for use of these methods in several

European countries (Ketting and van Os 1985; Ketting and van Praag 1985). Finally, numerous previous researchers have tried to assemble and rationalize survey and other data, either over time for a given country or for international comparisons (e.g., Berent 1982; Cliquet and Lodewijckx 1986; Kols et al. 1982; Leridon 1981, 1987; Liskin and Rinehart 1985; Ross, Hong, and Huber 1985; United Nations 1984).

The discussion in the present analysis centers mainly around the three most effective methods of contraception—sterilization, including both male and female operations, the pill, and the IUD. These modern medical methods currently account for the greater part of contraceptive use in a large majority of developed countries. Although it is recognized that other methods, especially barrier methods like the diaphragm and condom, can also achieve a high level of effectiveness with careful use, most studies have shown that they have considerably higher failure rates in practice than the former three methods (see Bone 1978, table 8.1; Cliquet et al. 1983, table 55; Grady, Hayward, and Yagi 1986; Vaughan et al. 1980).

Using all the materials described above, an assessment can be made of the broad pattern of contraceptive use with a fair degree of confidence for each of the twenty countries. The measure distinguishes five categories and takes into account both overall use of the three effective methods and the predominant method used. The categories are: countries where more than 30 percent of women use one of the three methods, and reliance is placed mainly (1) on sterilization, (2) on the pill, or (3) on the IUD; countries where (4) from 10 to 30 percent and (5) fewer than 10 percent use one of the three effective methods. The base for this measure is women of all marital statuses aged 15–44.

The distribution of countries according to this variable is shown in table 2.4 in combination with an evaluation of the quality of the data. Data quality, as assessed here, includes such considerations as coverage of the sample in terms of age and marital status and the suitability of the form in which the data were available to this analysis, as well as problems in the design and execution of the surveys. The Austrian and Swiss data are rated as poor because their surveys were restricted to recently married women, although they can be considered adequate for the measurement of use among young women.

The results reveal substantial variation in patterns of use. Even so, in as many as half of the twenty countries, use of the most effective methods is very widespread, and the pill is the principal one. Sterilization is the most common method in both countries of North America and, insofar as the data permit inferences about practice among women of all ages, also in Switzerland. The IUD predominates in two countries of Scandinavia. Use of the modern, highly effective methods appears to be relatively low in Ireland and in all the southern European

Table 2.4   *Distribution of countries by pattern of contraceptive use among women aged 15–44, according to quality of data*

	Percentage using effective methods				
	> 30% Principal method			10–30%	< 10%
Quality of data	Sterilization	Pill	IUD		
(Countries)					
Good	Canada United States	France Netherlands Sweden Great Britain	Norway	Spain	
Fair		Belgium Denmark	Finland	Italy Portugal	Greece
Poor	Switzerland	Australia Austria F.R.G. New Zealand		Ireland	
(Number of countries)	3	10	2	4	1

countries, including Greece, the only country where fewer than 10 percent of all women of reproductive age rely on an effective method.

Fortunately, data quality appears to be to some extent independent of the pattern of use. In particular, all five categories are represented among the countries having good or fair data. The analysis that follows is largely confined to these fourteen countries for which the data can be considered adequate (this is expanded to sixteen when the Austrian and Swiss data on younger women are included). In interpreting the results in later chapters, however, it is important to keep in mind that the data for five of the fourteen are far from ideal (for younger women, six out of sixteen).

More specific measures were developed for the countries with survey data. These are: the proportions of women using any method, the combined proportions using one of the three highly effective methods, and the proportions using selected individual methods. Attention is focused on use of the most effective methods as a group and on use of sterilization and the pill individually. The IUD has not been examined in detail because it had been withdrawn by its major manufacturers in the United States at the time of the study. The condom has been added to the list of individual methods considered, as it is very widely used in a number of the countries.

Preparing these measures required constant balancing of the goals of accuracy, comparability, and breadth of coverage. In view of the very small potential number of observations, the policy adopted here was to include the maximum number of countries and to get as close to a common basis for comparison as possible, even if this involved some sacrifice of precision. The measures for women aged 15–44 reflect use among women of all marital statuses, which is appropriate for the all-inclusive nature of the other sets of variables used in the analysis. Where survey samples were more narrowly defined, as was frequently the case (see table 2.3), approximations had to be made, sometimes involving substantial subgroups of women. Such approximations were based on various supplementary sources of information or, occasionally, on inference from countries where there was reason to believe the situation was similar. On the other hand, the measures for women aged 20–29 and 35–44 are based in most cases on data for currently married women only, mainly because the ECE tabulations, from which most of the detailed data by age were taken, were limited to currently married women in their first marriage. Although these measures are less general than desired, especially for the age group 20–29, most countries could be covered, and intercountry comparability was maximized.

Taking into account the possibility of inaccuracy in the quantitative estimates of use, the final variables were grouped in three categories, representing high, medium, and low levels of contraceptive use. The authors examined the distributions of the relevant estimated proportions of women with a view to maximizing the contrast between categories and at the same time achieving the best balance among them. Inevitably some decisions were arbitrary.

Table 2.5 shows the coding of the variables. The mean of the proportions underlying each category and the number of countries in the category are also given. The level of use of any method of contraception is fairly high everywhere, so that there is little contrast between categories for this variable. The United States, where 54 percent of all women of reproductive age use some contraceptive method, falls into the low category, along with Portugal and Spain. The range in the estimates of use of effective methods is much greater, and the differences between the category means are very large. Thirty-seven percent of all U.S. women were using one of the effective methods. This is the average of the six countries in the medium category of this variable. Comparison of the measures of use of any method and use of effective methods reveals that where fewer women use effective methods, less effective methods are widely used rather than no method at all. Examples are Greece and Italy, where many women report relying on withdrawal.

Table 2.5 provides further evidence of variation in the use of individual methods. In general, sterilization appears to be more acceptable in English-speaking countries and less acceptable in Scandinavian and Catholic countries. It is most prevalent, though not necessarily the principal method used, in Canada, the Netherlands, Great Britain, and

Table 2.5 *Level of contraceptive use*

Country	Year fertility survey	Any method Ages 15–44	Effective methods Ages 15–44	Ages 20–29	Ages 35–44	Sterilization Ages 15–44	Ages 20–29	Ages 35–44	Pill Ages 15–44	Ages 20–29	Ages 35–44	IUD Ages 15–44	Condom Ages 15–44
Austria	1981	u	u	H	u	u	L	u	u	H	u	u	u
Belgium	1976	H	M	M	M	L	L	M	H	H	H	L	L
	1982	H	H	H	H	M	L	M	H	H	H	M	L
Canada	1984	H	H	H	H	H	H	H	M	M	L	M	L
Denmark	1975	M	M	u	u	M	u	u	M	M	M	M	H
Finland	1977	H	M	M	M	L	L	M	L	L	M	H	H
France	1978	H	M	M	M	L	L	M	H	M	H	M	L
Greece	1983	H	L	L	L	L	L	L	L	L	L	L	H
Italy	1979	M	L	L	L	L	L	L	L	L	L	L	M
Netherlands[a]	1982	H	H	H	H	H	M	H	H	H	M	M	L
Norway	1977	M	M	H	H	L	L	M	L	L	H	H	M
Portugal	1980	L	L	L	L	L	L	L	M	M	H	L	L
Spain	1977	L	L	L	L	L	L	M	L	L	M	L	L
	1985	L	L	L	L	L	L	L	L	L	L	L	M
Sweden	1981	M	M	M	M	L	L	L	L	M	M	H	H
Switzerland	1980	u	u	H	u	u	M	u	u	M	u	u	u
Great Britain	1976	H	H	H	H	M	M	H	H	H	H	M	H
	1983	H	H	H	H	H	M	H	H	H	M	M	M
United States	1982	L	M	M	H	H	H	H	M	M	L	L	L
Mean Percentages[b]													
H		65	52	55	55	21	12	42	28	45	16	19	22
M		60	37	44	36	8	7	8	20	30	8	6	11
L		50	15	20	14	2	1	2	10	15	2	3	5
Number of countries[b]													
H		7	4	7	6	4	2	5	4	4	6	3	4
M		4	6	4	3	2	3	4	5	7	5	6	4
L		3	4	4	4	8	10	4	5	5	3	5	6

Key: H = high use; M = medium use; L = low use; u = data not available.
[a] Older age group restricted to ages 35–37.
[b] For Belgium, Spain, and Great Britain only the later survey is included.

the United States—the four case-study countries—where the average proportion sterilized among women aged 15–44 is 21 percent. Only in Canada and the United States, however, do significant proportions of couples resort to sterilization while the female partner is still in her twenties; the estimates for women aged 20–29 years are 12 and 13 percent, respectively. The proportion of married women using the pill tends to be very much lower at ages 35–44 than at ages 20–29, although it remains an important method at older ages in several countries. In the United States, the proportion of currently married women aged 20–29 using the pill is 28 percent, a little below the mean for the seven countries in the medium category, while at ages 35–44 it is 2 percent, equal to the mean for the three countries in the low category. Use of the IUD is widespread in the Scandinavian countries other than Denmark and is rather low elsewhere. The pattern of variation in use of the condom is similar to that for the IUD, but condom use is common also in Greece and Great Britain. Four percent of U.S. women were using the IUD and 7 percent the condom at the time of the survey, placing the United States somewhat above the average level for the low-use category in both cases.

Where the absolute differences in the mean values between categories of a given measure are small, the measure has little discriminating power. This is the case for the comparison between the medium-use and low-use categories in several instances and for all categories of use of sterilization among younger women.

RELATIONSHIP OF FERTILITY AND PREGNANCY TO CONTRACEPTIVE USE

Contraceptive use can be assumed to reduce the incidence of unplanned pregnancy. Because it leads to a higher proportion of planned pregnancies among wanted pregnancies, it should raise the planned pregnancy rate as well. It also seems natural to suppose that contraceptive use reduces the incidence of unwanted childbearing, although it would not necessarily be expected to have any direct effect on desired childbearing.

Contraceptive use is measured only in terms of level or volume. Its outcome, as expressed in the birth and abortion rates, actually reflects the efficacy of the various methods as well, but for practical reasons, this has not been taken into account. In effect, it is assumed (unrealistically) that not only exposure to risk of conception but also efficacy of contraceptive use is nearly the same from country to country.

To examine the relationship of fertility and pregnancy to contraceptive use, the mean values of the dependent variables for countries in the low, medium, and high categories of contraceptive use were compared. Because of the margin of uncertainty in some of the measures, results are shown rounded to one decimal place so that, for many of the rates, only rather large relative differences can be observed. Absolute differences must round to over 0.05 to be observable, representing a minimum contrast of three percent if the comparison is based on a rate of 1.8, but 17 percent when the base rate is 0.3, and even more when the base rate is lower. Whenever a given comparison involves fewer than thirteen countries, contraceptive use has been collapsed into two categories.

Two sets of results are presented concerning the use of the three effective methods and of individual methods. The first set includes every country with adequate data on all variables underlying the comparison in question. The maximum range of experience is thus covered, although continuity is lacking from one comparison to the next because of the changing composition of the sample of countries. Where the average value of a dependent variable has clearly been affected by one outlying case, it is shown both including and excluding the data from that particular country. The second set of results represents eight core countries with data on the full range of variables in all the tables. These eight countries are Belgium (1976), Canada, Finland, France, the Netherlands, Sweden, Great Britain (1976), and the United States. The one major exception is that the Netherlands and Great Britain do not provide data on unwanted births. Although the number of cases in the core group is very small, these are the only countries for which it is possible to quantify the effects of contraceptive use across the various fertility measures.

The more recent of the two surveys for Belgium, Spain, and Great Britain have been used in the comparisons of overall use. In order to maintain consistency within the core group, the earlier surveys for Belgium and Spain have been used in all of the more detailed comparisons. For Spain, which is not included in the core group, the later survey was used in comparisons of total fertility rates for all ages, and the earlier survey in comparisons for the two age subgroups and in all comparisons involving data on births by planning status.

For each country, the aim has been to utilize fertility and abortion data for the year following to the survey from which the data on contraceptive use were taken, assuming that this procedure provides the most appropriate temporal correspondence between the two variables. In the some cases, fertility or abortion data were not available either for the target year or for an adjacent year, and data for the closest alternative year had to be substituted. For Spain, the total fertility rate for 1983 rather than 1986 is used in conjunction with the level of use among women of all ages as measured in the 1985 fertility survey. For Canada and Greece, the abortion data precede the survey

Table 2.6   *Total fertility rate by pattern of contraceptive use*

Pattern of use among all women aged 15–44	All countries	Countries with adequate data on contraceptive use	Core countries
		Average total fertility rate	
> 30% using effective methods			
Main method sterilization	1.7	1.7	1.7
Main method pill	1.7	1.7	1.7
Main method IUD	1.7	1.7	1.6
10–30% using effective methods	2.1	1.8	—
< 10% using effective methods	1.8	1.8	—
Number of countries			
> 30% using effective methods			
Main method sterilization	3	2	2
Main method pill	10	6	5
Main method IUD	2	2	1
10–30% using effective methods	4	3	0
< 10% using effective methods	1	1	0
Total	20	14	8

by two years (1982 and 1981, respectively) instead of following it by one. Abortion estimates for Italy and Belgium are three and two years too late, respectively (1983, 1979).

Table 2.6 shows the average total fertility rate by pattern of contraceptive use for three progressively selective sets of countries: the twenty covered in the project, the fourteen for which adequate data are available, and the eight that compose the core group. In addition to a preliminary view of the association between fertility and contraceptive use, this table indicates the results of narrowing down the countries considered.

Starting with the largest set, the average level of fertility is the same, 1.7 births per woman, for countries where more than 30 percent of all women use highly effective methods, regardless of which method is most heavily relied upon. The average is markedly higher only for the countries where approximately 10 to 30 percent use an effective method, due principally to the inclusion of Ireland in this group. Ireland is excluded when the comparison is limited to countries with adequate data, and both categories characterized by lower levels of use of effective methods then have average total fertility rates just slightly higher than those where use of effective methods is relatively common. The core group includes only countries where the use of effective methods is fairly widespread, and the average level of fertility remains similar among the three categories.

Even though data quality is not closely associated with pattern of use, reducing the number of countries does narrow the diversity of experience represented with respect to both fertility and contraceptive

Table 2.7 Average total fertility, abortion, and pregnancy rates by use of effective methods of contraception and by age

Effective method use	Total fertility rate			Total abortion rate			Total pregnancy rate		
	All ages	Ages 20–29	Ages 35–44	All ages	Ages 20–29	Ages 35–44	All ages	Ages 20–29	Ages 35–44
Countries with adequate data on contraception									
Low	1.8	1.3 / 1.2ᵃ	0.2 / 0.2ᵃ	0.8 / 0.6ᵇ	0.3	0.1	2.5 / 2.3ᵇ	1.4	0.3
Medium	1.7	1.1	0.1	0.3	0.2	0.1	1.9	1.2	0.2
High	1.6	1.1	0.1	0.3	0.2	0.1	1.9	1.2	0.2
Core countries									
Medium	1.7	1.1	0.1	0.6	0.3	0.1	2.3	1.4	0.3
High	1.6	1.1	0.1	0.3	0.1	0.1	1.9	1.2	0.2
(Number of countries)									
With adequate data on contraception									
Low	4	4 / 3ᵃ	4 / 3ᵃ	9 / 8ᵇ	5	4	9 / 8ᵇ	5	4
Medium	7	5	4	3	5	4	3	4	5
High	3	6	5	3	4	5	3	5	4
Core countries									
Medium	5	5	4	5	5	4	5	5	4
High	3	3	4	3	3	4	3	3	4

ᵃExcluding Spain.
ᵇExcluding Greece.

Table 2.8 *Average percentages of births unplanned and unwanted by use of effective methods of contraception*

Use of effective methods of contraception (by level)	Unplanned	Unwanted
(Percentage of births)		
With adequate data		
Low/medium	26	7
High	18	8
Core Countries		
Medium	30	8
High	18	u^a
(Number of countries)		
With adequate data		
Low/medium	7	7
High	3	1
Core countries		
Medium	5	5
High	3	u

[a]*u* indicates data not available.

use, and availability of data tends to be inversely associated with the level of fertility. Nevertheless, variation in the total fertility rate according to pattern of contraceptive use appears to be rather minor.

Consistent with the findings above in relation to the overall pattern of use, the first panel of table 2.7 shows that, among all women of reproductive age, greater use of the effective methods of contraception is associated with a slightly lower average total fertility rate—1.6 children per woman in countries with high use compared to 1.7 in countries with medium use and 1.8 in countries with low use. Use of effective methods is much more strongly linked with the average abortion rate—0.3 abortions per women in countries with high use compared to 0.8 or 0.6 in those with low-to-medium use (second panel). Among the core countries, the average abortion rate for the medium-use category, into which the United States falls, is twice that of the high-use category. Because the comparison goes in the same direction for both components, the average pregnancy rate is inevitably negatively associated with the level of use of effective methods of contraception (third panel). Again, the contrast in the average pregnancy rate between the medium-use and high-use categories is substantial for the core countries. The volume of both births and abortions is much greater among young women, and these differences tend to emerge more clearly at ages 20–29 than at ages 35–44, although at all ages the pregnancy rates are lower in countries where use of effective methods is high than in those where it is low.

The proportions of all births reported as unplanned and unwanted are presented in table 2.8. In general, unplanned births occur reasonably often, while births that are not only unplanned but also unwanted at any time are relatively uncommon. The percentages of births that are unplanned are distinctly lower where more women use effective methods of contraception. Contraception, however, appears to make no difference in the proportions of births that are unwanted. These results, like the abortion ratios, cannot really be taken as indicative of the success of contraceptive practice because they also depend on the overall level of fertility, including planned births. Other things being equal, the lower the level of fertility, the greater the degree of fertility control required to achieve the same proportion of unplanned births.

Average fertility and pregnancy rates by planning status are shown in table 2.9. Because pregnancies that are unplanned but not unwanted tend to occur relatively early in reproductive life, the unplanned fertility and planned pregnancy rates are shown for women aged 20–29. Unwanted births are concentrated among older women, and the unwanted and wanted birthrates are given for ages 35–44. Because unwanted pregnancy rates cannot be calculated, and unplanned pregnancies among older women are presumably largely unwanted, the unplanned pregnancy rates are presented for both age groups.

The unplanned fertility rate differs considerably according to how much effective methods of contraception are used. Adding abortions to unplanned births increases the contrast; unplanned pregnancies occur almost twice as frequently in core countries that are in the medium-use as opposed to the high-use categories, regardless of age. Consistent with the above comparison of the proportions of births that are unwanted, however, the rate of unwanted childbearing seems to be equally low in both categories of countries. The average rate of planned pregnancies may be higher where there is greatest use of effective methods, while wanted fertility is, if anything, lower where effective methods are used more.

The implications of the results by planning status are not very clear cut, due largely to varying samples of countries and their small number. But the inverse association between use of effective methods and unplanned births—and especially unplanned pregnancies—and the possible direct association between use of effective methods and planned pregnancies do conform to expectation.

Methods of contraception vary not only in effectiveness but also with respect to the age and other characteristics of the women for whom their use is most appropriate, and fertility and pregnancy may be affected by how much particular methods are used. At the aggregate level, any effects of individual methods are blurred by use of other methods. They can be observed only when they are strong enough to dominate.

Table 2.9 *Average total unplanned, unwanted, and wanted fertility and unplanned and planned pregnancy rates, by use of effective methods of contraception*

Level of effective method use	Total unplanned fertility rate		Total unwanted fertility rate		Total unplanned pregnancy rate			Total planned pregnancy rate		Total wanted fertility rate	
	All ages	Ages 20–29	All ages	Ages 35–44	All ages	Ages 20–29	Ages 35–44	All ages	Ages 20–29	All ages	Ages 35–44
Countries with adequate data											
Low/medium	0.5	0.3	0.1	0.0	1.1	0.6	0.2	1.4	0.9	1.7	0.2
High	0.3	0.2	0.1	0.0	0.6	0.3	0.1	1.2[b]	0.8[b]	1.6[b]	0.1[b]
	0.4[a]	0.2[a]			0.7[a]	0.4[a]	0.1[a]	1.3	0.9	1.6	0.1
Core countries											
Medium	0.5	0.3	0.1	0.0	1.1	0.6	0.2	1.2	0.8	1.6	0.1
High	0.3	0.2	—	—	0.6	0.3	0.1	1.3	0.9	—	—
(Number of countries)											
With adequate data											
Low/medium	7	6	7	5	6	5	4	7	6	7	5
High	3	3	1	2	3	3	4	6[b]	5[b]	6[b]	4[b]
	2	2			2	2	3	3	3	1	2
Core countries											
Medium	5	5	5	4	5	5	4	5	5	5	4
High	3	3	—	—	3	3	4	3	3	—	—

[a] Excluding the Netherlands.
[b] Excluding Spain.

Table 2.10 *Average total fertility, abortion, and unplanned pregnancy rates, by use of sterilization*

Sterilization use	Total fertility rate		Total abortion rate		Total unplanned pregnancy rate	
	All ages	Ages 35–44	All ages	Ages 35–44	All ages	Ages 35–44
Countries with adequate data						
Low	1.8	0.2	0.8		1.0	
			0.6ᵃ			
Medium	1.7	0.2	⎫	0.1	⎫	0.2
		0.1ᵃ	⎬ 0.5		⎬ 0.8	
					1.0ᵇ	
High	1.7	0.1	⎭	0.1	⎭	0.1
						0.1ᵇ
Core countries						
Low	1.7		0.5		1.0	
Medium	⎫	0.1	⎫	0.1	⎫	0.2
	⎬ 1.7		⎬ 0.4		⎬ 0.8	
High	⎭	0.1	⎭	0.1	⎭	0.1
(Number of countries)						
With adequate data						
Low	9	4	7		4	
			6ᵃ			
				5		4
Medium	2	6	⎫		⎫	4
		5ᵃ	⎬ 5		⎬ 5	
					4ᵇ	
High	3	4	⎭	4	⎭	4
						3ᵇ
Core countries						
Low	4		4		4	
Medium	⎫	4	⎫	4	⎫	4
	⎬ 4		⎬ 4		⎬ 4	
High	⎭	4	⎭	4	⎭	4

ᵃExcluding Greece.
ᵇExcluding the Netherlands.

Table 2.10 shows the average fertility rate, abortion rate, and un-planned pregnancy rate according to level of use of sterilization for women aged 15–44 and 35–44. Because sterilization is used most by older women, who typically have low fertility and pregnancy rates, only large relative differences are visible. In addition, the mean levels of use for the categories and the distribution of countries among categories need especially to be kept in mind in the case of sterilization (see table 2.5). The contrast in mean level of use of sterilization is large only between the high and medium categories for all women and older women, but the numbers are such that when it is necessary to collapse

Table 2.11 *Average total fertility, abortion, and unplanned pregnancy rates, by use of the pill*

Pill use	Total fertility rate		Total abortion rate		Total unplanned pregnancy rate	
	All ages	Ages 20–29	All ages	Ages 20–29	All ages	Ages 20–29
Countries with adequate data						
Low	1.8	1.2 / 1.1[a]	} 0.8 / 0.6[b]	} 0.3	} 1.0	} 0.6
Medium	1.8	1.1				
High	1.7	1.1	0.4	0.1	0.8 / 0.9[c]	0.3 / 0.4[c]
Core countries						
Low/Medium	1.7	1.1	0.5	0.3	1.0	0.5
High	1.7	1.1	0.4	0.1	0.8	0.3
(Number of countries)						
With adequate data						
Low	5 / 4[a]	5	} 8 / 7[b]	} 7	} 5	} 6
Medium	5	7				
High	4	4	4	3	4 / 3[c]	3 / 2[c]
Core countries						
Low/medium	4	5	4	5	4	5
High	4	3	4	3	4	3

[a] Excluding Spain.
[b] Excluding Greece.
[c] Excluding the Netherlands.

the categories into a dichotomy, those are the two that have to be combined. Although the fertility rate appears to vary little by level of use of sterilization, the total abortion rate for ages 15–44 is slightly lower where sterilization is relied on more, and unplanned pregnancy also tends to be lower.

Variation in use of the pill is more evenly distributed, and the division of countries among categories is better, so that its effects on pregnancy and fertility should be more easily discernible. No systematic change in the fertility rate occurs either for ages 15–44 or for ages 20–29 as pill use rises (table 2.11). Among all women, and especially among younger women, however, the abortion rate is much lower in countries where pill use is high compared to those where it is low or medium. Unplanned pregnancy as a whole is also much less common among younger women where pill use is high. This finding is particularly relevant to the United States, where the pill is used less than in many other Western countries.

3
Institutional Factors

DATA AND CURRENT SITUATION

The main independent variables in the analysis (see figure 1.1) fall into three groups, highlighting the major institutional means by which society influences reproductive behavior—through (1) laws and policies related to family planning, (2) the provision of contraceptive services, and (3) dissemination of information about contraceptive methods and services. Assessing the influence of these variables on contraceptive practice and, ultimately, on the incidence of unintended pregnancies is a principal objective of this study. The three groups of independent variables are closely related, and in many cases an individual item could fit just as well under another heading as under the one to which it has been assigned.

Fewer systematic data are available on institutional factors that affect reproductive behavior than on fertility, pregnancy, and contraceptive use (see chapter 2), and the information often does not lend itself to quantitative treatment. Assembling an appropriate range of variables and incorporating them into the analysis have required a different approach.

Existing international sources of up-to-date information in this area consist mainly of two International Planned Parenthood Federation publications, *Family Planning in Five Continents* (1983) and *Planned Parenthood in Europe: A Human Rights Perspective* (Meredith and Thomas 1986), and the United Nations' *Monitoring Reports* series on population trends and policies (1982, 1985). Some of the data collected for the earlier AGI study of adolescent pregnancy in developed countries are relevant to this study as well (Jones et al. 1986). Numerous publications cover individual countries or a few countries. Careful review of these materials indicated that they provide an adequate base for developing comparable indicators on most policy issues of interest and on some aspects of information dissemination. The data on service provision, however, are largely descriptive and do not deal with specific topics in the same format and detail. Except for that about young people, almost no information can be found concerning efforts to assist groups that could have special problems with family planning—an issue of particular interest in the present study.

To fill the information gap concerning service provision and also to round out the data on information delivery, the Alan Guttmacher Institute carried out a country-level survey. Its questionnaire dealt with three general areas: characteristics of contraceptive services as a whole, provision of individual methods, and specific activities directed toward target groups in the population. In the United States, publicly subsidized family planning services are directed primarily toward low-income women. Virtually all the other countries in the study have some form of national health program that includes family planning and provides for everyone regardless of income, and there is very little basis for comparison in this respect. Many countries, nevertheless, recognize certain population groups as disadvantaged in one way or another and in need of special assistance with family planning. An effort has been made here to include materials from other countries that bear on this issue. To minimize work for the respondent, questions were all multiple choice. The questionnaire went out in April 1986 to several people in each of the twenty countries who were knowledgeable about family planning and who were expected to have some different points of view. These included administrators of family planning associations, government officials with major responsibilities in this area, and heads of medical associations representing obstetrician-gynecologists and family physicians. Nearly 60 percent of the questionnaires were returned, including at least two from every country. Family planning associations and government officials were well represented. For the questionnaire, see appendix D.

The quality of the response was good. Most of the questionnaires were completed carefully, and answers from different persons in the same country tended to be consistent. The responses also tally reasonably well with the descriptive information in the sources described earlier. The fundamental aim of establishing a basis for the development of indicators representing basic characteristics of family planning service systems was fulfilled. At the same time, it is clear that it was often difficult to do justice to the situation in a particular country within the framework of the set questions and answers offered. For instance, one item asked whether the main contraceptive service was operated directly by the government, was subsidized or funded by it, or whether government was not involved. Relationships between government and private sector in providing family planning services can be more complex than this, and the most appropriate reply is not always obvious. In the United Kingdom, family physicians are the main providers, and they are paid by the government as part of the National Health Service; both direct operation and indirect funding of services by family physicians were checked by different respondents without necessarily implying any inconsistency. In the United States, on the other hand, the government pays for services only for low-income clients, and either subsidization or no involvement could be the most appropriate answer. The type of respondent also introduced some bias. Government officials tended to rate government efforts to inform and educate the public about family planning services as stronger than nongovernment respondents did. For reasons of this sort, as well as such practical considerations as language problems, there is a substantial level of "noise" in the results. The variables used below correspond closely to specific items in the questionnaire and attempt to represent the most accurate interpretation of all responses for a given country. Where there was no response, or conflicting views could not be reconciled, data were treated as missing.

Laws and Policies
Six variables refer to the official climate surrounding provision of family planning services and practice of contraception (table 3.1). The first concerns the government's overall policy on family planning, taken usually from the latest official response to the regular United Nations inquiry on this topic. The countries fall almost equally into those where the government supports family planning directly, including the United States, and those where family planning is supported indirectly. Only Ireland provides no government support.

The issue surrounding advertisement of contraceptive methods has attracted considerable attention. It is not a cut-and-dried matter, however, since the importance of advertising, the media involved in it, and the permissibility of advertising pharmaceutical products in general differ from country to country. The most systematic array of comparable information provided sufficient information to code a simple indicator for only thirteen countries (Meredith and Thomas 1986). In eight of the thirteen, any method may be advertised; the United States is one of three where general advertising is limited to nonprescription methods (the others are Italy and West Germany). In two countries, no advertising of contraceptives is permitted.

Closely related to contraceptive practice and fertility behavior is the

Table 3.1   *Distribution of countries by law and policy variables*

Variable and category	Number of countries
Overall family planning policy	
Direct support	10
Indirect support	9
No support	1
Advertising of contraceptive methods	
Not permitted	2
Permitted for nonprescription methods	3
Permitted for any method	8
Insufficient information	7
Abortion laws	
Minimum restrictions	4
Some restrictions	8
Substantial restrictions	6
Illegal	2
Recognition of target groups	
None	5
Young people only	9
Low-income people, with or without other groups	4
Other combinations of groups	2
Teaching of contraceptive methods in school	
Always done	3
Officially encouraged	6
No uniform policy	9
Officially discouraged	2
Sterilization laws	
Legal	11
Not illegal but not specifically legalized	8
Illegal	1

legal status of abortion. In a number of Western countries, abortion laws have been liberalized in recent years, and by the mid-1980s diverse laws were in effect. Abortion was available with very few restrictions in four countries, including the United States. In the largest group, eight countries, some relatively minor limitations were set, typically involving such conditions as procedural safeguards.[1] In six other countries, there were substantial limitations: abortion was permissible only in cases of incest or rape, or when the pregnancy endangered the life or health of the woman.[2] In two countries (Ireland and Belgium) it was illegal. The legal situation does not necessarily reflect availability: in Belgium, for instance, abortions can be obtained easily, especially in the French-speaking southern part of the country, in spite of the proscription.

1. Austria, Canada, Denmark, Finland, France, Italy, Norway, and the United Kingdom.

2. Australia, West Germany, Greece, New Zealand, Portugal, and Spain.

The AGI country survey inquired whether the government had recognized any of the following population subgroups as needing special assistance with contraceptive services: immigrants, low-income families, rural residents, or young people. In table 3.1 countries where no target groups were reported, those where young people were the sole group, those where low-income families were identified (with or without other groups), and those where any other combination of groups was reported are distinguished. Young people are clearly the main focus of attention; in nine countries this was the only group identified,[3] and in five of the six countries—including the United States—where other groups were mentioned,[4] young people were included. Because adolescents in every country constitute a continuing stream of potential first-time contraceptive users, the results are not surprising. Besides the United States, only Australia, Canada, and the Federal Republic of Germany singled out low-income women. The incorporation of family planning services into national health systems that are designed to provide care for all subgroups of the population presumably obviates the need for special attention to poor people in most cases. Immigrants were specified in several countries. Rural residents were rarely mentioned.

An additional variable relating specifically to young women reflected official attitudes on the teaching of contraceptive methods in school. The information came from the earlier country-level survey conducted in connection with the AGI study of adolescents and showed considerable variation (Jones et al. 1986). Although teaching about contraceptive methods was not prohibited anywhere, it was discouraged in Italy and New Zealand. In nearly half the countries, including the United States, the decision was left up to the individual school or to local authorities;[5] in an equal number, teaching was encouraged, including three countries (Denmark, Finland, and Sweden) where it was part of the regular curriculum.

Like abortion, sterilization is often the subject of specific legislation. The United States falls in the majority of countries where sterilization for contraceptive purposes has been legalized.[6] It is illegal only in Greece. In the remaining eight countries,[7] which tend to have largely

3. Austria, Finland, France, New Zealand, Norway, Portugal, Spain, Sweden, and the United Kingdom.

4. Australia, Canada, Denmark, West Germany, the Netherlands, and the United States.

5. Australia, Belgium, Canada, Greece, Ireland, the Netherlands, Portugal, and Switzerland (as well as the United States).

6. Australia, Austria, Denmark, Finland, West Germany, New Zealand, Norway, Spain, Sweden, and the United Kingdom (as well as the United States).

7. Belgium, Canada, France, Ireland, Italy, the Netherlands, Portugal, and Switzerland.

Catholic populations, sterilization is neither illegal nor formally legalized; therefore perceptions of its legal status differ.

Service Delivery

The first item in the AGI country survey questionnaire asked, "Where is the average person most likely to go to obtain contraceptive services?" Possible responses were: family physician, specialist physician, clinic, hospital, pharmacy, and other (respondents were asked to specify). Both a main source and an alternative source (if thought to provide for as many as one-third of contraceptive users) could be designated.[8] These data yielded two variables, the first referring to the main source of services and the second to the combination of principal sources. Family physicians were given as the main source in half the countries (table 3.2).[9] Specialists fulfill this function in several countries, including the United States. Clinics were mentioned as the main service source only in Finland, Portugal, and Sweden but were the alternative source mentioned most often (in nine of the seventeen where they were not reported as the main source).[10] The United States is one of six countries where there is no secondary source that serves at least one-third of contraceptive users.[11] Hospitals and pharmacies were not identified as a main source in any country, although they are unquestionably an essential part of the total delivery system everywhere.

The survey results showed that certain important characteristics are closely associated with each principal type of source. The variables representing these characteristics cannot add anything to the analysis, above and beyond the type of source, and hence have not been used as such. Because their distributions are essentially the same as those of the main source of services, they are not shown in table 3.2. They are discussed here, however, because they help to elucidate the meaning attached to the various types of source. The extent to which family planning is integrated into general health care may reflect familiarity with the service on the part of potential clients and the degree to which they feel at ease with it. When asked whether the main source reported was the same facility to which a person would go for routine health care, the reply was almost always affirmative if the source was a family physician and negative if it was a specialist or clinic. Since most coun-

8. Throughout this study, the terms *family physician*, *general practitioner*, and *family doctor* are used interchangeably and are distinguished from *specialists*, which refers mainly to obstetrician-gynecologists but may include others (e.g., urologists).

9. Australia, Austria, Canada, Denmark, France, Ireland, the Netherlands, New Zealand, Norway, and the United Kingdom.

10. Australia, Canada, Denmark, Ireland, Italy, New Zealand, Norway, Spain, and the United Kingdom.

11. The others are Finland, Greece, the Netherlands, Sweden, and Switzerland.

Table 3.2 *Distribution of countries by service delivery variables*

Variable and category	Number of countries
Main source of services	
Family physician	10
Clinic	3
Specialist	7
Combination of major sources	
Family physician only	1
Family physician and clinic	7
Family physician and specialist	3
Clinic only	2
Specialist and clinic	3
Specialist only	3
Insufficient information	1
Method recommended for termination of childbearing	
Sterilization	3
Pill	6
Pill or sterilization	3
IUD	8
Special efforts to assist young people	
Added clinics and reduced cost	2
Added clinics with or without other efforts, except reduced cost	5
Special training or outreach only	2
No special service efforts	5
Young people not recognized	6
Special efforts to assist low-income people	
Reduced cost and other efforts	1
Reduced cost only	1
No special service efforts	2
Low-income people not recognized	16
Special efforts to assist immigrants	
Special counseling and other efforts	3
Special counseling only	2
No special service efforts	7
Immigrants not recognized	8
Contraceptive access for unmarried minors	
Most restricted	6
Somewhat restricted	6
Unrestricted	8
Payment for female sterilization in hospital	
Free, or nominal payment	12
Cost usually reimbursed	3
Client pays	3
Procedure illegal or unavailable	2
Payment to obtain pill prescription	
Free, or nominal payment	10
Cost usually reimbursed	4
Client pays	6
Payment for pill supplies	
Free, or nominal payment	3
Cost usually reimbursed	4
Client pays	13

Table 3.2 (*Continued*)

Variable and category	Number of countries
Variation in access to sterilization	
Urban/rural variation	4
Regional variation	6
Both urban/rural and regional variation	3
Little variation	5
Procedure illegal or not available	2
Reasons for variation in access to sterilization	
Inconvenient location of cources	5
Negative attitudes of providers and/or local officials	6
Negative public opinion	2
Little variation or not available	7
Variation in access to the pill	
Urban/rural variation	2
Regional variation	3
Both urban/rural and regional variation	1
Insufficient information	14
Sterilization requirements	
None	7
Minor requirements	8
Major requirements	3
Procedure illegal or not available	2
Pelvic exam before pill prescription	
Regularly done	15
Not regularly done	5

tries have some form of national health service, the question about governmental operation of the principal contraceptive service (referred to above) is related to its integration into general health care. The sixteen countries whose response to this item could be coded break down as follows: where specialists are the main source, the government was reported to be uninvolved; where clinics are the main source, the service was reported to be operated directly by the government; and in five of the seven countries where family physicians are the main providers, it was reported that the government funds the service. This variable is not associated with the variable on overall family planning policy described above. A question concerning the level of training and sex of principal service personnel showed that specialist physicians are almost always men, family physicians are often but not always men, and clinic personnel, both physicians and other professionals, tend to be women. No way was devised of inquiring about the geographic distribution and density of the main service sources, but it stands to reason that family physicians would be located closer to most people than either specialists or clinics.

To assess the climate of opinion among providers concerning individual methods, questions asked which method was most likely to be recommended at the main source, first to a woman aged twenty who wanted to postpone childbearing and second to a woman aged thirty-two who was seeking to terminate childbearing. The pill is the overwhelming choice for postponement, regardless of the source, and the distribution is therefore not shown in table 3.2. For termination, responses were spread out among the three efficient methods. Both the pill and sterilization were mentioned in the United States. In the United States, restricted availability of the IUD, the method mentioned in eight of the twenty countries,[12] clearly reduces women's options in the final stage of their reproductive lives.

Many countries whose governments have identified population groups with particular family planning needs reported that steps had been taken, either privately or under government auspices, to address these needs. Options referring to special information and education efforts and to communication in other languages are described under information delivery. Other options listed in the questionnaire were provision of additional or special clinics, opening of clinics during additional or special hours, special training of regular clinic personnel, making special counseling available, contacting subgroup members through outreach workers, reducing cost, and incorporating family planning in a broad program designed to meet the health and welfare needs of the specified group. The indicators presented here cannot do justice to the detail in the response but are intended to portray the principal patterns. Nine of the fourteen countries where young people were recognized as having special needs reported that some effort was being made to address them.[13] Special clinics constitute the most common approach, which fits in with the observation made in the AGI adolescent study that young people often prefer services tailored to their needs (Jones et al. 1986). Only the United States and Australia offer reduced cost as well as special clinics. Two of the four countries where low-income people were recognized as having special needs (the United States and the Federal Republic of Germany) said they had taken extra steps to assist such people. Reduced cost was mentioned in both cases. In the United States, this is one part of a multifaceted effort. Four of the five countries where immigrants were singled out (including the United States) mentioned efforts other than information, education, and language assistance. All four include special counseling, and in the United States special clinics are also provided. Because few

12. Austria, Denmark, Finland, France, Greece, Italy, Norway, and Spain.
13. Australia, Canada, the Netherlands, New Zealand, Norway, Portugal, Sweden, the United Kingdom, and the United States.

countries identified rural residents as having special needs, programs directed toward them are not considered here.

The AGI adolescent study (Jones et al. 1986) provided one additional variable related to young people. An index was made from responses to a set of questions concerning possible restrictions on access to contraception for unmarried women under eighteen which do not apply to older women or married women. Although this is partly a question of official policy, it is included under service provision because the question referred to practical as well as legal considerations, and practicality may often be the determining factor. The United States fell into the intermediate category (together with Australia, Austria, Ireland, Italy, and Switzerland) with some restrictions but fewer than in several other countries.[14]

Cost, accessibility, and special requirements associated with specific methods of contraception were also investigated. Although the questionnaire was designed to collect parallel information about common aspects like cost with respect to female and male sterilization, the pill, IUD, and condom, more attention is given here to sterilization and the pill, which are the predominant methods in the United States. The patterns of response for female and male sterilization were so similar that they could be covered together.

Cost of the method was assessed according to whether the client receives the service free or makes only a nominal payment, pays but is later reimbursed, or bears most or all of the cost. For sterilization, the evaluation of cost was based on responses to a question specifying payment for female sterilization operations taking place in a hospital. In sixteen of the twenty countries replies to a comparable question about male sterilization (taking place anywhere) were identical to those concerning female sterilization. Three countries that reported that female sterilization was essentially free gave different answers for male sterilization. Two said that clients had to pay for male sterilization themselves, and one said that there was insufficient information on payment for male sterilization. One country reporting that reimbursement was usual for female sterilization said that male sterilization was not available there. Female sterilization is provided free or at nominal cost in twelve countries.[15] In Belgium, France, and the United States, the client pays but is typically reimbursed by some form of insurance. The cost is borne by the client in Austria, Ireland, and Switzerland. Female sterilization is not available in Italy or Greece. For the pill, separate questions concerned the cost of obtaining a prescription at the

14. Belgium, Canada, Denmark, Greece, Portugal, and Spain had more restrictions.
15. Australia, Canada, Denmark, Finland, Federal Republic of Germany, the Netherlands, New Zealand, Norway, Portugal, Spain, Sweden, and the United Kingdom.

main service source and the cost of supplies. In half the countries, there is no payment for the medical service required to obtain a prescription for the pill,[16] whereas this is much less often true of pill supplies.[17] In the United States and four other countries (Austria, Greece, Ireland, and Spain), the woman usually pays out of pocket for both the pill prescription and supplies.

The query on access to methods of contraception focused on variation in availability between urban and rural areas or between regions of the country. If either kind of variation was reported, follow-up questions asked whether this is because of inconvenient location of sources, negative attitudes of service personnel or local officials, negative public opinion, lack of publicity, or lack of demand for the method. Most countries reported variation in access to male and female sterilization procedures. In the United States, urban/rural variation was specified. Variation in availability was more often attributed to negative opinion on the part either of providers or the general public than to inconveniently located facilities, although this was cited as a problem in the United States. Relatively little variation in pill accessibility was reported, but what there is seems to involve the urban/rural and regional dimensions fairly equally. Variation in access to the pill was not considered significant in the United States.

Special requirements concerning the provision of individual methods could be regarded as a policy matter, but again, since the formulation of the questions stressed the actual as well as the legal situation, they have been treated as an aspect of service delivery. A question on possible eligibility requirements for female sterilization specified age, number of children, and husband's consent. Responses fell into three categories distinguishing places where there are no prerequisites, where there is a lower age limit between twenty-five and thirty or the consent of the husband must be obtained, and where the lower age limit is over thirty or the woman must have a certain number of children. The United States and six other countries have no requirements.[18] They do exist, however, in more than half of the countries. When it comes to the pill, on the other hand, the United States is among the large majority of countries where a pelvic examination is the regular procedure before prescription. In five countries[19] a pelvic examination is not routinely required.

16. Canada, Denmark, Finland, Federal Republic of Germany, Italy, the Netherlands, Portugal, Sweden, Switzerland, and the United Kingdom.

17. The Netherlands, New Zealand, Portugal, and the United Kingdom.

18. Australia, Belgium, Canada, Federal Republic of Germany, the Netherlands, and New Zealand.

19. Ireland, New Zealand, Spain, Sweden, and the United Kingdom.

Table 3.3 *Distribution of countries by information delivery variables*

Variable and category	Number of countries
Overall information effort	
Weak effort	5
Moderate effort	12
Strong effort	3
Special information efforts for target groups	
Special effort for more than one group	3
Special effort for one group	8
No special effort	4
No recognition of target group	5
Proportion of female students receiving instruction on contraceptive methods	
< 1/3	5
> 1/3 < 2/3	6
> 2/3 < 9/10	3
> 9/10	4
Insufficient information	2
Advertising of condoms	
Common	14
Not common	6

Information Delivery

To gauge the emphasis put on provision of information related to contraception and contraceptive services overall, respondents to the country questionnaire were asked to rate the level of both governmental and nongovernmental information efforts. The results have been combined into one indicator, ranging from weak to strong effort (table 3.3). Most countries fall into the intermediate category. The United States is one of five countries[20] indicating that such efforts were relatively weak. Denmark, the Netherlands, and the United Kingdom were the only countries reporting strong efforts.

Special information and education efforts directed toward target groups have been treated as an individual item. Eleven of the fifteen countries that recognized at least one population subgroup as being in need of special family planning help reported that some effort was made to provide information and education geared to their needs.[21] In the case of immigrants, this almost always included communication in other languages. The United States is one of three countries (Canada and the Netherlands are the others) where special information and education programs are designed to reach more than one target group.

20. The others are the Federal Republic of Germany, Ireland, Italy, and Spain.
21. Austria, Canada, Denmark, Finland, France, the Netherlands, Norway, Spain, Sweden, the United Kingdom, and the United States.

The earlier AGI study on adolescent pregnancy (Jones et al. 1986) collected estimates of the proportion of female students receiving instruction on contraceptive methods. Among the eighteen countries providing estimates, substantial variation was reported, ranging from fewer than 33 percent receiving instruction in Belgium, Greece, Italy, Portugal, and Spain to more than 90 percent in Denmark, Finland, Sweden, and Switzerland. Survey data showed that over half of U.S. adolescents learned about specific methods in school (Jones et al. 1986, 58).[22]

Finally, although advertising of contraceptives may be legal in most countries, it does not always occur. The country survey inquired about the situation in practice regarding advertisement of clinic services, physicians' services, the pill, and condoms in several specified media. Advertisement of physicians' services and the pill appear to be quite rare. Advertisement of clinic services is more or less limited to countries where clinics are a main source of service. Hence, only the advertising of condoms is considered here. Newspapers and magazines are the typical media for condom advertising. The issue of advertising condoms on television does not arise where it is publicly operated and carries no advertising at all, as is the case in many of these countries. Condoms were reported to be advertised widely except in Belgium, Canada, Finland, Greece, Ireland, and the United States. Condom advertising may have increased very recently because of concern about the spread of AIDS; the circumstances relevant to the fertility and contraceptive-use data used in this study, however, are those prevailing at the time of the survey.

RELATIONSHIP OF CONTRACEPTIVE USE TO INSTITUTIONAL FACTORS

Because of limitations on the size of the sample and inadequacies in the measurement of the different variables, the ensuing discussion is necessarily impressionistic. No claims for empirical proof, let alone quantitative precision, can be offered. Tabulations have been made in the spirit of pointing the way toward probable explanations and are not intended to offer statistical proof.

The discussion is organized around the three groups of institutional factors introduced earlier: law and policy, service delivery, and information delivery. The approach taken was to prepare simple cross-tabulations of actual numbers and to look for possible patterns. Each independent variable was examined in relation to a variety of measures

22. A more recent estimate suggests this proportion has reached about 75 percent; see chapter 5.

of contraceptive use, including the overall pattern of use, use of any of the three effective methods, and use of sterilization, the pill, IUD, and condom individually. Use among women aged 20–29 and aged 30–34 as well as among those aged 15–44 was considered. The findings are reviewed briefly in the text, with presentation in tabular form limited to a few selected results. Except for the results concerning the pattern of contraceptive use, in which all twenty countries are represented, data are limited to the subset of countries with adequate data on contraceptive use. Cases missing data on either of the variables in a given tabulation were omitted.

A major drawback here is the disparity in the time reference of independent and dependent variables. The information on policy, service delivery, and information delivery was from the AGI's 1986 country survey, but the most recent survey providing data on contraceptive use is the 1985 Spanish fertility survey, and five of the surveys represented in the tables were carried out during the 1970s. The greater the time gap, the more likely that the comparison is inappropriate because of changes in policies and programs.

Laws and Policies
Neither overall family planning policy nor the legality of advertising contraceptives seems to be associated with the level of use of effective methods of contraception. The legal status of abortion, however, does appear to bear some relation to the use of effective methods. Except for Italy, all the countries where abortion is available without substantial restrictions[23] fall into the medium or high categories of effective-method use. Use is low in all three countries where abortion is substantially restricted (Greece, Portugal, and Spain). Belgium, the one country with adequate data on contraceptive use where abortion is illegal, is the exception that proves the rule, since use is high, but abortion is readily available there. Sterilization is infrequent in Greece, where it is illegal, but otherwise its legality and how much it is resorted to seem unconnected.

With respect to target groups, recognition of groups other than young people alone may be associated with higher levels of use. Use of effective methods is low in four of the ten countries where either no group or only young people were singled out,[24] whereas the level is medium or high where low-income people or other groups are recognized as needing special attention.[25] Among older women, use of

23. Canada, Denmark, Finland, France, Netherlands, Norway, Sweden, the United Kingdom, and the United States.
24. Greece, Italy, Portugal, and Spain.
25. Canada, the Netherlands, Sweden, and the United States.

effective methods is high in all countries where low-income people, immigrants, or rural residents were targeted. Government sensitivity to the special needs of particular groups could reflect greater commitment to family planning in general.

Among women aged 20–29, use of effective methods does not seem to be higher where young people are the only group recognized as needing special attention, nor does it differ according to government policy on teaching contraceptive methods in school. This may be because policies concerning young people are usually directed primarily toward even younger women, especially unmarried teenagers, while the measure of use here is based on married women in their twenties.

Service Delivery

The most widely used methods of contraception differ markedly as to the most suitable means for their distribution and the skills needed to dispense them. Thus connections can be anticipated between the arrangements for provision of services in a country and the prevailing pattern of use. In developed countries, both male and female sterilizations are usually performed by highly trained specialists working in sophisticated technical settings. Insertion of the IUD also requires considerable expertise, but there is less need for technical backup. The diaphragm must be fitted and prescribed by a person with at least some training. Although a doctor's prescription is needed to obtain the pill in virtually all developed countries (Meredith and Thomas 1986), it is increasingly the accepted view that only very elementary medical skills are called for. Unless the doctor who prescribes the diaphragm or pill works in a clinic, filling these prescriptions brings in a pharmacist, who has less extensive training and is usually located in another facility. Many over-the-counter contraceptive products, for example, spermicidal foams and jellies, are mainly provided in pharmacies and clinics. Condoms are for sale in a wide variety of highly accessible places, including vending machines, which do not require even the intervention of a shop clerk. These service-related characteristics, which affect both access and cost, may be as important as those pertaining to the methods themselves in determining individual contraceptive choices.

Table 3.4 shows the overall pattern of contraceptive use according to the main sources of service delivery for all twenty countries. In two of the three countries where use of effective methods is high and sterilization is the most common method (Switzerland and the United States), specialists dominate service provision, although in the other (Canada), specialists are neither the main nor the supplementary source. Reliance on specialists for the provision of family planning services could make it easier to obtain sterilization operations since they are presumably qualified to perform such procedures themselves,

Table 3.4 *Sources of service and pattern of contraceptive use*

	Pattern of contraceptive use					
	> 30% using effective methods					
	Principal method			10–30% using effective methods	< 10% using effective methods	
Main sources of services	Sterilization	Pill	IUD			N
Main source of services						
Family physician	1	7	1	1	0	10
Clinic	0	1	1	1	0	3
Specialist	2	2	0	2	1	7
Combination of main sources						
Family physician only	0	1	0	0	0	1
Family physician and clinic	1	4	1	1	0	7
Family physician and specialist	0	3	0	0	0	3
Clinic only	0	1	1	0	0	2
Specialist and clinic	0	0	0	3	0	3
Specialist only	2	0	0	0	1	3

whereas family physicians generally have to refer sterilization candidates to specialists or appropriate facilities. The willingness of family physicians to make such referrals is undoubtedly a critical determinant of the frequency of use of this method, especially where the client does not have direct access to specialized medical services.

Women in countries where use of effective methods is high and the pill is the most widely used method are very likely to be served mainly by family physicians. The pill is an easy method for general practitioners to deal with. As mentioned above, they must usually refer for sterilization operations, and, unless the IUD is very widely used in the country, they are unlikely to have sufficient practice to feel confident about inserting it. Use of the pill also requires ongoing supervision, and a relatively small input of time and effort may be of continuing financial benefit to the physician.

In both Finland and Norway, where use of effective methods is high and the IUD is the most common method, clinics play a major role, even though in Norway family physicians are the main providers. Family planning clinics are perhaps an ideal setting for dispensing the IUD since one staff member can specialize in this method. Where the IUD is popular enough, however, family physicians may also have enough patients using it to become quite expert.

In three of the five countries where fewer than 30 percent of women rely on the most effective methods (Greece, Italy, and Spain), the main source is specialists, and in four of them (Ireland, Italy, Portugal, and Spain) clinics also play a prominent role. The impression is that in these countries family planning remains set apart from normal health care. It is either the province of gynecologists, who may be difficult to reach, or is available through a clinic system that is possibly less than adequately developed. Ireland is the one country where use of effective methods is low and family physicians are the principal source. Only a small fraction of doctors there do, in fact, provide contraceptives.

Cross-tabulations according to several more refined measures of use and the basic service delivery variables are presented in table 3.5 for the fourteen countries having adequate data on contraceptive use. In no country where family physicians are the main providers is use of effective methods low.[26] Among the eight countries where specialists or clinics are the main providers,[27] however, only Belgium has high use of effective methods. The results for the combination of main sources reveal that low use is associated more with specialists than with clinics. Specialists play an important role in all countries where use is low,[28] but clinics often provide significant services in countries where use of effective methods is medium or high.[29] Provision of services by family physicians appears to be even more strongly linked with higher levels of use among young married women than among all women of reproductive age (not shown).

The association between provider type and individual method (table 3.5) amplifies some of the observations made in discussing the overall pattern of use. Extensive use of sterilization is confined to countries where family physicians and specialists are the main providers. The pattern for the pill is very similar to that observed for the three effective methods together. Where family physicians are the principal service source, use tends to be high; where specialists are the principal source, it is usually low; and where clinics are the principal source, it typically falls in between. Use of the IUD appears to be linked with clinic services but, somewhat unexpectedly, it may be less common where specialists are the main providers than where family physicians play that role. Although many couples also rely on the condom in countries where clinics are the main source of services, this method seems to be used infrequently where family physicians are the main providers.

In the section on laws and policies, it was noted that use of effective methods appears to be higher in countries where target groups other than young people are recognized as being in need of special help with family planning than in countries where they are not. There is no

26. Canada, Denmark, France, the Netherlands, Norway, and the United Kingdom.
27. Belgium, Finland, Greece, Italy, Portugal, Spain, Sweden, and the United States.
28. Greece, Italy, Portugal, and Spain.
29. Canada, Denmark, Finland, Norway, Sweden, and the United Kingdom.

Table 3.5 *Sources of service and level of contraceptive use*

Method and sources	Level of use			N
	High	Medium	Low	
Main source				
Effective methods				
Family M.D.	3	3	0	6
Clinic	0	2	1	3
Specialist	1	1	3	5
Sterilization				
Family M.D.	3	1	2	6
Clinic	0	0	3	3
Specialist	1	1	3	5
Pill				
Family M.D.	3	2	1	6
Clinic	0	2	1	3
Specialist	1	1	3	5
IUD				
Family M.D.	1	5	0	6
Clinic	2	0	1	3
Specialist	0	1	4	5
Condom				
Family M.D.	1	2	3	6
Clinic	2	0	1	3
Specialist	1	2	2	5
Combination of main sources				
Effective methods				
Family M.D. only	1	0	0	1
Family M.D. and clinic	2	2	0	4
Family M.D. and specialist	0	1	0	1
Clinic only	0	2	0	2
Specialist and clinic	0	0	3	3
Specialist only	0	1	1	2

evidence that the existence or nonexistence of efforts to meet the needs of these groups makes any further difference. Only two of the four countries where the government has singled out low-income people have adequate data on contraceptive use, and use of effective methods is actually lower in the one that reported having services specifically for this group (the United States) than in the one that does not, Canada (not shown). Similarly, no relationship is evident between special service efforts for immigrants and use of effective methods.

Effective methods may be more widely used by women in their twenties in countries with special services for young people. Use is high for women aged 20–29 in four of the seven countries with some kind of program,[30] but in only one of the four (Belgium) that do not make such efforts (not shown). Use of effective methods of contraception among young women also tends to be positively associated with unre-

---

30. Canada, the United Kingdom, the Netherlands, and Norway.

Table 3.6 *Service delivery characteristics and level of contraceptive use*

	Level of use			
Method and characteristic	*High*	*Medium*	*Low*	N
Sterilization				
Reasons for variation in access				
Source inconveniently located	2	0	1	3
Negative attitudes of providers and officials	1	1	2	4
Requirements				
No special requirements	3	1	0	4
Minor requirements	1	1	3	5
Major requirements	0	0	3	3
Pill				
Payment for prescription				
Essentially free	2	4	2	8
Cost usually reimbursed	2	0	1	3
Client must pay	0	1	2	3
Payment for supplies				
Essentially free	2	1	0	3
Cost usually reimbursed	1	1	1	3
Client must pay	1	3	4	8

stricted access to contraceptives for unmarried minors, even though it is common in two (Belgium, Canada) of the six countries where access is most restricted (not shown).

Turning to the delivery of sterilization services, there is no evidence of any link between its popularity and the client's liability for payment, nor does variation in access to sterilization appear to be a deterrent. Where access is uneven, low use may be associated more often with negative attitudes on the part of providers or local officials (France and Spain) than with inconvenient location of sources (Portugal) (see table 3.6). In none of the countries with information on sterilization was public opinion thought to be the main problem. Because sterilization involves one or at most a few visits to the provider, inconvenience of location would not necessarily be a substantial obstacle to use. As might be expected, sterilization is much more apt to be widespread where few or no requirements must be met before the operation, and vice versa.

With respect to the pill, its use appears to be somewhat more likely to be low where the client must pay to obtain a prescription (Greece and Spain versus the United States) than where it is essentially free.[31] The pill is clearly less likely to be used where the client must pay for supplies. Both of these relationships are stronger among older than among younger women, possibly because there are more alternative contraceptive options for women who wish to terminate childbearing

31. Finland and Italy, versus Canada, Denmark, the Netherlands, Portugal, Sweden, and the United Kingdom.

Table 3.7 *Information delivery and use of effective methods of contraception*

	Level of use			
Age and variable	High	Medium	Low	N
All ages				
Overall information effort				
Weak	0	1	2	3
Moderate	2	4	2	8
Strong	2	1	0	3
Special information efforts for target groups				
More than one group	2	1	0	3
One group	1	5	1	7
No special effort	0	0	1	1
Ages 20–29				
Overall information effort				
Weak	0	1	2	3
Moderate	5	3	2	10
Strong	2	0	0	2
Proportion of female students receiving instruction on contraceptive methods				
< 1/3	1	0	4	5
> 1/3 < 2/3	3	1	0	4
> 2/3 < 9/10	1	1	0	2
> 9/10	1	2	0	3

than for those who are still postponing births. Uneven access to the pill may also deter use, and again this makes sense since return trips must usually be made at regular intervals, both to renew the prescription and to get supplies. The requirement of a pelvic examination before obtaining a prescription does not have the expected negative effect on pill use, perhaps because adolescents are not included here.

The method recommended for termination of childbearing seems to have some association with use of both sterilization and the pill among older women (not shown). Use of sterilization is common in this age group in all three countries where it is likely to be recommended, either alone or on an equal footing with the pill (Canada, the Netherlands, and the United States). In addition, pill use is high among women aged 35–44 in three of the four countries where it is regarded by providers as the most appropriate method for those terminating childbearing (Belgium, Portugal, and Sweden versus the United Kingdom), although it is low in the United States, which is the one country where it might be recommended on an equal footing with sterilization.

Information Delivery
The results concerning provision of information about contraception suggest that provision can contribute significantly to use (table 3.7). There is a modest positive relationship between use of effective meth-

ods of contraception and information effort. Similarly, use is apt to be higher when an effort is made to direct information specifically toward groups needing special assistance with contraception, although, as noted above, no such connection appears for other initiatives for these groups. The association between use of effective methods and the overall information effort may be somewhat stronger among young women than among women of all ages. Use of effective methods among young people is often higher also in countries where more than one-third of female students receive sex education that includes instruction in contraceptive methods. Use of the condom is low in only two of the nine countries where this method is commonly advertised (Denmark and Finland). Reliance on the condom is low in four of the five countries where it is not commonly advertised (Belgium, Canada, France, and the United States, versus Greece).

4

Background for the Country Reports

Four of the twenty Western countries included in the overview analysis were selected for detailed examination and visited by teams of researchers. These were Canada, the Netherlands, the United Kingdom, and the United States. Choice of the three foreign countries was based on the anticipated relevance of their circumstances to the United States, on such outstanding features as low abortion rates and pregnancy rates in the Netherlands, and on data availability, especially data on contraceptive practice and abortion. These countries were also examined in detail in the earlier AGI adolescent study (Jones et al. 1986), so that a base of knowledge, contacts in the countries, and materials already existed.

In Canada, providing family planning is a provincial rather than a national responsibility. As a consequence, there is considerable diversity from one part of the country to another. Because of this Ontario and Quebec, the two most populous provinces, are focused on and treated as separate units. In 1982, 35 percent of the Canadian female population of childbearing age resided in Ontario, and 27 percent lived in Quebec. These two provinces also present a marked contrast with respect to social, economic, and cultural conditions.

The survey data that provide much of the background material for the case study of the United Kingdom pertain to Great Britain, so that it is the primary level of reference. Ninety-eight percent of all women in the United Kingdom aged 15–50 resided in Great Britain in 1982. Most of the information on service provision refers only to England and Wales, which represented 89 percent of women of reproductive age in the United Kingdom and 90 percent of those in Great Britain.

The principal area omitted is Scotland, where arrangements for service provision and background conditions differ to some extent from the rest of the country. The country visit was further restricted to England.

The materials presented in this chapter form a common body of information to serve as background for the individual country chapters that constitute the remainder of the report. They include that statistical material for the five study areas which lends itself to presentation in a common format. Detailed tabulations of the survey data on births by planning status and contraceptive use have been prepared for these five study areas. For definitions of the samples and other characteristics of the surveys see chapter 3. In the case of the Netherlands, measures including women over thirty-seven are based on the available survey data, which cover women up to this age only.

The tabulations extend to differentials by socioeconomic status. Income and education are used as indicators of status. In general, cross-national comparisons by socioeconomic status present many difficulties. In addition, each of these two status measures has its own problems. Current income tends to rise with age but may also fluctuate because of unemployment or other changes. The nature of the income distribution often differs widely between countries. For instance, income disparities are narrow in the Netherlands; a low-income Dutch woman is thus less disadvantaged, both in absolute and in relative terms, than her counterparts in the other countries. Although education is likely to be a constant characteristic throughout adult life, there has been a trend toward greater educational achievement among more recent cohorts of women that has affected these countries to varying degrees. There is also substantial variation in national educational systems and no adequate means of establishing real equivalence from one country to another.

Results by income are not presented for the two Canadian provinces. Information on income was collected in the 1984 Canadian fertility survey, but the nonresponse rate was very high. For the Netherlands, family income was estimated by summing the husbands' and the respondents' income. Unfortunately, the underlying data for both variables were in the form of broad categories. Values were assigned according to the midpoints of the categories, but the results are inevitably imprecise. Direct data on income were not obtained in either the 1976 or the 1983 surveys of Great Britain, and in both cases the respondents' "socioeconomic group," the standard British status variable, was substituted. The measure used for the United States was poverty status, which takes into account family size as well as income. Information on the respondents' education is available for all four countries. For Canada it represents number of years of schooling, and for the other three countries it represents the highest level of education completed.

Comparisons by income and education are limited to women currently in union. The samples for all four countries were divided as evenly as possible into two categories representing the lower and upper halves of each distribution without regard to comparability across countries. Because of the specific interest in poor women in the United States, results are also shown for the lowest income category that could be distinguished in each data set and had descriptive meaning. The lowest income group is a subset of the lower income half rather than the last of a series of three categories. For the United States, the lowest income category covers up to 150 percent of the federally established poverty level. This very simple approach was dictated by the necessity of including an age control. Results are presented for younger and older women, with the division again made according to criteria that vary from country to country. The lack of common definitions of categories lends further weight to the caution that comparisons of a given category across countries are not appropriate; the purpose of the socioeconomic differentials tables is to establish the direction of any relationships with status, and to compare patterns across countries.

Most information for the country profiles was collected during site visits to the four foreign case-study areas during late 1986 and early 1987. Teams of two staff members spent one week each in Ontario and Quebec and ten days each in the Netherlands and England. Some months before the visit the teams contacted a strategically situated local person whom they asked to arrange a schedule of appointments. They conducted interviews with representatives of all major elements of the service delivery system, with persons in the media and information services, and with government officials responsible for service evaluation and policy formulation. One difficulty that arose in all study areas was appraising the role of physicians, who constitute an important element of service provision but practice as individuals within guidelines that are typically quite loosely drawn up. The teams could meet only with leaders of appropriate professional organizations, interview one or two practicing doctors, and collect information on doctors' performance from other providers. Although a great deal of quantitative material was collected during these visits, it serves mainly descriptive not analytical, purposes. The country reports naturally contain much that is subjective and nonverifiable.

To gain better perspective on the reasons for variation in contraceptive practice, a special effort was made to find data on attitudes and perceptions concerning individual methods. Couples who fear the side effects of a method or doubt its reliability may use it irregularly and hesitantly. The information collected did not permit presentation in a comparative format, but it is discussed in the individual profiles. Some recent, reasonably comparable data concerning the pill and other methods appear in the reports of the International Health Foundation surveys in France, the Federal Republic of Germany, Italy, Spain, and Great Britain (Riphagen, Van der Vurst, and Lehert 1984, 1985, 1986a, 1986b, 1986c).

The country profiles follow a common outline (see table 4.1). Adherence to the same plan facilitates comparisons of specific topics across countries, although it entails redundancy in some reports. The sections on provider types are devoted to detailed descriptions of the components of the family planning services system, one component per section. The same format is used for the presentation of all components, although their number and ordering varies to accommodate different service arrangements. The major headings appear in the country profiles, whereas the subheadings are not necessarily specifically labeled.

FERTILITY

In all five study areas, the total fertility rate has been below the level required for population replacement in the long term at least since the mid-1970s (figure 4.1). Nevertheless, there are appreciable differences between the areas with respect both to trends in the rate and to its composition by age.

Around 1975 the level of fertility was very much the same, with rates close to 1.8 births per woman except in the Netherlands, where it was slightly lower (1.7). After 1975 rates dropped fairly regularly in Ontario and less regularly in the Netherlands, whereas they declined steeply in Quebec, especially at the beginning of the 1980s. In Great Britain, the rate fluctuated, decreasing rapidly to 1977, then rising equally sharply until 1980 and dropping off again. The break in the downward trend from 1978 to 1980 in the Netherlands and in Great Britain came at a time of declining use of oral contraceptives that has been associated with a wave of negative publicity about them (Ketting and van Praag 1985, 234; Wellings 1986b, 16). In the United States, the total fertility rate rose modestly up to 1978 and then stabilized at or just over 1.8. Around 1983, total fertility was still about 1.8 births per woman in Great Britain and the United States, just under 1.7 in Ontario, and below 1.5 in the Netherlands.

Comparison of the age-specific fertility rates for 1982 indicates that variation in the level of total fertility is determined mainly by differences below age thirty (figure 4.2). Childbearing drops off rapidly after that, and the rates are almost indistinguishable in the five areas. Early childbearing is an outstanding feature of the U.S. situation, with much

Table 4.1 *Outline of the country reports*[a]

I. General description
   A. Overall health system
      1. Provision of care
      2. Payment, insurance
   B. Family planning services
      1. What they are and how they fit into general health care
      2. Overall policies
      3. Abortion policy and services
   C. Target groups for family planning

II. Provider type(s)[b]
   A. Geographic distribution and accessibility
   B. Funding and fees
   C. Role: active/passive
      1. Characteristics of clientele
      2. Outreach
   D. Contraceptive service: personnel (male/female, doctors/nurses), schedule (opening hours, etc.), medical policies and procedures, provider method preferences, time spent with client, referral, follow-up
   E. Counseling: personnel, schedule, content, time spent with client
   F. Client's overall expenditure of time
   G. Information and literature (package inserts)
   H. Other services offered

III. Client preferences
   A. Providers
   B. Methods

IV. Information and education
   A. Organized communication efforts: information and education in general, sex education, government role, target groups
   B. Advertisment of methods and services
   C. Media treatment of contraception: radio and television, newspapers and magazines
   D. Climate of opinion concerning sex

V. Assessment
   A. Proportion of need met
      1. General public
      2. Target groups
   B. Barriers to service
   C. Relation of services to method use

[a]Major headings appear within each country profile, whereas all subheadings may not necessarily appear or be labeled.

[b]There are as many entries for this section as there are provider types. Thus, the outline for this section is reepated for each major provider type for the individual country. Provider types include physicians, family planning clinics, pharmacies, specialized services, private and nonprofit agencies, domiciliary services, and other facilities.

higher rates at ages 15–24 and a somewhat lower rate at ages 25–29. Women below age twenty-five contribute almost one-half of the U.S. total fertility rate, compared to approximately one-third in Ontario, Quebec, and Great Britain, and only one-quarter in the Netherlands. The differences in absolute numbers of births follow a similar pattern. Births to women less than twenty-five years old made up 27 percent of

Figure 4.1. Total fertility rates, 1975–84

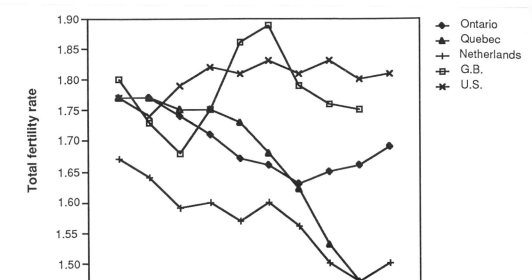

all births in the Netherlands, 35 percent in Quebec, 36 percent in Ontario, 40 percent in Great Britain, and 47 percent in the United States.

ABORTION AND PREGNANCY

Official statistics on abortion are most complete and accurate for Great Britain. For the three other countries, the ages of a certain proportion of the women undergoing abortions have been estimated on the assumption that the distribution is the same as that for women whose age at the time of abortion is known. Age is not reported for Dutch women who obtain abortions in hospitals; however, it has been

Figure 4.2. Age-specific fertility rates, 1982

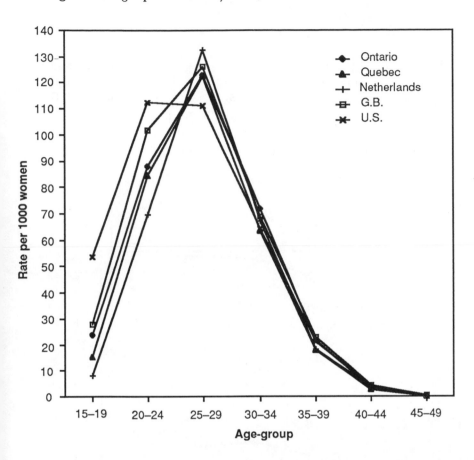

shown that the age distribution resembles that of women who obtain abortions in clinics (Ketting 1983). In the United States, the age of the woman is unknown for one-third of all abortions, which are not reported to state health departments. For Canada the national data used incorporate estimates of the ages of women obtaining abortions in clinics and of Canadian residents going to the United States for abortions. The information on abortions taking place at clinics pertains exclusively to Quebec, and these abortions are included in the figures for the province. Data on abortions Canadian women receive in the United States are available by state of occurrence but not by province of residence, and they have been excluded from the provincial data. Because abortion is easily available in Quebec, it is unlikely that many women from Quebec go to the United States to have abortions. If all Canadian women who obtained abortions in New York State, Massachusetts, Michigan, and Minnesota in 1982 had been from Ontario (and no Ontario women had gone to other U.S. states), the total abortion rate for Ontario would have been four percent higher than that shown (0.432 compared to 0.415), which would not have a substantial impact on the comparisons.

The data show considerably more international variation in abortion rates than in fertility rates (figure 4.3). In recent years, the total abortion rate has been almost twice as high in the United States as in the next highest country, Great Britain, and about four times as high as in the Netherlands. The relative position of the countries remains the same as for the total fertility rates except that the level of abortion is

Figure 4.3. Total abortion rates, 1975–84

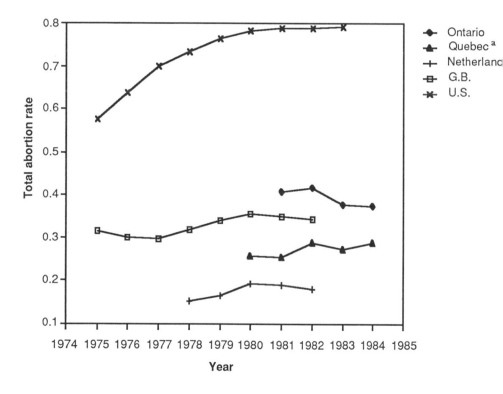

[a] Adjusted for clinic abortions.

lower in Britain than in Ontario. Although trends cannot always be traced over many years, the British and Dutch rates do not appear to have changed very much, while the U.S. rate leveled off around 1980, following a rapid rise.

Differences in the age-specific abortion rates persist at least up to age forty (figure 4.4). There is again an enormous gap between the United States and the other countries at ages 15–24. As the level of abortion decreases, the age curve also flattens out, further reducing the percentage of abortions occurring to younger women. Women under age twenty-five account for 61 percent of the total abortion rate in the United States, 57 percent in Ontario, 51 percent in Great Britain, 48 percent in Quebec, and 40 percent in the Netherlands.

Adding the fertility and abortion rates together to obtain estimated

Figure 4.4. Age-specific abortion rates, 1982

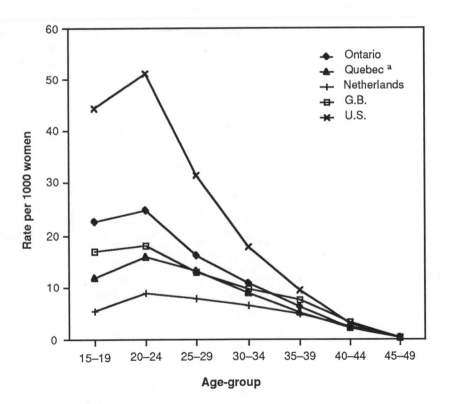

[a] Adjusted for clinic abortions.

pregnancy rates highlights the exceptional situation in the United States (figures 4.5 and 4.6). The pregnancy rates vary more than the fertility rates because of the wide differences in the level of abortion. The incidence of pregnancy is also much higher in the United States than in any of the other four study areas, and virtually all of the "excess" pregnancies in the United States occur before age twenty-five. Pregnancy rates for women over twenty-five are similar. Abortion accounts for an especially large proportion of the U.S. total pregnancy rate (30 percent) compared with other study areas: 20 percent in Ontario, 17 percent in Great Britain, 15 percent in Quebec, and only 10 percent in the Netherlands (see figures 4.1 and 4.3). Although abortion represented a considerably smaller component of all preg-

Figure 4.5. Total pregnancy rates, 1975—84

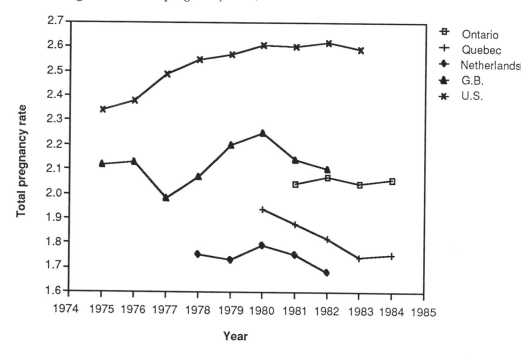

nancies in Great Britain than in Ontario in the early 1980s, the pregnancy rates in the two areas were much the same. The incidence of
pregnancy is lowest in the Netherlands, and differences are concentrated among younger women.

UNPLANNED AND UNWANTED FERTILITY

For each of the study areas, special tabulations of births by planning
status were obtained from the fertility surveys. The data are restricted
to experience within the five years preceding the survey. This reduces
but by no means eliminates the inappropriateness of the time sequence
for observing contraceptive use and unintended fertility. The tabula-

Figure 4.6. Age-specific pregnancy rates, 1982

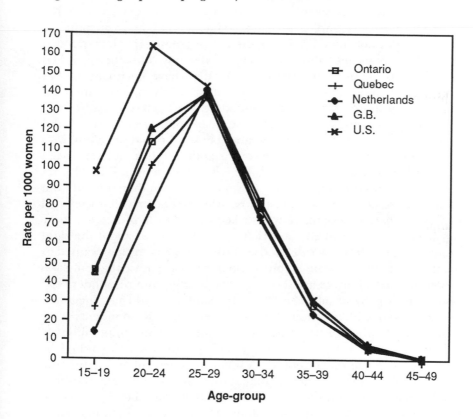

tions also include women of all marital statuses. For Britain, the most recent survey containing any data on planning status is the 1976 Family Formation Survey.

In Canada, Great Britain, and the United States, questions about unintended pregnancies came in a series concerning the circumstances surrounding each pregnancy. In each case, they followed questions on whether a contraceptive method was being used at the time the pregnancy occurred (although planning status was not determined on this basis). The Canadian questionnaire asked each respondent directly, "Did you want to become pregnant at that particular time; would you have preferred to become pregnant at some other time; would you have preferred not to have a child?" The first response has been classified as planned, the second as wanted but unplanned and the third as unwanted. The British questionnaire first asked the respondent whether she was trying to become pregnant at the time she conceived. If the answer was no, she was then asked whether the pregnancy was "a complete accident, a kind of accident on purpose" or she "just did not mind" whether she got pregnant. If she responded that she was trying to get pregnant or did not care, the birth was classified as planned. Both types of accident have been classified as unplanned, and no attempt has been made to distinguish unwanted births from those that were unplanned. In the United States, women who were not using a method at the time of conception were asked if they had wanted to become pregnant. Those who said no, along with respondents who were practicing contraception at the time, were asked whether they had wanted "a(nother) baby at some time." Finally, respondents who had not wanted to become pregnant then but did want a baby at some time, as well as those who said at first that they had wanted to become pregnant, were asked whether the pregnancy came "sooner than . . . wanted, later than . . . wanted or at about the right time." Planned births are defined as those coming later than wanted or at the right time; unplanned but wanted births are those that came too soon; unwanted births are those that came when the respondent did not want a baby at all. The Dutch questionnaire did not include a separate series of questions for each pregnancy. Respondents were asked simply whether they had ever become pregnant unintentionally and, if so, how many times. Each such pregnancy is identified by outcome and year of conception. A follow-up question on whether the respondent had not wanted a child at that time or not wanted (more) children was asked only in reference to the first unintended pregnancy. Although the number of respondents who had more than one unintended pregnancy was not very large, it was decided not to try to break down unplanned births into those that were wanted and unwanted.

Clearly, there is enough variation in the way planning status was addressed to raise questions about the comparability of the data. To evaluate how the results may have been affected is not easy. The wording of the follow-up question in Britain makes it uncertain how best to draw even the basic distinction between planned and unplanned births. While only about 2 percent of all births were reported as "a kind of accident on purpose," as many as 12 percent occurred when the women "just did not mind." The Dutch approach, in which each pregnancy was not discussed separately, might well have led to underestimation of unplanned pregnancies. In addition, because only the year of conception and the outcome are known, there was some difficulty determining those that fell into the five-year period. The U.S. format is by far the most detailed and specific.

The estimated proportions of all births occurring in the five years preceding each survey that were unplanned are shown in figure 4.7 for women aged 15–44, 20–29, and 35–44. In the three cases where the subgroup of unplanned births that were unwanted can be distinguished, these proportions are also shown. The proportion that is unplanned varies considerably among young women, whereas among older women, differences in the proportions unwanted are striking. The United States almost always has the highest percentages of births both unplanned and unwanted. Ontario comes second, and both proportions are consistently lower for Quebec than for Ontario. Except among older women, the percentage of births that is unplanned is still lower in Britain, and it is lowest of all by a considerable margin in the Netherlands. The overall incidence of unplanned childbearing in the United States reflects the much higher fertility rates at young ages as well as the relative frequency of unplanned births.

It is hard to evaluate the results shown in figure 4.7 without reference to the relative levels of fertility and abortion. Although the comparison must be made very cautiously, table 4.2 shows the fertility and pregnancy rates by planning status that result from applying the distributions of births shown in figure 4.7A to the levels of fertility and abortion in the year following each survey (that is, at the time when the impact of contraceptive practice as observed in the survey would most appropriately be measured). Differences in the level of planned pregnancy are small, and most variation in total fertility and pregnancy rates is due to differences in unplanned births and abortions. The U.S. unplanned fertility rate is about one-third higher than Ontario's, almost twice as high as Quebec's and Great Britain's, and as much as six times as high as the Netherlands'. Its elevated abortion rate contributes substantially to making the U.S. unplanned pregnancy rate more than half again as high as that of Ontario, the next highest, and nearly five times as high as that of the Netherlands, the lowest. The total planned pregnancy rate tends to vary inversely with the overall level of fertility,

Figure 4.7. Proportions of all births occurring during the five years previous to the survey that were unplanned and unwanted

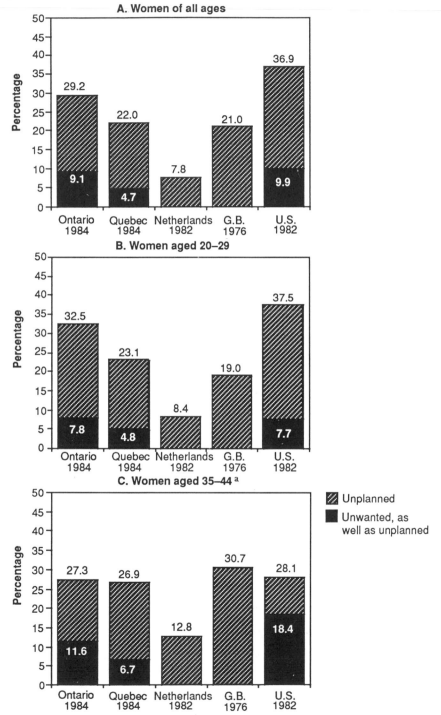

A. Women of all ages

B. Women aged 20–29

C. Women aged 35–44 [a]

Unplanned

Unwanted, as well as unplanned

[a] For the Netherlands, the planning status of births to women aged 35–44 was determined on the basis of data for women 35–37.

Table 4.2 *Total fertility and pregnancy rates by planning status*

Rate	Ontario[a] 1984	Quebec[b] 1984	The Netherlands[c] 1982	Great Britain 1976	United States 1982
Total fertility rate	1.7	1.5	1.5	1.7	1.8
Total wanted fertility rate	1.5	1.4	u[d]	u	1.6
Total planned pregnancy rate	1.2	1.1	1.4	1.3	1.1
Total unplanned fertility rate	0.5	0.3	0.1	0.4	0.7
Total unplanned but wanted fertility rate	0.3	0.3	u	u	0.5
Total unwanted fertility rate	0.2	0.1	u	u	0.2
Total abortion rate	0.4	0.3	0.2	0.3	0.8
Total pregnancy rate	2.1	1.7	1.7	2.0	2.6
Total unplanned pregnancy rate	0.9	0.6	0.3	0.7	1.4

[a]Fertility and abortion data for 1982 rather than 1985.
[b]Abortion data for 1982 rather than 1985.
[c]Abortion data for 1982 rather than 1983.
[d]Indicates data not available.

but the opposite may be true of the wanted fertility rate. This suggests that many unplanned births are wanted births that come too soon, and lack of success in postponing childbearing is a major factor in the association between early childbearing and the total fertility rate noted in connection with figure 4.1.

Tables 4.3 and 4.4 show the proportions of births that were unplanned or unwanted according to income and education. The results are very clear. For both dependent variables and both measures of status in all areas, unplanned births compose a consistently higher

Table 4.3 *Percentage of births unplanned or unwanted, by age and income*

Area and planning status	Younger ages			Older ages		
	Lowest income group	Lower income half	Upper income half	Lowest income group	Lower income half	Upper income half
(Percentage of births)						
The Netherlands, 1982						
Unplanned	10	8	4	9	7	3
N	633	1308	209	302	804	339
Great Britain, 1976						
Unplanned	25	21	12	32	35	26
N	277	993	549	37	110	94
United States, 1982						
Unplanned	35	32	23	42	33	17
Unwanted	8	7	4	16	19	13
N	864	1340	525	65	125	84

Table 4.4 *Percentage of births unplanned or unwanted, by age and education*

Area and planning status	Younger ages		Older ages	
	Less educated	Better educated	Less educated	Better educated
(Percentage of births)				
Ontario, 1984				
Unplanned	28	21	36	18
Unwanted	8	5	18	4
N	447	247	106	97
Quebec, 1984				
Unplanned	21	18	31	22
Unwanted	5	3	10	3
N	409	142	71	36
The Netherlands, 1982				
Unplanned	8	7	7	5
N	616	525	446	515
Great Britain, 1976				
Unplanned	21	13	37	19
N	966	619	138	80
United States, 1982				
Unplanned	30	28	32	20
Unwanted	7	4	18	15
N	1335	530	118	91

fraction among women with lower incomes and less education than among those better off and more educated. Women in the lowest income group also have higher proportions of unplanned births than those in the lower half of the income distribution as a whole, except for older women in Great Britain.

CONTRACEPTIVE USE

Finally, contraceptive use, which is assumed to be the main determinant of pregnancy rates is reviewed. Comparisons are made for women aged 15–44 and for three subgroups representing successive stages in reproductive life, which are characterized by differences in sexual activity, fecundity, and reproductive intentions. They are: (1) never married and not cohabiting women aged 20–29, who may or may not be sexually active, are generally highly fecund, and who intend for the most part to postpone childbearing; (2) currently married or cohabiting women aged 20–29, who are both sexually active and likely to be highly fecund, and whose intentions vary from postponement to conception, spacing, and even termination of childbearing; (3) currently married or cohabiting women aged 35–44, who are sexually active but usually less fecund and who intend almost exclusively to terminate childbearing. Although teenagers are in many ways distinct even from unmarried women aged 20–29, they could not be considered because of the variation in the lower age limit of the survey samples. Consistent with the earlier analysis, no attempt has been made to reduce the base for measurement of contraceptive use by eliminating women not exposed to the risk of pregnancy, other than the use of marital status. The denominators include women who were infecund, pregnant, or wanting to become pregnant. The fundamental differences in survey questioning procedures prevented any further refinement. Moreover, the goal is to establish a link with measures of fertility that are also influenced by variation in nonexposure to conception.

The distinction between contraceptive and noncontraceptive sterilization operations was drawn differently in the various surveys. This is particularly important because the countries included in the case studies are those where sterilization is commonly chosen as a method of terminating childbearing. In Canada, the classification was done on the basis of the type of operation. Vasectomy and tubal ligation are considered to be contraceptive operations, and all others are assumed to be noncontraceptive. In the Netherlands, women who said that they were unable to have children because they and/or their partner had been sterilized were classified as contraceptively sterilized, as opposed to those who said it was due to "illness, accident, or an operation." In Britain, the first question asked concerning fecundity and contraception was whether the respondent or her partner had had a sterilizing operation "intended to prevent pregnancy," and those replying affirmatively were classified as contraceptively sterile (unless there had later been a successful reversal). In the United States, respondents who reported that they were unable to have children because of a sterilizing operation were asked whether "one reason for the operation [was that they] had all the children [they] wanted," and those replying yes were considered contraceptively sterilized. Contraceptive sterilization may be understated in Canada compared to the other countries, because desire to avoid further childbearing might well have been at least a partial motive for some women who had operations other than tubal ligation (four percent of the sample). In the United States, however, an exceptionally high proportion of women reported themselves as surgically sterile for noncontraceptive reasons, including a substantial proportion of the women who had had tubal ligations. If the U.S. classification were based only on type of operation, as in Canada, the proportion of the total sample classified as contraceptively sterilized would rise from 17.8 percent to 19.6 percent. In general, the exclusion of women who were compelled to avoid childbearing solely for health reasons from the contraceptively sterilized category would tend to bias the U.S. results downward. Such women are presumably included among users of other contraceptive methods in all four countries.

For Great Britain, the 1983 General Household Survey is used in this section in preference to the 1976 Family Formation Survey because it is so much closer in time to the observation of family planning services. The only exception is the comparison of fertility and pregnancy rates by planning status in table 4.2. The very small percentage of respondents in the 1983 General Household Survey who reported current use of more than one contraceptive method has been distributed among users of condoms and users of other methods.

A much higher proportion of all women of childbearing age use no method of contraception in the United States than in any of the other study areas: 46 percent compared to 35 percent in the Netherlands, and close to 30 percent in Ontario, Great Britain, and Quebec (table 4.5 and figure 4.8). Some part of this gap is undoubtedly accounted for by less exposure to the risk of pregnancy among nonusers in the United States, due both to the frequency of sterilization for noncontraceptive reasons and to the high incidence of marital disruption. As suggested in the comparisons for the age and marital-status groups that follow, however, this does not wholly explain the difference. There is also greater reliance in the United States on nonmedical, less effective methods than in any other study area except Great Britain, where the condom, the most effective of such methods, is particularly popular.

With respect to the three effective methods, the high level of sterilization in the two Canadian provinces is fairly well balanced by extensive use of the pill in the Netherlands and Great Britain, so that the differences between these study areas in the combined use of effective methods are not very great. In the United States, however, use of the pill is about the same as in Quebec (16 percent compared to 15 percent), and the prevalence of sterilization is no higher than in the Netherlands and Great Britain (18 percent, 19 percent, and 20 percent, respectively). The combined use of effective methods is appreciably lower among U.S. women. The IUD is not particularly popular in any of these countries, but it is used less in the United States than anywhere else. (It was generally available in the United States at the time of the 1982 survey.)

Among women aged 20–29 who had never been married and were not living with a male partner, the level of use of contraceptives is relatively low but nevertheless differs substantially from country to country (table 4.5 and figure 4.9A). Use of any method ranges from 64 percent in Britain down to 43 percent in the United States. Although variation in the proportions sexually active is a potentially important determinant of the level of use among this group of women, the

Table 4.5 *Percentage distribution of all women aged 15–44 and selected age and marital status groups by current contraceptive use[a]*

Age group and method	Ontario (1984)	Quebec (1984)	Netherlands (1983)	Great Britain (1982)	United States (1982)
All women 15–44[b]					
Any method	68.9	71.3	65.3	70.0	54.5
Total effective	54.9	60.0	56.3	52.0	37.4
Sterilization	36.5	39.0	19.1	19.6	17.8
Pill	12.2	15.3	30.2	27.1	15.6
IUD	6.3	5.7	7.0	5.3	4.0
Less effective	14.0	11.3	9.0	18.0	17.1
Condom	8.9	7.3	7.0	11.8	6.7
Other	5.2	4.0	2.0	6.2	10.4
None	31.0	28.6	34.7	29.9	45.5
Never married and not cohabiting, 20–29					
Any method	57.5	49.2	56.7	63.7	43.4
Total effective	52.0	42.6	48.2	50.9	28.7
Sterilization	1.5	0.0	0.2	0.0	1.6
Pill	48.4	39.4	44.2	49.4	25.0
IUD	2.0	3.3	3.8	1.5	2.1
Less effective	5.5	6.6	8.5	12.8	14.7
Condom	3.1	4.4	4.4	2.5	3.8
Other	2.4	2.2	4.2	10.3	10.9
None	42.6	50.8	43.2	36.3	56.6
Married or cohabiting, 20–29[c]					
Any method	69.0	71.6	76.3	78.5	68.9
Total effective	52.2	54.8	66.4	60.4	44.5
Sterilization	13.9	11.4	5.6	6.4	11.9
Pill	31.9	35.1	51.6	46.3	27.5
IUD	6.4	8.4	9.2	7.6	5.2
Less effective	16.8	16.8	9.9	18.1	24.4
Condom	9.4	11.1	7.2	12.9	9.0
Other	7.5	5.7	2.7	5.3	15.3
None	30.9	28.4	23.7	21.4	31.1
Married or cohabiting, 35–44[d]					
Any method	77.4	82.6	78.4	80.2	67.0
Total effective	67.0	73.6	67.5	54.4	47.8
Sterilization	59.0	64.8	41.9	40.2	41.8
Pill	3.2	4.5	18.4	7.5	1.9
IUD	4.9	4.2	7.3	6.7	4.2
Less effective	10.4	9.0	10.9	25.8	19.2
Condom	6.3	4.2	7.1	14.9	9.0
Other	4.0	4.8	3.8	10.9	10.3
None	22.6	17.4	21.6	19.8	32.9
Total	100.0	100.0	100.0	100.0	100.0

[a]Percentage totals may differ slightly because of rounding.

[b]Data for Canada and Great Britain are adjusted to include ages 15–17; data for the Netherlands are adjusted to include ages 15–17 and 38–44.

[c]For Great Britain, women aged 18–29.

[d]For the Netherlands, women aged 35–37; for Great Britain, women of all marital statuses.

finding in the earlier AGI study of similar patterns of sexual activity for
teenagers in these same countries strongly suggests that such variation
is not very important. The United States stands out particularly for its
low use of the pill (25 percent of women in this subgroup as opposed to
39 percent in Quebec, 44 percent in the Netherlands, 48 percent in
Ontario, and 49 percent in Great Britain). Because few women in this
subgroup depend on sterilization or the IUD in any of the countries,
this translates into substantially less reliance on any effective method in
the United States than elsewhere.

Among 20–29-year-olds who were living in a sexual union at the
time of interview, both overall use of any method and combined use of
the three most effective methods are again lowest in the United States

Figure 4.8. Percentage distribution of all women aged 15–44[a] by contraceptive use

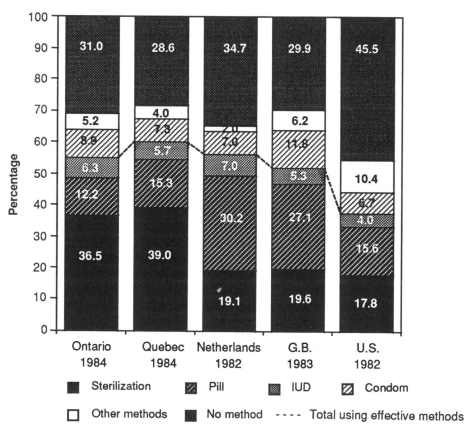

[a] Data for Canada and Great Britain are adjusted to include women aged 15–17;
data for the Netherlands are adjusted to include those aged 15–17 and 38–44.

Figure 4.9. Percentage distribution of women in selected age and marital status groups by current contraceptive use

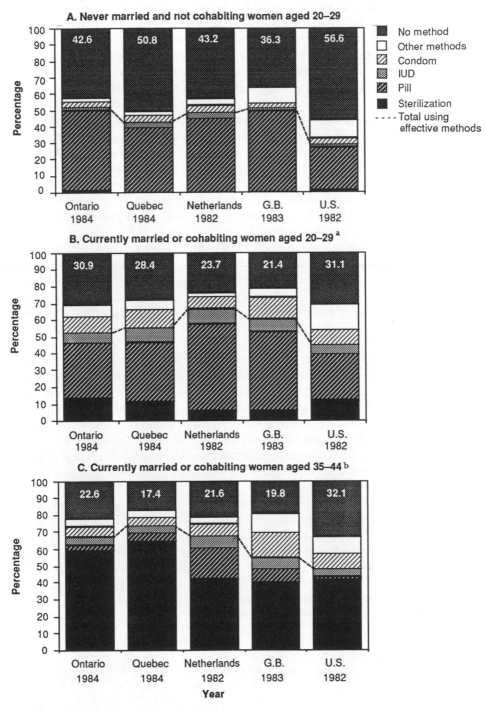

A. Never married and not cohabiting women aged 20–29

No method
Other methods
Condom
IUD
Pill
Sterilization
- - - - Total using effective methods

B. Currently married or cohabiting women aged 20–29 [a]

C. Currently married or cohabiting women aged 35–44 [b]

[a] For Great Britain, women aged 18–29.
[b] For the Netherlands, women aged 35–37; for Great Britain, women of all marital statuses.

(69 percent and 45 percent, respectively; see table 4.5 and figure 4.9B). Overall use approaches 80 percent in Britain, and as many as 66 percent of Dutch women rely on one of the three most effective methods. The proportions of married or cohabiting women aged 20–29 who rely on oral contraceptives (ranging from 28 percent in the United States to 52 percent in the Netherlands) do not differ greatly from those for never married women except in Ontario, where the percentage is actually considerably lower. Moderate proportions of women living in a sexual union use the IUD. As many as 14 percent of couples where the female partner is in her twenties have already opted for sterilization in Ontario, as have 12 percent in the United States and 11 percent in Quebec. Early sterilization is not so common in the Netherlands and Britain. Substantial condom use occurs in all of the study areas, especially in Britain, but use of other less effective methods is significant only in the United States.

Finally, among married or cohabiting women in the later stages of reproductive life, close to 80 percent use contraceptives everywhere except in the United States, where the figure is 67 percent (table 4.5 and figure 4.9C). The large proportion of U.S. women reporting non-contraceptive sterilization is concentrated among nonusers in this group. Because of greater reliance on the condom and other less effective methods, combined use of the highly effective methods is relatively low in Great Britain as well as in the United States. Very few older women continue to use the pill in the United States (2 percent), and this method is prominent at older ages only in the Netherlands (18 percent). The IUD tends everywhere to be somewhat less popular among older women than among younger women living with a partner. About 40 percent of all couples aged 35–44 rely on sterilization in the Netherlands,[1] Great Britain, and the United States, and this proportion reaches approximately 60 percent in the two Canadian provinces.

The association between income and contraceptive use among currently married women varies in many respects among the three countries for which measures of income are available (table 4.6). There is no clear pattern relating income to use of the most effective methods as a group, although sterilization is often more prevalent among low-income women than among high-income women. In general, married women who are better off rely more on ineffective methods than those who are less well off. There is a strong positive association between income and condom use in Great Britain.

1. A 1985 survey in the Netherlands indicates that there was a small decline in the proportion of couples protected by sterilization after 1982, probably reflecting the trend toward later childbearing rather than a decline in the proportion of couples who will eventually choose contraceptive sterilization (van de Giessen 1987, table 1).

Table 4.6 *Percentages of currently married women practicing contraception, by age and income*

Area and use category	Younger ages			Older ages		
	Lowest income group	Lower income half	Upper income half	Lowest income group	Lower income half	Upper income half
Netherlands, 1982						
Effective methods	64	64	71	70	68	70
Less effective methods	8	10	10	9	11	11
Any method	72	74	81	79	78	82
Sterilization	8	6	4	32	31	37
Pill	47	49	58	29	25	23
IUD	10	9	9	9	12	10
Condom	6	7	7	5	7	8
Other methods	2	3	3	4	4	4
Great Britain, 1983						
Effective methods	61	62	57	64	61	57
Less effective methods	14	15	25	21	26	29
Any method	75	77	82	85	87	86
Sterilization	7	7	5	46	44	34
Pill	45	46	48	11	11	14
IUD	9	9	5	7	7	8
Condom	11	10	18	12	15	18
Other methods	4	5	6	10	11	10
United States, 1982						
Effective methods	53	48	43	41	47	48
Less effective methods	16	22	26	18	21	18
Any method	69	70	69	59	68	67
Sterilization	23	22	17	38	42	42
Pill	24	21	21	1	2	2
IUD	6	6	5	2	3	5
Condom	7	9	11	7	9	9
Other methods	10	13	15	10	12	9

The comparisons by education give a somewhat different view of the relationship between contraceptive use and socioeconomic status and one that lends itself a little more easily to generalization (table 4.7). Among younger married women, use of effective methods is strongly and negatively linked, and use of less effective methods is strongly and positively linked, with education in Ontario, Quebec, and the United States. In the Netherlands and Great Britain, both of these associations are weaker and usually positive. Overall contraceptive use is somewhat higher among younger women with more education than among those with less education in the Netherlands, Great Britain, and the United States. At older ages, differentials by education in the use of effective methods, less effective methods, and any method all suggest greater use among more educated women. They are marked only with respect to effective methods (and any method) in Quebec, as well as less ef-

Table 4.7 *Percentages of currently married women practicing contraception, by age and education*

Area and use category	Younger ages		Older ages	
	Less educated	*Better educated*	*Less educated*	*Better educated*
Ontario, 1984				
Effective methods	60	50	68	66
Less effective methods	13	24	7	17
Any method	73	74	75	83
Sterilization	30	16	60	56
Pill	23	23	3	5
IUD	7	12	5	6
Condom	7	15	4	10
Other methods	6	9	3	7
Quebec, 1984				
Effective methods	62	54	71	78
Less effective methods	11	21	9	11
Any method	73	75	80	89
Sterilization	28	10	63	67
Pill	27	30	5	4
IUD	7	14	3	7
Condom	7	13	5	6
Other methods	4	8	4	6
Netherlands, 1982				
Effective methods	66	67	68	67
Less effective methods	8	11	10	13
Any method	74	78	78	80
Sterilization	8	3	36	29
Pill	49	54	24	23
IUD	8	10	8	15
Condom	6	9	7	9
Other methods	3	3	4	4
Great Britain, 1983				
Effective methods	59	62	59	59
Less effective methods	17	20	27	27
Any method	76	82	86	86
Sterilization	8	5	42	34
Pill	43	51	11	16
IUD	8	7	7	9
Condom	12	14	16	17
Other methods	5	6	11	10
United States, 1982				
Effective methods	50	39	46	51
Less effective methods	18	33	16	24
Any method	68	72	62	75
Sterilization	22	16	41	43
Pill	22	19	2	2
IUD	6	5	3	6
Condom	8	13	7	12
Other methods	10	20	9	11

fective methods (and any method) in Ontario and especially the United States.

Sterilization is much more commonly relied on by less educated than by more educated women. This negative association is consistent at the younger ages, where the contrast is very sharp in both Canadian provinces and only a little less so in the United States. It persists at older ages except in Quebec and the United States. Most of the other associations of any consequence for individual methods are positive, although the differential in condom use by income that was evident for Great Britain does not emerge here.

SUMMARY COMPARISON OF THE FIVE AREAS

The Netherlands. Fertility was the lowest of the five study areas until 1983, when Quebec's total fertility rate dropped slightly below that of the Netherlands. Childbearing below age twenty-five is less common than elsewhere. (Above age thirty, the age-specific fertility rates of all the study areas are similar.) The Dutch have the lowest total abortion rate of any of the five areas, hardly one-quarter of the recent level in the United States. Like the other countries, the incidence of abortion peaks in the Netherlands at ages 20–24, but the age-specific rates are much lower than elsewhere at all ages below thirty-five. Hence the total pregnancy rate is relatively low, with especially low age-specific pregnancy rates up to age twenty-five.

A far smaller proportion of births is unplanned (1982) than in the other countries, particularly among young women. There are only minor differences among the countries with respect to the level of planned pregnancy. However, the Dutch unplanned fertility and unplanned pregnancy rates are much the lowest in the group. All the comparisons suggest a consistent negative association between socioeconomic status and the proportions of births that are unplanned and unwanted in all five study areas.

Overall use of the three most effective methods of contraception is quite similar in the Netherlands (1982), Quebec (1984), Great Britain (1983), and Ontario (1984), and considerably higher than in the United States (1982). The pill is widely used in the Netherlands. Young married women of higher socioeconomic status are more likely than those of lower status to use one of the three highly effective methods, especially the pill; no consistent pattern emerges among older married women.

Quebec. The total fertility rate was relatively high in the late 1970s, but it dropped rapidly to become the lowest in this group by 1984. In

1982, the age-specific rates up to age twenty-five were lower than anywhere else except the Netherlands. Quebec has also had the second lowest total abortion and total pregnancy rates in recent years. Young women have had fewer abortions and fewer pregnancies than in Great Britain, Ontario, or the United States.

The proportion of births reported as unplanned is higher (1984) than in either Great Britain (1976) or the Netherlands (1982). The total unplanned fertility rate and unplanned pregnancy rate are both higher than those of the Netherlands but lower than those of Great Britain, as well as those of Ontario and the United States.

Contraceptive sterilization, which is quite widespread even among married women in their twenties, is more prevalent among married women aged 35–44 than in any other area. Among younger married women, education is strongly negatively associated with use of sterilization, while the association tends to be positive for sterilization among older married women, and for the pill and the IUD at all ages.

Great Britain. The total fertility rate has fluctuated recently but has tended to be among the higher ones in the group. In 1982, childbearing was more common among women younger than twenty-five than in any other area except the United States. The total abortion rate has been lower than in Ontario or the United States, however, with the greatest differences in the age-specific rates occurring below age thirty. Total pregnancy rate and age-specific pregnancy rates are similar in Great Britain and Ontario.

The proportion of births that is unplanned is lower (1976) than in any other country except the Netherlands (1982). The unplanned fertility and pregnancy rates fall around the middle of the range for the five areas.

Among older married women, the three most effective methods of contraception are used much less often than in the Netherlands and the two Canadian provinces and not much more than in the United States (1983). The pill is the most extensively used method of contraception. Among married women, use of the condom is exceptionally widespread. No clear pattern of socioeconomic differentials in the use of effective methods appears, although pill use is generally positively related to status.

Ontario. Here the total fertility rate fell after 1975, and by 1982 it was intermediate among the five areas. The age-specific fertility rates for women 15–19 and 20–24 (1982) are only slightly higher than those for Quebec. The total abortion rate is higher than Great Britain's, but very much lower than the United States', and the age-specific rates follow a similar pattern, with the Ontario rates exceeding those of

Great Britain by a larger amount among women aged less than twenty-five. Although abortion represents a larger component of the pregnancy rate than in Great Britain, the total pregnancy rate and the age-specific rates are nearly the same. The proportions of all births that are unplanned and unwanted are higher (1984) than in any other study area except the United States (1982), and the total unplanned fertility and pregnancy rates are likewise second only to the United States.

Sterilization is the most prominent method of contraception, and a good many couples turn to this option before the female partner reaches age thirty (1984). Pill use is also very high among younger unmarried women. Like Quebec, sterilization is far more likely to occur early among married women with less education.

The United States. In the early 1980s, due entirely to high birth rates below age twenty-five, the total fertility rate was the highest of the five areas. The total abortion rate has also been very much higher than elsewhere, with marked differences at all ages up to forty. Hence, the total pregnancy rate exceeds the others by a considerable amount, and differences are largely confined to women under age twenty-five.

More than one-third of all births are unplanned, and one out of ten is unwanted (1982). These proportions are higher than for any other area. The unplanned fertility and pregnancy rates also exceed those of the other countries.

Fewer women use one of the three highly effective methods of contraception than elsewhere (1982). The contrast is especially marked among never married women in their twenties. Women use the pill considerably less overall than in either the Netherlands or Great Britain. Although sterilization is almost as common among young married women as in Ontario and Quebec, the proportion sterilized at older ages is much lower. Use of sterilization is negatively related to socioeconomic status among younger married women.

5

United States

Overall Health System

The U.S. health care system is based on private physicians, the majority of whom are specialists. Patients usually pay the fee the physician sets for services, and if they are covered by private health insurance, they obtain reimbursement themselves. By offering clinics as alternate sources of care and providing coverage for health-care costs for some segments of the population, government has tried to help those who are unable to obtain private care either because they cannot afford it or because private doctors are not available to them.

Provision of care. About three-quarters of the population rely on an office-based private physician or a private clinic as their regular source of medical care. Others depend on hospital outpatient departments, emergency rooms, or public clinics (15 percent), or have no regular source of care (11 percent). A person's ability to consult a private physician varies according to his or her ability to pay. Among those who do not have private insurance, only six in ten go to a doctor as their regular source of medical care (calculated from Aday and Anderson 1984, tables 2 and 3).

About 174 private physicians work in patient care per 100,000 population (Roback et al. 1985, 36). The availability of doctors varies by state from 106–07 per 100,000 in Idaho and Mississippi to 242–47 in Maryland, Massachusetts, and New York (NCHS 1986, 160–61). Non-metropolitan areas of the country (where one-quarter of the people

78

live) are less well served than metropolitan areas. There physicians per 100,000 number only 60 percent of those in metropolitan areas (Roback et al. 1985, 28, 113–16, 274).

Most U.S. physicians are men (83 percent in 1983) and aged thirty-five or older (74 percent). General and family practitioners are more likely to be men (90 percent) than are obstetrician-gynecologists (84 percent). Women are much more common among the youngest physicians. Twenty-two percent of physicians under age thirty-five and one-third of the obstetrician-gynecologists under age thirty-five are women (Roback et al. 1985, 49, 51).

Most U.S. physicians are specialists. Only 16 percent are general or family practitioners, and only one-third of all office visits in 1985 were to general or family practitioners. Seven percent of doctors are obstetrician-gynecologists (NCHS 1986, 163). Specialists are less likely than general and family practitioners to locate their practices in nonmetropolitan areas. General and family practitioners represent one-third of all private office-based physicians in nonmetropolitan areas, compared to one-seventh in metropolitan areas of the country (Roback et al. 1985, 28).

Patients have direct access to specialists as well as to general and family practitioners, and, rather than one family physician, as in many other countries, many Americans see a number of specialists for treatment of different conditions. This means that people often see only the physician they need at that time for a particular service and either seek another doctor themselves or request referral to one when they need other care. It is not uncommon for a physician to be asked to treat a specific problem while knowing nothing more of the patient's medical history than what the patient has reported. When a sample of adults was asked what influenced their choice of physician for nonemergency office visits, the most common response was that this physician was the source normally used for nearly all medical care. Yet, people cited this reason for only 44 percent of all visits. For 29 percent of visits, the physician was chosen because the patient thought he or she was especially skillful at treating a specific condition. Fourteen percent of the respondents said another doctor referred them. Other less frequently cited reasons for choice of physician included convenience of the doctor's location, referral by friends or relatives, and insurance requirements. Respondents could give more than one reason; on the average they gave 1.3 reasons for their choice (Ries 1987, 30).

Because access to private physicians is based on paying for service, those who cannot afford the costs have historically had to depend on doctors to forgo some or all of the fee (out of goodwill or inability to collect it) or go without care from a private physician. Some people have not been able to get medical care even if they could have afforded it because they live where private physicians do not choose to practice. These are usually economically depressed inner-city areas or sparsely populated and generally poor rural ones.

In the early decades of this century public efforts directed at setting up alternatives to private physicians usually took the form of clinics and community health departments for the poor (Miller and Moos 1981). In the mid-1960s, public insurance systems were set up for the elderly (Medicare) and those on welfare or with very low income (Medicaid). Although Medicaid is aimed at providing access to private physicians, many of those covered by it still do not have such access, and they often turn to public clinics for their health care services. Fifteen percent of all U.S. citizens rely on clinics, public hospitals, or other publicly funded facilities for their regular medical care, including 20 percent of those with no health insurance and 28 percent of those covered by Medicare or Medicaid. Many who have no regular source of care (22 percent of those with no insurance have no regular source) also rely on such public sources when they need care (Aday and Anderson 1984).

The few federally run hospitals in the country are for special populations: primarily armed forces personnel, veterans, and Native Americans. About a quarter of the nonfederal, short-term general hospitals are run by state or local governments, six in ten are nonprofit, nongovernmental hospitals, and the rest are for-profit facilities (U.S. Bureau of the Census 1986, 89). Fifty-four percent of the 5,300 short-term general hospitals in the United States have organized outpatient departments where patients can receive ambulatory care for specific problems, but usually not general or comprehensive health care (AHA 1986, 186).

Each state has a state health agency responsible for public health. Besides environmental activities (like restaurant inspections and rabies control), and health education and immunizations, most state health agencies oversee the provision of some personal health services like family planning, prenatal care, and well-baby care. In five states, the state health agency provides health services at the local level. In the other forty-five approximately 2,000 to 3,000 local county or city health departments provide direct community health services. These often include the operation of one or more clinics, and many larger health departments offer extensive services that include such services as prenatal care and testing and treatment for sexually transmitted diseases (AGI 1984a, 44–45; ASTHO Foundation 1985; Public Health Foundation 1986).

In addition to health-department clinics, approximately 560 separately administered community and migrant health centers across the country extend a broad range of primary-care services to poor people in areas where there are not enough private physicians. They provide basic primary medical care—physician services, preventive health services, and dental care—as well as such ancillary services as laboratory tests, X-rays, and pharmacies.

Payment for health care. When someone visits a private doctor, he or she usually pays for the service at the end of the visit or sends payment by mail shortly afterward. Some physicians now accept credit-card payments as well. Patients must obtain reimbursement from their insurance company if they are covered for the service. Some weeks normally elapse before the patient receives the insurance reimbursement. The individual physician or physician group has the choice of accepting payment directly from an insurance company and taking the insurance reimbursement as full or partial payment for the fee. Most are reluctant to do so because of the time it takes to be paid and because the reimbursement usually does not cover the full fee. Unless the medical provider accepts the insurance reimbursement as full payment, the patient has to pay any amount that insurance does not cover.

Many physicians will not accept patients with public insurance through the Medicaid program primarily because the reimbursement levels are usually lower than the physician fees, and the doctor may not ask the patient to make up the difference. The physician is also responsible for completing the extensive paperwork needed to claim reimbursement, and the claims can be denied, for instance, because a patient has already made the maximum number of medical visits allowed in a particular state; or payment can be long delayed or never come if the state has already exhausted the funds budgeted for Medicaid.

Hospital bills, which most female sterilization procedures incur, are usually handled differently because they involve larger sums of money, and people are more likely to be insured for hospital care than for routine physician care. Although the patient is still ultimately responsible, hospitals usually claim reimbursement directly from the patient's health insurance company and bill the patient later for any uncovered costs. Before admission to a hospital, patients must give proof of insurance or, if they have none, document how they will pay their bills. Although recently passed legislation requires hospitals to admit poor, uninsured patients whose lives are in danger and women in active labor, nonpublic hospitals can and do refuse admittance to patients with non-life-threatening conditions who need care but cannot pay.

Publicly funded clinics, which mainly provide services to those who cannot afford private physicians, offer free services or charge a fee based on the patient's income. If a patient has Medicaid coverage, that program is generally billed for the services rendered.

The cost of personal health care (including physicians, hospitals, dentists, and drugs and supplies, but excluding long-term nursing-home care) averaged $1,361 per person in the United States in 1985. Six in every ten health-care dollars came from private funds—26 percent ($361 per capita) came from direct patient payments, and private insurance paid 34 percent—and four in ten came from government funds, primarily health-care coverage for those over age sixty-five and for the military or veterans. Medicaid coverage for the poor accounted for 7 percent of the total.

Expenditures for physician care alone averaged $335 per person in the United States in 1985. Seven of every ten dollars spent for this came from private funds—26 percent was paid directly by patients and 45 percent by private insurance. The government insurance program for the elderly (Medicare) paid 21 percent, and eight percent came from other government funds like Medicaid. Hospital expenditures are less likely to be paid by the patient directly (9 percent) or by private insurance (36 percent) and more likely to be paid by such funds as Medicare and Medicaid (Waldo, Levit, and Lazenby 1986).

People in the United States are quite conscious of the costs of medical care and generally feel they are too high. Medical-care expenditures account for 11 percent of the gross national product (Arnett et al. 1985, 8). When asked to identify the main problem facing health care and medicine today, 68 percent of adults polled in 1984 said cost. Only 12 percent said quality and 5 percent access (Shapiro and Young 1986, 427).

In recent years, the health-care system in the United States has been in considerable flux. Legal pressures and malpractice insurance costs have affected the ways doctors practice medicine, and those paying for health insurance have tried to control costs. If a medical-care provider harms someone, that person's primary recourse for obtaining compensation for additional expenses, disability, or "pain and suffering" is through the courts. The frequency of suits has been seen as causing many physicians and other health professionals to practice "defensive medicine," sometimes ordering more tests or more intensive care than may be necessary to bolster their defense against a possible malpractice claim. The litigious climate is one factor leading to a general crisis in the insurance industry in the United States. One result has been steep increases in what physicians must pay for malpractice insurance, costs that they pass on to their patients in the form of higher fees. Obstetrician-gynecologists are charged some of the highest malpractice fees, ranging in 1987 from less than $20,000 to more than $100,000, depending on the state and the insurance company (ACOG 1987a).

Insurance companies, businesses with their own health plans, and federal and state governments that provide health insurance for some groups (particularly the poor or the elderly) have exerted strong pressure to limit the costs of health care. Pressure has taken forms like encouraging use of health-care providers other than private physicians (for example, health-maintenance organizations [HMOs]), limits on how much insurers will pay for specific services, and limits on the services they will cover.

Even though people feel that medical care costs too much, most expect that they will be able to receive all the care they need without limitation. Attempts to lower costs by reducing reimbursements and by reducing the amounts of care given have generally not been matched by consumers' willingness to accept less care. Both government (which manages Medicaid and Medicare) and employers are urging patients to become more informed users of medical care and are trying to place more of the costs of care and insurance on the consumers directly instead of paying them through third-party insurance plans.

Insurance coverage. A large majority of Americans have private health insurance (AGI 1987). In 1984, 76 percent of civilians under age sixty-five had private insurance (NCHS 1986, 202). Ninety-two percent of those sixty-five and over are covered for health care under the federal government's Medicare plan (U.S. Bureau of the Census 1986, 18, 89).

Nine out of ten people covered by insurance are in group plans provided through employment. Of these, 49 percent must pay part or all of their health insurance costs (AGI 1987). For most of the others, the employer or the union pays all insurance costs (U.S. Bureau of the Census 1986, 89). Workers in small firms and part-time workers are less likely to be offered insurance coverage and are more likely to be asked to pay a higher proportion of the charges. Some employers do not offer health insurance at all.

For those who pay part of employment-related insurance or purchase their own insurance, the cost is often considerable. People with work-related group plans pay an average of $490 annually for family coverage and $156 for individual coverage. The cost of insurance for those who do not have employment-related coverage averages $2,400 (Gold 1987). Most people—71 percent of those polled in 1982—believe that the price of health insurance is getting too high for the average family to afford (Shapiro and Young 1986, 425).

How much and what kinds of health care insurance covers varies from one plan to another. Materials describing insurance coverage are often written in unfamiliar technical language, and many people do not have a clear idea of exactly what their plans cover. While almost all private policies cover surgery, hospital care and diagnosis, and treatment of illness, more than 80 percent do not include office visits or such services as contraception (HIAA 1986, 12).

Health insurance usually covers a family, that is, spouse and children into their late teens or early twenties, depending on whether they are in school or not. The policyholder is the person who deals with the insurance company for all family members and must sign an application for any reimbursements.

Most insurance policies require that each person covered pay some amount, called a deductible (often $100 to $150 each year), of covered medical bills. The insurance company reimburses some portion, often about 80 percent, of any costs above that amount for covered care during the year. The policyholder must pay the full charges for any noncovered medical care.

Medicaid is a joint federal and state government program under which states reimburse health-care providers that participate in the Medicaid program for certain services individuals with a Medicaid identification card receive from them. The states in turn are reimbursed by the federal government for part of those costs, ranging from 50 to 78 percent of the states' expenditures (Gold and Kenney 1985, 107–08). The federal government reimburses 90 percent of state expenditures for contraceptive services.

Medicaid is viewed as part of the welfare system rather than as a health program. People on welfare are the main group eligible for it, and because the welfare system focuses on providing assistance to very poor unmarried mothers and their children, Medicaid does not cover all the poor. States determine the criteria for welfare eligibility, which vary between and sometimes within states. For example, in 1985 only California set the income criterion for eligibility above (by three percent) the federal poverty level of $10,850 annual income for a family of four, while almost one-half of states set public assistance cutoffs at less than half the poverty level (AGI 1987).

To limit costs for welfare and for Medicaid, states—and especially the federal government—have incentives to limit the number of people who are eligible. In addition, Medicaid reimbursement levels are often set below the health-care provider's normal charges. If a physician or other provider serves a woman whose eligibility has lapsed or provides a service that is not covered (some states limit the total number of covered visits per year, for example), the provider is not reimbursed. Medicaid forms often entail extensive paperwork, especially if a woman's eligibility or service coverage is challenged. Reimbursements come some time after the services have been rendered, and some states simply stop paying when they have exhausted the funds set aside for Medicaid. Initially the health-care providers bear the burden of care for which they are not paid in full or at all. Many, especially private physicians whose care Medicaid is supposed to make possible, choose not to accept Medicaid patients. These people must then turn to other sources, primarily public clinics, or forgo care.

Most women (73 percent) in the reproductive ages 15–44 are covered by private insurance, and 10 percent by public sources (primarily Medicaid), but 17 percent have no health-care coverage (Gold and Kenney 1985, 103; Singh 1985). Private insurance coverage is higher among married women (84 percent, versus 62 percent of the unmarried), older women (about 80 percent of those thirty and above compared to less than 66 percent of those under age twenty-five) and women with higher family incomes (91 percent of those with incomes at or above 250 percent of the poverty level, but only 26 percent of those below 100 percent of poverty) (Singh 1985). Because most private insurance is linked to employment, the proportion of women covered is highest among couples where both partners work, followed by women who are not employed but married to a man who is, and by employed single women; it is lowest among unemployed single women (Singh 1985). Among women with family incomes below the federal poverty standard, who represent 17 percent of all women of reproductive age, four in ten depend on Medicaid for access to medical care. One in ten women with slightly higher incomes (100–49 percent of poverty) is covered by Medicaid. Medicaid coverage is more common (14 percent) among those who are unmarried.

One in six women of reproductive age has no health insurance. This generally is because the woman is not married to someone working or does not work herself, or because the employer does not offer health-care coverage. Sometimes the expense of contributing toward an employer's plan for oneself and/or for one's dependents or of coverage through an individual plan, is unaffordable. Also, as discussed above, Medicaid eligibility is limited almost entirely to those on welfare. About one in four unmarried women and women under age twenty-five have no coverage for health care, and one in three of those under 150 percent of poverty level has none.

Family Planning Services
The delivery pattern for family planning services in the United States reflects the way the general health-care system is organized as well as some differences specific to family planning. Private doctors offer most but not all reproductive health services in the United States. Seven in ten women who made a medical family planning visit between 1979 and 1982 went to private physicians, primarily general and family practitioners and obstetrician-gynecologists (Orr and Forrest 1985). Women with higher incomes are more likely than poorer ones to see a

private physician for family planning: 77 percent of women with family incomes over 150 percent of the federal poverty standard who made a family planning visit went to a private physician, compared with 53 percent of lower-income women. Teenagers are less likely to visit a private physician for family planning (49 percent) than are women aged twenty or older (73 percent) (Forrest 1987a). Almost all tubal sterilizations and vasectomies are performed by private physicians (Forrest and Henshaw 1983, 164).

Access to private physicians for family planning services depends not simply on whether the woman or man can afford the charges, but also on whether the doctor will provide the services. Eighty-four percent of general and family practitioners provide reversible contraception, but only one-third offer infertility or obstetrical care, and one-quarter or fewer perform male or female sterilization. For these services, many women and men either go directly to an obstetrician-gynecologist, urologist, or general surgeon, or they are referred by another physician. Almost all obstetrician-gynecologists provide all contraceptive services as well as obstetric care (Orr and Forrest 1985, 64). The provider of reproductive health services is usually not the physician one sees for general health care. Often a woman's first visit on her own to a physician is to an obstetrician-gynecologist to obtain a prescription for contraceptives (Lieblum and Burnhill 1987).

The first family planning clinics were developed in a few areas of the country in the 1920s by private organizations such as the Planned Parenthood Federation of America (PPFA) to provide women with contraceptive information and diaphragms at a time when physicians would not do so. As private physicians began to offer contraceptive advice and services, these private clinics came to serve mainly poor women who could not obtain contraceptives from public health clinics because they did not offer these services.

A number of factors came together in the late 1960s to bring about federal funding of family planning services in both public and private clinics. These included the introduction of oral contraceptives; heightened concerns about poverty and a belief that it could be greatly reduced if not eliminated in a "War on Poverty"; fear of the "population bomb"; and social science data indicating that poor women wanted to have smaller families but were less apt than higher-income women to use contraceptives. Federal funds went not only to the small number of existing clinics, but also were used to introduce family planning services in public health clinics and to start up new facilities.

As in other public health efforts, the initial goal of publicly supported family planning services was to serve poor women who could not afford to see private physicians. As time went on, it became clear that many unmarried and adolescent women were using the clinics because they wanted confidential services that they believed a private doctor would not provide. The federal mandate was eventually broadened to include services not only to women who need financially subsidized services, but also to women, especially adolescents, who need an alternative to private physician care.

Clinics are generally seen as complementary to private physicians rather than in competition with them. Physicians have little reason to want to serve clinic patients, who would not be able to pay full fees for service. Many clinics, such as those run by the private Planned Parenthood organizations, employ private physicians as part-time staff in their clinics. A woman who cannot pay for services in a private physician's office may be referred to a clinic, but otherwise such referrals are seldom made. Because family planning clinic services are usually limited to fairly routine primary care, however, patients with special problems are referred from clinics to other providers, often to private physicians.

Approximately 53,000 general and family practitioners in the United States provide office-based patient care. Of these an estimated 45,000 provide reversible contraceptive services, 10,000 perform female sterilization, and 14,000 do vasectomies. About 23,000 obstetrician-gynecologists provide reversible and permanent contraceptives to women. In addition, 6,000 general surgeons perform tubal ligations. Vasectomies are available from 12,000 general surgeons and 6,000 urologists (AGI 1984c, 48, 71; NCHS 1986, 163; Orr and Forrest 1985, 64–65). Contraceptive services are provided at 5,100 family planning clinics (Torres and Forrest 1985). There are probably more than 58,000 pharmacies in communities across the country where prescription supplies and nonprescription methods can be obtained (AHA 1986, 183; NABP 1987).

Among all women in 1982 who relied on contraceptive sterilization or the IUD and had made a medical family planning visit in the last three years, or who were using another reversible contraceptive method, 63 percent had last visited a physician (21 percent visited a general or family practitioner or general surgeon and 42 percent an obstetrician-gynecologist or urologist), 25 percent a clinic, and 12 percent some other nonmedical source such as a pharmacy (AGI 1984c; Forrest 1987a).

Policies. In the United States, it is generally up to the medical provider to decide what services to offer. Some general and family practitioners offer no contraceptive services. Those clinics that receive federal support for their contraceptive services are free to offer other services as long as other funds are used. The federal administration has tried, to date unsuccessfully, to withhold family planning funding from any organizations that also provide abortion. Recently it has proposed barring organizations that counsel or make referrals regarding abortion from receiving family planning funds (*Washington Memo* 1988a).

Private physicians are permitted to set conditions for rendering their services, such as requiring minors to obtain parental consent before they will prescribe contraceptives or requiring spouse consent for sterilization. Historically clinics have been less likely to set conditions for their services and have often led the way in providing care under less restrictive conditions. The federal administration has tried to require parental notification or consent for minors obtaining contraceptives in family planning clinics (Kenney, Forrest, and Torres 1982), but Congress has not approved such restrictions, and an attempt to impose them by administrative regulation was overruled by the courts in 1983 (*Washington Memo* 1988b).

The availability of a particular contraceptive depends not only on whether a provider will offer it but also on approval from the U.S. Food and Drug Administration (FDA) and private industry's willingness to market it. For example, no injectable is approved for contraceptive use in the United States. FDA consideration of the Depo-Provera injectable steroid generated questions about the applicability of some negative animal research findings and considerable pressure against its approval from feminist and other consumer groups. No organization has even attempted to gain approval of the morning-after pill, used in many other countries, presumably because of concern over the threat of boycotts organized by antiabortion groups.

Even after a drug or device receives FDA approval, the FDA continues to review and approve patient package inserts and claims made for the method. For instance, the FDA must approve the package inserts that accompany oral contraceptives and only recently allowed manufacturers to include claims regarding prevention of AIDS on condom packages. Oral contraceptives, intrauterine devices, and diaphragms must be obtained by prescription from or insertion by a physician or by a nurse-practitioner supervised by a physician. Condoms and spermicides—for example, foams, jellies, and the contraceptive sponge—are available without prescription.

Even if a method is approved by the FDA it will be available to U.S. women only if a company markets it. The costs are set by the manufacturer or marketer. In 1985 and 1986, companies stopped marketing nonmedicated intrauterine devices in the United States primarily because of the high costs of defending lawsuits brought in the wake of the much-publicized dangers of a device already removed from the market (the Dalkon Shield), and because they could not obtain product liability insurance at a time of crisis in the insurance industry (Forrest 1986). From the beginning of 1986 to mid-1988, while copper-bearing IUDs were not being sold in the United States, only a hormonal IUD (the Progestasert) with a one-year life span could be purchased. Women had to choose other methods or go out of the country, to Canada, for example, to obtain IUDs. (A new copper-bearing IUD, the TCu380A, or ParaGard, became available in mid-1988. The cervical cap was also approved by the FDA in 1988 and began to be marketed in late fall 1988.) Prices of contraceptives tend to be high in the United States, partly because companies must pay high fees for product liability insurance or, more generally, put aside money to cover potential product liability costs.

Abortion policy and services. Abortion services in the United States are usually provided outside the regular system of health-care and reproductive health services. Abortion was made legal in a few states in 1970 and throughout the nation in 1973 by the Supreme Court. The Supreme Court decisions prohibit states from restricting abortion in the first trimester and allow states to regulate abortion to assure its safety in the second trimester and prohibit it, except to save the pregnant woman's life or health, after viability. Many private physicians and hospitals, however, will not provide abortions. In 1983, only 3 percent of office-based general and family practitioners and general surgeons and 42 percent of obstetrician-gynecologists performed abortions (Orr and Forrest 1985, 64). As a result, special clinics have been established for abortions. At present, although no more than 31 percent of abortion providers are nonhospital clinics, they provide 83 percent of all induced abortions (Henshaw, Forrest, and Van Vort 1987, 67). Most abortion clinics provide contraceptives as part of their postabortion services.

Although a majority of Americans believe abortion should remain legally available, there is very vocal opposition to abortion and abortion services ("Average of 63% Approve of Legal Abortions" 1987). Almost half of all abortion providers and more than eight in ten large abortion clinics, which provide the majority of all abortions in the country, report that they have been subject to one or more types of antiabortion violence or harassment, some of which has been illegal (Forrest and Henshaw 1987, 9).

Because of the geographic concentration of abortion providers and their limits on service at certain gestational stages, women often must find and travel to one outside their home areas. In 1985, 98 percent of abortion providers were located in urban areas (where three-quarters of the U.S. population live). Forty-three percent of abortion providers offer services after twelve weeks' gestation; about 90 percent of women have their abortions at twelve weeks' gestation or earlier (Henshaw 1987; Henshaw, Forrest, and Van Vort 1987).

Current administrative regulations for federally funded family planning clinics require that pregnant women be offered information about all their options, including having the baby and parenting, having the baby adopted, and having an abortion. If a woman wants a referral for abortion, the clinic must give her names and addresses of abortion providers. In fall 1987, the federal administration proposed to reverse this policy and to prohibit federally supported family planning clinics from discussing abortion with patients or giving referrals for abortion but was prevented from doing so by federal court decisions which have now been appealed (*Washington Memo* 1988c). It is not clear whether current policies will be changed.

The Medicaid program is supposed to provide coverage for necessary medical care to indigent individuals. Legislation to bar abortion services from Medicaid funding was enacted in the 1970s, but was in litigation until 1980. Since then, federal Medicaid funds have been available only for abortions needed to save the life of the mother. Fourteen states and the District of Columbia continue to use state Medicaid funds to subsidize abortions, but in the majority of states women cannot receive free abortions through Medicaid (Gold 1987).

Target Groups for Family Planning
Private physicians primarily serve patients who can pay their fees. Family planning clinics, like other public health services, focus on groups who have difficulty getting services from private physicians. These are low-income women who cannot afford private services and adolescents who cannot afford physicians' fees or who are concerned about confidentiality. In some areas of the country, other special groups are also targeted, such as non-English-speaking immigrants, Native Americans, and rural residents. Usually these are also low-income groups.

PRIVATE PHYSICIANS

Nearly all private physicians who provide reversible contraceptive services prescribe oral contraceptives. Most who provide services will also fit a woman for a diaphragm and write a prescription for it. Those who do not fit diaphragms—perhaps because they see few patients who request this method—will instead refer the woman to another doctor, usually an obstetrician-gynecologist. Not all physicians, especially those who are not obstetrician-gynecologists, know how to or will insert IUDs. Many women who might wish to use the IUD must also be referred by their private physicians to some other provider.

For all medical contraceptive services, a prospective patient must first find a private physician willing to provide the service. This is relatively simple for reversible contraception, especially the pill, but is more difficult when a woman or her husband is ready for sterilization. The patient may be asked to satisfy certain conditions before receiving the service, usually including the patient's ability and willingness to pay the physician's fee.

Obstetrician-gynecologists and general and family practitioners are most likely to provide contraceptive services. About 68,000 physicians in these two specialities (84 percent) provide reversible contraceptives in the United States. Because there are many more general and family practitioners in the country than there are obstetrician-gynecologists, they account for two-thirds of those offering reversible contraception (Orr and Forrest 1985, 65). More than two-thirds of all reversible contraceptive patients visiting private physicians, however, are served by obstetrician-gynecologists, because these specialists see on average four times more contraceptive patients than general and family practitioners do (AGI 1984b, 9).

Private physicians who offer reversible contraceptives will generally serve any patient who can pay their fee, but only 73 percent of them will provide contraceptives to minors without parental consent. Three in 10 general and family practitioners and two in ten obstetrician-gynecologists who provide contraceptive services will serve minors only with parental consent (AGI 1984b, 80). In a community with few physicians (especially in nonmetropolitan areas, where there are few obstetrician-gynecologists) a minor may have difficulty obtaining confidential services.

If patients cannot pay the full fee, they often cannot get contraceptive services from a private physician even if they are covered by Medicaid. Fifty-six percent of physicians who provide reversible contraception accept Medicaid reimbursement, and only 17 percent will reduce their fees for patients who cannot pay the full amount.

Female sterilization is available from fewer physicians (approximately 38,000) than are reversible contraceptives. Six out of ten physicians who provide reversible contraceptive services also perform female sterilizations, almost all of which take place in a hospital either on an inpatient or outpatient basis. Among the 82 percent of general and family practitioners who do not perform female sterilizations, most refer women either to obstetrician-gynecologists (94 percent of whom provide tubal ligations) or to general surgeons (26 percent of whom do them). Obstetrician-gynecologists account for 58 percent of doctors providing female sterilizations and perform about 80 percent of all procedures (Orr and Forrest 1985, 64–65; Orr et al. 1985, 218).

Vasectomies are available from 26 percent of general and family practitioners, half the general surgeons, and 89 percent of urologists. Of the 32,000 physicians providing vasectomy services, four in ten are

general or family practitioners, and the same number are general
surgeons (Orr and Forrest 1985, 64–65). Urologists account for one-
fifth of providers but do almost one-half of all vasectomies. Sixty-four
percent of vasectomies are performed in the physician's office, and 28
percent are done in hospitals on an outpatient basis. Only 8 percent are
done in hospitals on an inpatient basis (Orr et al. 1985, 218).

Of those private doctors performing sterilizations, 83 percent set
one or more conditions for female sterilization, and 95 percent set
conditions for vasectomy. The most common is spouse's consent, required by half the doctors who perform tubal ligation and by eight in
ten of those who perform vasectomy. Other considerations include
minimum age or number of children, a waiting period, or that the man
or woman be an established patient. Only 12 percent of the private
physicians who do male or female sterilizations will reduce their fees
for patients who cannot afford to pay the full cost. Six in ten providers
will accept Medicaid for female sterilization, and half will accept it for
vasectomy (Orr and Forrest 1985, 67–68). Medicaid reimbursement
for sterilization covers only eligible individuals who are mentally competent and aged twenty-one or older who gave informed consent at
least 30 days, but not more than 180 days, before the sterilization,
except in the case of premature delivery (when consent must have been
given at least thirty days before the expected delivery date) or emergency abdominal surgery (when consent must have been given at least
seventy-two hours earlier). Consent may not be obtained when an
individual is in labor or is seeking to obtain or obtaining an abortion (42
CFR 1978).

Funding and Fees
Average fees for a woman's first visit to a doctor for contraceptives fall
between the average rates for a first office visit and for a history and
physical examination. In 1985, an initial contraceptive visit to a general
or family practitioner cost $39; a first visit to an obstetrician-gynecolo-
gist cost $66 (estimated from AGI 1984b, 82, D–15; and Kirchner 1986,
126, 130). The charge for a revisit for a continuing patient is generally
20 percent less for general and family practitioners and 40 percent less
for obstetrician-gynecologists (Kirchner 1986, 130). Charges generally
are higher in cities and suburbs than in rural areas and in the West and
are generally lowest in the Midwest (AGI 1984b, 82; Kirchner 1986,
128, 134). A national survey found that fees for first office visits ranged
from less than $15 to more than $100 for general practitioners and
from less than $25 to more than $100 for obstetrician-gynecologists
(Kirchner 1986, 130).

Medicaid reimbursements are usually much less than the physician's fee. In 1983, the average reimbursement for an initial contracep-

tive visit was 25 percent less than the average fee charged by a general or family practitioner; 40 percent of these physicians charged $10 to $61 more than their state Medicaid program would reimburse. The difference was even greater for obstetrician-gynecologists, whose Medicaid reimbursement was half their average fee; 83 percent charged from $20 to $116 more than Medicaid reimbursed. It is not surprising that physicians whose fees were so much higher than Medicaid reimbursement rates were significantly less likely to accept Medicaid patients (AGI 1984b, 82, 88–89).

In addition to the doctor's fee, contraceptive patients must pay for supplies. With one cycle of pills priced at $13 or more, the annual cost of pills is at least $170 (MEC 1988). The one IUD available in 1986 and 1987, the Progestasert (which must be reinserted annually) costs physicians $84, and the recently introduced ParaGard costs about $140; the amount that patients are charged for IUD insertion is not known but is probably higher.

In the short term, surgical sterilization costs much more than reversible methods. In 1983, physician and hospital charges for an inpatient or outpatient tubal ligation were around $1,300, and the fee for an office vasectomy averaged $240 (Orr et al. 1985, 219). But if this amount is amortized over a patient's remaining reproductive years, the price of sterilization is usually at least comparable to other methods.

Role of Private Physicians

Characteristics of clientele. Because access to private physicians is limited to those able to pay for services, or to those covered by Medicaid who can find a physician who will accept it, the majority of patients who rely on private physicians for family planning services are not poor (80 percent have annual incomes above 150 percent of the poverty level). White women, who are less likely than black and Hispanic women to be poor, are overrepresented among private physicians' family planning patients. Older women are more likely than younger ones to go to private doctors both because they are more likely to be able to afford it and because they are less likely to be concerned about confidentiality than younger women (Forrest 1987a).

Outreach. Private physicians can be characterized as passive health-care providers. Patients normally must seek them out, because few physicians advertise or actively try to obtain new patients in general or contraceptive patients in particular. Doctors' names, addresses, and phone numbers are listed in the classified sections of telephone books, usually by specialty. A few words describing their services are sometimes included, but contraceptive services are seldom mentioned. Only recently has it been considered ethical for private physicians to put paid advertisements in newspapers, and only a small minority of physicians advertise this way.

Many physicians put restrictions on the patients they will see; this information is generally not in telephone book listings or advertisements. To find out a doctor's policies and fees, a patient must either consult other patients or phone or visit the doctor's office. Some physicians who accept Medicaid reimbursements do mention this in their listings, however.

Contraceptive Services

Personnel. A private physician's office is usually staffed by a receptionist who makes appointments and collects information on medical history and insurance coverage of new patients. The receptionist usually gives the patient a bill for services at the end of the visit and accepts payment. A nurse usually records the patient's height, weight, and blood pressure. Traditionally, a nurse has been in the room when a male physician made a pelvic exam, but costs have made this practice less common. Nurses and receptionists are almost always female, and most physicians are male.

Schedule. Most physicians see patients in their office on weekdays. A survey of obstetrician-gynecologists in four cities in 1986 found that 32 percent see patients some weekday evenings and 13 percent have office hours on Saturdays (Silverman and Torres 1987).

Medical policies and procedures. Whether and how physicians provide contraceptives is influenced by professional standards and guidelines (such as those developed by the American College of Obstetricians and Gynecologists [ACOG]), by their own preferences and patient demands, and by concern over potential malpractice suits. Pelvic examinations (usually including a Pap smear) are normally required before a medical method is prescribed.

The ACOG (in a 1987 "Technical Bulletin") recommends that physicians give pill users the formulation containing the lowest dose of estrogen and progestogen consistent with the prevention of pregnancy and with continued use (ACOG 1987b, 4). The previous "Technical Bulletin" on oral contraceptives had recommended using "the lowest reliably effective dosage that is compatible with the needs of the individual patient." Based on data available at that time, however, it stated that "A 50 mcgm. dosage of estrogen in a combined oral contraceptive appears to be the minimum dose necessary for consistent protection from pregnancy" (ACOG 1976). Many women use pills with 35 or fewer micrograms of estrogen, but higher-dose pills are still used by a sizable number of women, especially older women who began pill use some time ago (Ory, Forrest, and Lincoln 1983, 47). In 1982, 44 percent of all oral contraceptive prescriptions dispensed through retail pharmacies and office-based physicians were for formulations with 35 micrograms of estrogen or less, 45 percent included 50 micrograms of estrogen and 11 percent, more than 50 micrograms. In 1986, 71 percent of new prescriptions were for formulations containing 35 micrograms of estrogen or less (Kennedy 1987). A recent ACOG "Technical Bulletin" identifies nonsmokers over forty and smokers over thirty-five as women at potentially higher risk of complications with the use of oral contraceptives and recommends annual blood tests and reassessments for these women. A recent survey of physicians who subscribe to a monthly newsletter about contraceptives (and who may be more liberal in their prescribing practices than other physicians) found that most prefer patients with no contraindications to stop oral contraceptive use no later than age forty, but almost one-fourth will prescribe pills up to age forty-five and nearly 10 percent will prescribe them to women fifty or older. Seventeen percent of physicians would not prescribe oral contraceptives to a sexually active fourteen-year-old who had had only one menstrual period (American Health Consultants, Inc. 1987).

Physicians give varying degrees of time and attention to counseling patients about possible side effects of the drugs they prescribe. The ACOG and the pharmaceutical companies produce informational materials for physicians to give to their pill patients. Information for the patient is included with each package of oral contraceptives.

The companies marketing intrauterine devices in the United States now require physicians to obtain documented informed consent on a form prepared by the company before they insert the device. The forms are specific about risk factors that should rule out a woman's using the device and about its possible side effects. The woman is asked not only to sign it but also to initial each section to verify that she has read and understood it. The heightened attention to the need for informing the patient adequately about her risks has undoubtedly made women more aware of potential side effects. The emphasis on being sure the woman knows what could go wrong also increases the time and cost of providing contraceptives and may add to a woman's fear about using a medical method.

Provider method preferences. The pill is the reversible method most commonly provided by private physicians. It is generally viewed as the most effective reversible method and as quite safe for suitable patients.

Private physicians generally consider sterilization to be the most appropriate method for couples who want no more children, especially for couples where the woman cannot use the pill.

Time spent with client. A private physician's income depends on how many patients he or she sees and what types of services are rendered. One study (Waitzkin 1985) of office visits to internists in the United States found that the appointments averaged 16.5 minutes, with most of the time spent in the physical examination. Doctors apparently believe they spend more time giving information to patients than they really do. One study found that although doctors spent an average of 1.3 minutes giving information to a patient, the physicians themselves thought that they spent an average of twelve minutes doing so.

Referral. About one in six general and family practitioners does not provide reversible contraceptive services. Sixty percent of these physicians refer patients, and 12 percent have never been asked for a referral, but the remaining 28 percent (who account for only 4 percent of all general and family practitioners) do not make referrals for contraceptive services. All those who make referrals will refer patients to another physician; 47 percent will also refer women to a clinic or hospital for services; 10 percent will refer them in another way, such as by providing a list of physicians (AGI 1984b, 21–22). Eighty-seven percent of physicians who do not perform female sterilizations and 94 percent of those who do not perform male sterilizations will provide referrals for patients wishing these procedures (Orr and Forrest 1985, 64).

Follow-up. There is seldom any follow-up of patients who do not make a return visit. Some physicians, however, do send patients reminders that they are due for a follow-up visit and ask them to call to make an appointment.

Counseling

Personnel. The physician generally does any counseling that he or she thinks is necessary directly with the patient. Sometimes the physician's nurse may answer questions over the phone.

Schedule. The patient is expected to bring up questions and issues for discussion with the physician before, during, or after the examination, depending on the office scheduling practices.

Content. Discussion with the physician usually covers alternative methods of contraception if the patient requests such information or if the physician does not approve of the method that the patient desires. Otherwise the discussion with the physician consists primarily of information about how to use the method for patients who have not used it before, its risks, and what side effects should trigger a call to the physician.

Time spent with client. As noted earlier, doctor visits are short and there is little time for counseling beyond brief discussion of potential problems. Part of the reason may be that U.S. physicians receive little training in counseling during their medical education.

Client's Overall Expenditure of Time
Patients are usually given a set time for their appointment and the receptionist will try to find out in advance what service is needed in order to know how much time to set aside for the visit. Because appointment times are estimated, and since physicians try to see as many patients as possible in the time available and therefore schedule little slack time, doctors are often delayed when a patient needs more time than has been planned or is late. Between forty-five and sixty minutes may be necessary in order to make a 15-minute physician visit.

Information and Literature
Physicians may have informational literature produced by pharmaceutical companies or the ACOG available for their contraceptive patients. Such booklets usually contain a description of how to use the method, what to do if pills are missed, what side effects might occur, and when to call the physician about side effects. In addition, each pill package comes with an extremely detailed insert describing contraindications to pill use. This covers who should not use oral contraceptives; what oral contraceptives are, and how they work; typical pregnancy rates for users of oral contraceptives and of other nonsurgical contraceptive methods; the risk of circulatory disorders, tumors, and gall-bladder disease; potential dangers to a developing fetus; and other side effects. It gives a comparison of the risk of death for all methods of contraception in graph form. The insert also lists signs of serious adverse effects that should signal a woman to call her physician and includes information on drugs that might reduce pill effectiveness to the extent that users should rely on an additional method for contraceptive protection. Although the package insert explains when to take the pill, it does not discuss what to do if one or more pills are missed.

Other Services Offered
Private physicians offer a variety of services other than contraception. General and family practitioners who provide contraceptive care re-

port that family planning patients account for only 6 percent of their total case load, whereas obstetrician-gynecologists estimate that 31 percent of their patients come for contraceptive services (AGI 1984b). General and family practitioners provide primary health care, and some perform inpatient surgery. Only a minority, however, offer other reproductive health services like obstetric care, infertility services, vasectomy, prenatal genetic screening, tubal ligation, or abortion (AGI 1984b). Obstetrician-gynecologists are specialists in the female reproductive system. In addition to reversible contraception, more than 90 percent also provide tubal ligation, infertility care, obstetric care, and prenatal genetic screening. About forty percent will perform abortions (Orr and Forrest 1985, 64).

FAMILY PLANNING CLINICS

Family planning clinics prescribe oral contraceptives and diaphragms. They often also provide these supplies. Before 1986, most inserted IUDs. The clinics give out information and usually supplies for nonprescription contraception as well. Most do not perform sterilizations but refer patients to other providers who do. The United States has 5,100 family planning clinics run by 2,500 different agencies (Torres and Forrest 1985). Clinics are located in every state, but metropolitan areas are better served than nonmetropolitan areas. About one in eight women living in a nonmetropolitan area has no family planning clinic in her county.

Family planning clinics are run by various public and private organizations. Public health departments run the majority (57 percent). Fourteen hundred health departments operate family planning clinics, and these have an average of two sites each, with each site serving an average of 674 patients annually. Approximately four in ten family planning clinic patients are served in health department clinics.

The next most common provider is the Planned Parenthood Federation of America (PPFA), a private, nonprofit organization. The approximately 180 independent agencies that make up PPFA operate an average of four clinic sites per agency and serve the largest number of patients annually, averaging 1,989 patients per site in 1983. Planned Parenthood clinics account for about 28 percent of all family planning patients.

Almost three hundred hospitals offer family planning clinic services. Most operate at only one site and hospital clinics represent only about seven percent of all family planning clinics. They serve an average of 1,462 patients per site, accounting for 11 percent of all patients.

About six hundred other organizations—neighborhood health centers, women's health centers, and community action groups—also operate family planning programs. They average 899 patients at two sites per agency, representing 23 percent of all clinics and 21 percent of all family planning clinic patients.

Most smaller counties have only one clinic site, but more populated areas and larger cities usually have more than one. The types of providers running family planning clinics vary considerably across regions of the country. Some states and areas have no clinics of certain types, and others have fairly even distributions. Services in rural non-metropolitan areas are more likely than those in cities to be run by health departments, while PPFA and hospital clinics are more common in metropolitan sections of the country (Torres and Forrest 1987, 55).

Like other clinic services, family planning clinics tend to be located in lower-income areas of communities. They are often located in buildings with other health services, sometimes using a medical facility that provides other services at other times. In these cases, clinic services may be available only a few times a week (Silverman and Torres 1987, 126–134).

Clinics are much less likely than private physicians to require parental consent before serving teenagers. In 1979–80, 80 percent of agencies would serve teenagers fifteen or younger without parental consent, and 90 percent would serve sixteen and seventeen-year-olds. Hospital clinics are most likely to require consent or notification (80 percent will serve sixteen and seventeen-year-olds confidentially). PPFA clinics usually offer confidential services (Torres, Forrest, and Eisman 1980, 287).

Funding and Fees
Few, if any, family planning organizations have only one source of funding (Torres 1984), and agencies must often patch together funds from a variety of sources. About one-third of family planning agency income comes from federal grants provided under Title X of the Public Health Service Act. The program is administered by the Department of Health and Human Services, and the funds are allocated by the department's ten regional offices to public and nonprofit private organizations to provide contraceptive and related services. About eight in ten family planning agencies receive Title X funding. Organizations usually apply for Title X grants annually. In many cases, an agency receiving the Title X project grant serves as an umbrella agency or coordinator for many other organizations as well. Title X has fairly detailed guidelines for agencies receiving funding, including a requirement that priority in service provision be given to persons from low-income families; teenagers are also singled out for program attention. Since Title X is the only nationwide program specifically funding family planning clinic services, and because it initially represented the

major source of funds for family planning, its program guidelines are generally relied on by other funding sources and are often followed by non–Title X funded agencies as well.

Ninety percent of all agencies are reimbursed by Medicaid for serving eligible patients. On average, however, only 10 percent of their total income comes from this source (although one-quarter of hospital clinics' income comes from Medicaid). Funds are also available through the Maternal and Child Health block grants under Title V of the Social Security Act. Federal monies are given as grants to states for maternal and child health care, and the states must match federal funds. The monies are usually administered by the state's health agency, and the amount used for family planning services is up to the state. About two-thirds of the states use some of their Maternal and Child Health block-grant funds for family planning (Gold and Macias 1986, 260). How states use these funds varies. Some use them to support outreach workers and nurse-practitioners, some fund services for women in targeted areas of the state, and some pool these funds with those from Title X to support general clinic services. Across the country, about three in ten family planning agencies have some Maternal and Child Health funds, which represent 7 percent of all clinic income.

About half the states (Gold and Macias 1986, 260) also use Social Services block-grant (Title XX of the Social Security Act) funds for family planning. Like the Maternal and Child Health block grant, federal funds are given to each state and matched with state funds. These are usually administered by the state's social services or welfare agency. Some states use the money to provide family planning counseling and educational services, information and referral for family planning by welfare workers, or else to fund family planning clinics to provide services to eligible women, often on a reimbursement basis. About half of all family planning agencies have some funding from the Social Services block grant, representing, on average, 13 percent of all clinic income.

About half the family planning agencies receive income from state or local governments, which represent 17 percent of total income. These funds are most likely to be used by public health departments and may be part of general funding rather than specifically designated for contraceptive services. They account for almost one-quarter of health department clinic income.

Other agency income comes from fees. In 1983, some or all patients at 92 percent of the family planning agencies were charged for services. Patient fees represent 13 percent of all agency income and about one-third of PPFA clinics' income.

Private contributions from the general public and from private foundations are also made to about four in ten family planning agencies, including almost all PPFA agencies and over half of family planning agencies run by those other organizations noted earlier. Such contributions account for 7 percent of all family planning agency income.

Clinics with Title X funding must serve at no charge any patient with a family income under 100 percent of the poverty standard. In other clinics, the median fee (for a first visit and a three-month supply of pills) in 1983–84 was $14 (Torres 1984). The median fee for a woman with an income at 125 percent of poverty was $15 in a Title X clinic and $28 if the clinic relied on other funds. Charges for women at 250 percent of poverty were similar in Title X and non–Title X clinics, about $50. Teenagers are served free or charged less than are older low-income women in about half of Title X–funded clinics and in about one-third of those without Title X funding. While costs are likely to differ by whether Title X funding is involved, few if any women seeking services have ever heard of Title X or are aware that they might get cheaper services in a Title X clinic. In general, hospital and Planned Parenthood clinics charge more than others. All public health-department clinics serve patients under the poverty level gratis.

In 1983, two-thirds of all clinic patients received free services, including 79 percent of adolescent patients and 61 percent of older women. About one in four clinics will not accept the patient's own statement of her income as a qualification for free care or reduced fees. They require some form of verification, such as a payroll stub, an income tax return, a Medicaid card, or a rent receipt. Planned Parenthood clinics are most likely to rely on the patient's own report, hospitals are most likely to ask for proof of income (Torres 1984).

In addition to offering medical examinations for contraceptives free or at less cost than most private physicians, almost all family planning clinics also provide contraceptive supplies free or at below-market price. Many agencies are able to keep their visit fees relatively low because, even though they charge less than pharmacies, their charges for supplies are much above what they had to pay for them in special purchasing arrangements negotiated by large groups of family planning agencies and contraceptive suppliers. Although most patients receive free supplies, some are charged $6 to $7 for a cycle of pills (Torres 1984).

Role of Clinics

Characteristics of clientele. Almost all family planning clinic patients are women, and they are largely poor: 83 percent have incomes below 150 percent of the poverty standard, and 13 percent receive welfare. Twenty-six percent of all clinic patients are black, and 11 percent are

Hispanic. Thirty-two percent of all patients are under twenty, and 14 percent of patients are under eighteen (Torres and Forrest 1985).

Outreach. In general, clinics are much more active in trying to attract patients than are private physicians, but the amount and the type of outreach vary. Eight in ten agencies running family planning clinics provide community education, and about half do special outreach focused on bringing teenagers into the clinic (Torres 1984, 137). Outreach activities may focus on the general importance of contraception or on specific information about clinic services. Teen recruitment may include putting up posters, giving speeches to teenage audiences, or placing advertisements or special news stories in newspapers and on radio or even local television.

Advertisements for family planning clinics do not appear in every community, and those that are run usually do not say specifically what the clinic charges are, or that poor women can get free services. They may note that services are confidential. Private, nonprofit organizations, especially Planned Parenthood, are more likely to seek public recognition and to advertise their services than are public health departments or hospital providers. Because private clinics are often freestanding and run by an organization that focuses primarily on providing contraceptive services, they are also more likely to be listed in the telephone book. Hospital and health department family planning clinics are usually not listed separately, and one must call the main hospital or health department number to get information about family planning clinic services. Information about local family planning clinics is available to women who are on welfare through social service counselors and brochures, but otherwise the onus falls on the woman to be aware of or seek out family planning clinics.

Contraceptive Services

Personnel. Family planning clinics must be supervised by physicians, but because of the expense of employing full-time or part-time doctors, many clinics rely on nurse-practitioners to provide services under standing orders from a supervising physician. When nurse-practitioners are employed as clinicians, physicians develop and monitor the medical protocols, see high-risk and problem patients, and in clinics or at times when there is no nurse-practitioner, perform pelvic examinations and write prescriptions. A study of clinics in four cities found that about four in ten relied on nurse-practitioners for clinical care (Silverman, Torres, and Forrest 1987).

Depending on the management model used by the clinic, a patient may see as few as two staff members during her visit (usually a nurse-practitioner and a receptionist, a counselor, or an educator) or as many as five or more, in a clinic where tasks are quite specialized (Winter and Goldy 1987, 103–04). Other than physicians and nurse-practitioners, staff members can include some or all of the following: receptionist, educator, counselor, lab technician (to take blood and urine samples), nurse or nurse's aide, and financial clerk or exit interviewer (to determine and accept fees and schedule revisits). Except for physicians, staff members are almost always female.

Schedule. The times a clinic is open for business depends on the individual provider, but many are not open every day. On average, clinic sites are open for about thirty hours each week (Torres 1984, 137). One study of clinics in four cities found that about half are open evenings, and fewer than one-third have Saturday hours (Silverman and Torres 1987, 138).

Most clinics give patients appointment times. The four-city study found that fewer than one-third of all clinics will see a patient for routine services without an appointment, but two-thirds will see a patient with a problem even if she does not have an appointment (Silverman and Torres 1987, 139).

The length of time a patient must wait between making an appointment and coming to the clinic varies according to how busy the clinic is, but averages between one and two weeks (Chamie et al. 1982, 137; Silverman and Torres 1987, 95, 139).

Medical policies and procedures. Title X guidelines represent the most typical policies and procedures, although Planned Parenthood clinics must adhere as well to very detailed standards set by a national committee of medical advisors. According to the Title X guidelines (BCHS 1981), all contraceptive patients are required to have the following at their first visit: general history and general physical exam, including pelvic exam, weight, blood pressure, blood test, Pap smear, education, and counseling. Patients choosing nonprescriptive methods may defer the physical examination, but they are encouraged to have an examination at a return visit. Pap smears are required every year for pill and IUD patients and every two years for those using the diaphragm or nonprescriptive methods. Other tests and examinations are given if indicated. Title X guidelines require return visits three months after the first prescription.

Before a clinic patient can receive any medical services, she must sign a form documenting that she is voluntarily consenting to that care. The form has to cover all procedures and medications that she receives. That form, or a separate one that she must sign, includes a statement that she has been told and understands the risks and benefits of this and alternative methods and has been informed about the safety, effectiveness, potential side effects, complications, and danger signs of the method she is receiving. Although such forms are supposed to be in language familiar to the patient, legal requirements often have great influence, and many are long, difficult to read, and even frightening.

Providers that perform or arrange for sterilization and receive Title X funding must follow policies similar to those for Medicaid individuals receiving sterilization. The patient must be mentally competent, twenty-one or older, and must have given informed consent at least thirty days but not more than one hundred eighty days before the procedure, except in cases of unanticipated surgery or premature delivery.

Provider method preferences. Family planning clinics usually provide counseling, prescriptions, and supplies for all contraceptive methods. If they do not provide a particular method themselves, they must make arrangements with another provider to accept referrals and may pay for that service by another provider. This is sometimes done for periodic abstinence. Some clinics will arrange with other providers for sterilization.

Family planning clinics provide primarily prescription methods, usually the pill. Most patients request this method, and two-thirds of all patients receive pill prescriptions (Torres and Forrest 1985, 35). Most clinicians working in family planning clinics prefer triphasic pills. Preferences for specific brands are influenced by contracts some providers have with pharmaceutical companies (American Health Consultants, Inc. 1987, 113). The majority of clinics set the upper age limit for pill use by women with no contraindications at age forty or below, and almost half set it at age thirty-five or lower. The medical standards of the PPFA consider oral contraceptives contraindicated for heavy smokers over thirty-five. Women over thirty-five who do not smoke heavily are considered as potentially high-risk. They are given blood tests for cholesterol levels and must sign a high-risk consent form if they will not accept an alternative contraceptive method (PPFA 1987). No upper age limit is set for women who do not have contraindications to pill use, but many Planned Parenthood clinics set an automatic age cutoff at forty (Tyrer 1987). One-third of nurse-practitioners, who usually work in family planning clinics, will not prescribe oral contraceptives to a sexually active fourteen-year-old who has had only one menstrual period (American Health Consultants, Inc. 1987).

Although staff spend most of their time providing oral contraceptives, they may, in fact, be less likely to use pills than other women. A study in the late 1970s suggested that half as many clinic staff used the pill as women in the general population and that staff were more likely than other women to use the diaphragm or the IUD (Hatcher and Trussell 1981, 22–23). Some have suggested this reflects the emphasis on the risks of contraceptives in the information given at clinics and that a lack of confidence in the safety of the pill comes through to the patients seen by staff members who have questions about its safety.

Time spent with client. The amount of time the clinician spends with a patient is determined not only by the woman's needs but by the structure of the clinic. In some clinics, the clinician conducts education and counseling functions; in others, clinicians see the patient only for the time needed to perform the physical examination. In a study of eighty-three family planning clinics in four cities, clinic directors reported that clinicians usually spent slightly less than twenty minutes with each patient (Silverman and Torres 1987, 139).

Referral. Clinics refer patients to other providers for services they do not provide, such as sterilization, prenatal care, and abortion, as well as for conditions outside the scope of their specific program, such as treatment of infections, cervical dysplasia and malignancy, and treatment of sexually transmitted diseases. They are required to offer pregnancy diagnosis and counseling and to refer pregnant women, on request, to sources of prenatal care and delivery, infant care, foster care, adoption, and abortion.

Clinics usually have lists of other health-care providers in the community, which patients can use to pick another provider. Lists can include private physicians, health departments, hospitals, and other agencies in the community. Clinics sometimes make an appointment with the other provider for the patient and follow up to see that she made a visit. They need not, however, cover the cost of care for services their patients get from other providers.

Follow-up. Most clinics do not follow up patients who miss appointments or who do not come back for a revisit. If clinic personnel do call or send reminder cards, or if they need to contact a patient about a positive Pap smear or other test result, they try to be sensitive to a patient's need for confidentiality. At the initial visit, patients, especially teenagers, are usually asked how they can be contacted by the clinic after the visit.

Counseling

Personnel. Most clinics have personnel whose specific job is to discuss with the patient the available methods, their risks, benefits, and effectiveness, and their proper use. Most clinics used to have group sessions for education about reproductive physiology and method alternatives and individual counseling in which the woman made her choice and went over any questions about it. More recently, many providers have moved to individual education and counseling, in which more attention is given to answering the woman's specific questions about contraception and about her method. This change was made to save time and cut costs as well as to be more responsive to each client's situation.

Schedule. General education and counseling and provision of specific information about the contraceptive method the woman chooses are done at the time of her initial visit to a clinic. In most clinics, she can have a medical exam and get a contraceptive at the same visit.

Content. The emphasis of education and counseling in family planning clinics is on helping the patient make an informed decision and learn how to use the method effectively. It is not considered the counselor's role to suggest a specific method but to give the patient information to help her select. The Title X Guidelines (BCHS 1981, 9–10) state,

> Education services should provide clients with the information they need to make informed decisions about family planning, to use specific methods of contraception, and to understand the procedures involved in the family planning clinic visit. . . . The primary purpose of counseling in the family planning setting is to assist clients in reaching an informed decision regarding the choice and continued use of family planning methods and services. The counseling process is designed to help clients resolve uncertainty, ambivalence, and anxiety in relation to reproductive health and to enhance their capacity to arrive at a decision that reflects their considered self-interest.

Time spent with client. The amount of time spent in actual counseling depends not just on the patient's needs but also on the structure of the clinic. In clinics with group education sessions, time spent on education and counseling is often as much as 45 minutes. Less time is spent where group sessions are not used because counseling is geared more to the individual's needs and less general information is reviewed (Johnson 1985).

Client's Overall Expenditure of Time

Patients spend an average of an hour or more at the clinic in the course of one family planning visit (Silverman and Torres 1987, 95, 139; Winter and Goldy 1987, 104). Initial visits usually take much more time than return visits. A 1981 study found that, on average, a new teenage patient spent more than an hour and a half at the clinic for an initial contraceptive visit (Kisker 1984a). More than half of this time is spent waiting to see a staff person for services (Silverman and Torres 1987, 139; Winter and Goldy 1987, 104).

Information and Literature
Clinics usually have available patient information prepared by their agency, the federal government, or a pharmaceutical company. Brochures are usually in languages other than English in areas where there are many non-English-speaking clients. This material generally covers such topics as alternate methods of contraception, specific methods, clinic or agency services and hours, and other matters related to reproductive health, for example, vaginal infections, sexually transmitted diseases, and prenatal care.

Other Services Offered
Most family planning clinics offer a variety of reproductive health services other than contraception, and many are involved in providing other services and programs as well. These services may be considered by the agency or their funder as part of the family planning program or as separate from it. Such distinctions are usually not clear or not relevant to the client. Sometimes services are offered at the family planning clinic site, and in other cases they are provided at another location run by the same agency. Because clinics usually do not provide a full range of reproductive health services, women must find different providers when they need other care. Clinics are not, and are not designed to be, places where women obtain complete reproductive health care.

More than 90 percent of all family planning agencies provide pregnancy testing and counseling as well as testing for sexually transmitted diseases. About three-quarters offer treatment for sexually transmitted diseases. Six out of ten clinics provide infertility counseling, but only two in ten offer infertility treatment. Between one-quarter and one-half offer prenatal care services, genetic counseling, and programs for adolescent mothers. Fewer than one-quarter provide either female or male sterilization services and programs for males (Torres 1984, 137). Some hospitals and private agencies (but not health departments) provide abortion services, but strict guidelines preclude using Title X family planning funds to provide abortion.

PHARMACIES

Whether they are using oral contraceptives, the diaphragm, or nonprescription contraceptives such as condoms, foam, or the sponge, the majority of women who visit a private physician to obtain such methods must also visit a store in order to obtain supplies. In most cases they go to a pharmacy, although some supermarkets stock spermicides among feminine hygiene supplies. In response to the publicity about AIDS, more facilities besides pharmacies are selling condoms.

Pharmacies tend to be quite large and offer a wide variety of products, from cosmetics to books to picnic supplies. A pharmacy, therefore, is a place that a consumer of any age can plausibly visit. Condoms and spermicides used to be kept out of sight even in pharmacies, and a customer had to ask for them. Most pharmacies now display them in plain view. Spermicides are usually sold in the feminine hygiene section. Condoms are often on a rack near the checkout area, in part because there is no comparable male hygiene section, perhaps to discourage shoplifting. The price of condoms varies, but they generally cost about $6.00 for a package of 12. Each contraceptive sponge generally costs more than $1.00.

Two-thirds of the 150,000 pharmacists are men, but 59 percent of current pharmacy students are women (Parade 1987, 23). Pharmacists do not receive any special training in handling questions about contraceptives. Sometimes the drugstore has informational material from pharmaceutical companies available for customers.

CLIENT PREFERENCES

Women generally say they prefer to visit private physicians for family planning care, in part because they see physicians as providing more personal and higher-quality care than clinics (Silverman, Torres, and Forrest 1987). Physicians are the usual source of care for those who can afford to choose.

Lower-income women who go to clinics instead of private physicians do so primarily because they cannot afford private physicians' fees or because the clinic will accept Medicaid. Adolescents who go to family planning clinics do so because of the free or low-cost services and because they are afraid the physician will tell their parents (Chamie et al. 1982, 133). In addition, some, especially teens who have never been to a physician on their own, go to clinics because they do not know a private physician who would serve them.

Clinic patients usually shift to private physicians when their incomes rise and as they become older. A switch may also occur when they become pregnant and must look elsewhere for obstetric care.

A 1982 survey (Forrest and Henshaw 1983, 158), asked women their attitudes about a variety of contraceptive methods. The methods about which the highest proportions of women reported favorable attitudes were sterilization and oral contraceptives. Between 62 and 65 percent of women of reproductive age said their attitude about even these methods was favorable. Only 30 to 40 percent had positive attitudes about the condom and the diaphragm. Few felt positively about the IUD, foam, periodic abstinence, or withdrawal.

Data suggest that some who choose sterilization, the most prevalent method today in the United States, later regret it. Sterilization is presented as a permanent method to women and men considering it, yet one-quarter of all women who rely on sterilization of themselves or their partners say they want more children, and 10 percent report that they, and if they are married, their spouses, want to have the sterilization reversed (Henshaw and Singh 1986).

Those who switch from using the pill to another method or to using no method do so primarily because they are worried about side effects and health risks, while those who switch from the condom, diaphragm, or spermicides do so because of concerns about effectiveness, interference with intercourse, and the inconvenience these methods entail. Those switching from periodic abstinence or withdrawal are chiefly concerned about effectiveness (Silverman, Torres, and Forrest 1987).

Even though oral contraceptives are looked upon more favorably than any other reversible method, fears about the pill's health risks are pervasive in the United States. Three-quarters of adult women and about two-thirds of men think that pill use involves "substantial risks," primarily from cancer or blood clots. These proportions differ little by educational level (Gallup 1985). When it was introduced in 1960, the pill was hailed as the answer to women's contraceptive needs. Reports of adverse health effects of oral contraceptives, widely covered in the press and other media in the early 1970s, promoted pill discontinuation (Jones, Beniger, and Westoff 1980). The last decades have seen a growth of interest in personal fitness and health as well as in exercise and natural foods, and an astounding decrease in smoking, in part because of public health campaigns. Fears about oral contraceptives appear to reflect both broad concerns about health and medications and specific worries about contraceptives.

The pill was rated most favorably in a recent survey of single women in their twenties (Tanfer and Rosenbaum 1986, 271). While it received the most favorable ratings on effectiveness, lack of interference, and convenience, however, it received the lowest score (after the IUD) on safety.

Often women are not very confident that they will not become pregnant even if they are using a contraceptive. Less than two-thirds of low-income current users surveyed by Silverman, Torres and Forrest (1987) were "very sure" they would not become pregnant. The proportions who were very sure they would not become pregnant while using their method ranged from a high of 72 percent among pill users to 58 percent of IUD users, 55 percent of those using the diaphragm, half of the spermicide users and only 46 percent of those relying on the condom.

INFORMATION AND EDUCATION

Organized Communication Efforts

The U.S. mass media include sexual relationships in their entertainment programming, especially in soap operas, and sexual innuendo is often used to attract attention in advertisements. The sexual content of programming does not include graphically explicit portrayal of intercourse, but rather kissing, embracing, and verbal references to intercourse and implicit intercourse, and references to deviant or discouraged sexual practices such as incest, rape, and prostitution. Since the late 1970s, the amount of explicit sexual content in television programming has increased (Louis Harris and Associates, Inc. 1987a). This occurred even though the rising influence of fundamentalist Christian groups in the late 1970s and early 1980s increased media coverage of their teachings against any sexual relationships outside marriage. The focus of sexual content in entertainment programming is more often on nonmarital, extramarital, and problem relationships than on sex within marriage or a committed relationship. Sixty-four percent of adults think television encourages teenage sexual behavior, and 66 percent think that television exaggerates the importance of sex (Louis Harris and Associates, Inc. 1987b). Contraception is almost never mentioned in entertainment programming and is relegated to coverage in news or information programming and a few advertisements, if it is seen at all.

The messages conveyed through the media reflect tensions or ambivalence in the country about the role of sexuality and its expression. One report (Jones et al. 1985, 61) summed it up this way:

American teenagers seem to have inherited the worst of all possible worlds regarding their exposure to messages about sex: Movies, radio and TV tell them that sex is romantic, exciting, titillating; premarital sex and cohabitation are visible ways of life among the adults they see and hear about; their own parents or their parents' friends are likely to be divorced or separated but involved in sexual relationships. Yet, at the same time, young people get the message good girls should say no. Almost nothing that they see or hear about sex informs them about contraception or the importance of avoiding pregnancy.

The recent emergence of AIDS has increased public discussion about the risks of sexual transmission of the virus. AIDS has been discussed in news and special feature programs on television and radio as well as in newspaper and magazine articles. Coverage has generally included identification of sexual intercourse as a risk factor and discussion of avoiding intercourse with someone who might have the virus or using condoms as preventive behaviors. As a result, recently much more open discussion about condoms has taken place, almost all of it focusing on disease prevention, however, not contraception.

Sex education. Most adults did not receive any sex education when they were in school, beyond possibly having one or two movies or lectures about sexually transmitted disease (for boys) and about menstruation and childbirth (for girls). The situation is quite different today. About six in ten girls and half of all boys have taken a specific sex-education course before they leave high school (Marsiglio and Mott 1986). Sex education is often taught as part of other courses instead of being a specific course. Not all schools include contraception as a topic in their sex education (Dawson 1986; Marsiglio and Mott 1986; Orr 1982; Sonenstein and Pittman 1984). About three-quarters of girls have had some instruction about contraceptive methods before they leave school (Dawson 1986).

In all but the few states that require it, whether or not to teach sex education is up to the local town or city school district. What to teach and how to teach it is almost always left up to the particular school district or school, and courses of instruction and their goals differ widely. The most commonly cited goals of sex education are to promote rational, informed decisionmaking about sexuality and to present facts about sexual intercourse. Moral and personal values are included as often or more often than information about contraceptive methods or their sources (Orr 1982; Sonenstein and Pittman 1984).

Government role. Federal and state governments do little to inform and educate the public about family planning. Title X–funded family planning agencies are supposed to provide community education programs and to carry out activities to make their services known to the community (BCHS 1981). As described above, such activities generally focus on the target groups: low-income women and teenagers. Women receiving welfare are also supposed to be told about where they can obtain family planning services.

There is disagreement within the federal government, as well as the country as a whole, over the appropriate government policy concerning prevention of AIDS. The basic dispute is whether to tell people that they can lower their risk of contracting AIDS by using condoms if they have intercourse with someone who might have the virus or whether to tell them only that they should abstain from sex outside marriage and not use drugs.

Target groups. To the extent that the most common information and education effort about sexuality and contraception is school sex education, the primary target group is adolescents. Even so, instruction including contraception often is not given until the upper grades of school, when teens are sixteen and older (Dawson 1986; Marsiglio and Mott 1986; Orr 1982; Sonenstein and Pittman 1984). Many teenagers initiate sexual intercourse before this age.

Advertising of Methods and Services

Advertisement of contraceptive methods is limited in the United States. Prescriptive drugs generally cannot be advertised to the public. Television, radio, newspapers, and magazines have had long-standing policies against advertising contraceptives. In the past few years, magazines have increasingly allowed ads for spermicides, spurred by the submission of advertisements for the contraceptive sponge, and condom ads have begun to appear as well. They must be "tastefully" done, which means seldom showing the method. Attempts by pharmaceutical companies and other private organizations to place advertisements for contraceptives on television and radio have been strongly resisted. They do exist, but are limited to a few stations and are often broadcast at hours when the audience is small. Analysis of afternoon and evening programming on stations affiliated with a representative sample of one hundred hours of the three major television networks in fall 1986 found no commercial advertisements or public-service announcements for contraceptives (Louis Harris and Associates, Inc. 1987a). The ACOG tried to place television advertisements aimed at adolescents, talking about the importance of preventing unintended pregnancy in order to achieve one's goals in life. No contraceptive methods were mentioned in the ad, but a toll-free number was given, which a viewer could call to receive a pamphlet about how to prevent pregnancy, including both abstinence and contraceptive methods. After much discussion with officials of the major television networks, the spots were accepted by some, but only after the word *contraceptive* was removed.

Advertisements for family planning services are limited to those placed and paid for by service providers. They are not widespread, and those that do appear are usually rather small ads in local newspapers. Some providers use posters and placards in public transportation. Local providers may be unable to afford such ads or may believe that they do not represent a good use of scarce funds. Private physicians and organizations that provide family planning services—especially hospitals and health departments—do not normally advertise any of their services. Some family planning agencies put low priority on expanding their case loads because they are already at capacity and do . not have the staff or funds available to serve more patients (Chamie et al. 1982, 138).

Media Treatment of Contraception

Radio and television. As noted above, there are few advertisements for contraceptives or for family planning services on radio or television. Contraceptive advertisements are restricted by the policies of national and local networks. Those for private physician services are limited by custom, and ads for clinic services are also limited by the ability of family planning agencies to pay for advertisements and absorb more clients.

Although contraception is seldom mentioned in the entertainment programming of television or radio, the topic is covered in broadcast news and feature stories. Such stories may report information about contraceptive use, safety, or effectiveness, or about research into development of new contraceptive methods. They sometimes also touch on contraception within the broader context of stories on adolescent pregnancy or AIDS.

Newspapers and magazines. News articles in the print media cover contraception in much the same way as news and feature programming on radio and television. Feature articles, especially in women's magazines and women's or health sections of newspapers, sometimes review the range of methods, treating such topics as safety, side effects, and how to use contraceptives. Articles are straightforward and informational.

Climate of Opinion Concerning Sex

The media reflect, as well as form, the climate of opinion in the United States about many topics, including sex. It is a rather ambivalent or mixed climate. On the one hand, premarital intercourse and divorce are common and often accepted. A strong theme of entertainment in television, pop music, movies, and popular literature is the attraction of nonmarital sex. Sexual innuendos are common in advertisements for all kinds of products.

On the other hand, media representatives continue to claim that including references to contraceptives in entertainment programming or in advertisements will offend their audiences. There is a strong religious tradition in the United States that condemns sexual relationships outside marriage.

Another theme that is part of public opinion in the United States is that sexual behavior is a private matter, not an appropriate area for legislation. The definition of the behavior that should be covered under the umbrella of privacy has resulted in some controversy in recent years, including often heated discussions about the appropriateness of legal abortion, the government's role in promoting chastity, and parental notification of minors' obtaining prescription contraceptives from family planning clinics.

ASSESSMENT

Proportion of Overall Need That Is Met

General public. Among all women aged 15–44 who are at risk of unintended pregnancy because they are fecund, not pregnant, post-partum, or seeking pregnancy, and have had sex within the last three months, 12 percent use no method of contraception (Bachrach 1984, 255). The most common reason such women give for not using contraceptives is that they are concerned about side effects or health risks (Forrest and Henshaw 1983; Silverman, Torres, and Forrest 1987). It has been estimated that almost half of all unintended pregnancies that occur in the United States are to these 12 percent of women at risk who use no method (Forrest 1987b). Nonuse is greatest among unmarried women. Among those at risk of unintended pregnancy who have never married, 22 percent use no method and 16 percent of women who are separated, divorced, or widowed use none, compared to only 7 percent of currently married women.

If one looks at all women in the country who are of reproductive age, one in every ten women who is not currently married is at risk of unintended pregnancy but is not using any contraceptive, and one in twenty married women is fecund, does not want to become pregnant, but uses no method to prevent it (Bachrach 1984, 255).

Of those who do use contraceptives, as many as 31 percent use the less effective methods, compared to the 69 percent relying on sterilization, pill, or IUD (Forrest 1987b). As discussed above, such methods are often chosen because of fears of health problems and side effects from the pill and IUD, and because of the desire for reversibility.

Target groups. Nonuse is higher among those groups that are the special focus of organized family planning efforts. Among those at risk of unintended pregnancy, 18 percent of women with family incomes at or below 150 percent of poverty level do not use contraception, compared to 10 percent of higher-income women. Younger women are the least likely to use contraceptives; 29 percent of girls aged 15–19 who are at risk of unintended pregnancy use no method, compared to 13 percent of those aged 20–24 and 9 percent of women aged 25 and older (Bachrach 1984).

Differences are greater by poverty status and age among unmarried women than among those who are married. Among all unmarried women with incomes below 150 percent of the poverty standard, 87 percent use a contraceptive, compared with 92 percent of higher-income women. The levels among currently married women are 93 and 94 percent, respectively (Forrest 1987a). Younger women and poor women are less likely to be married than their older, richer counterparts. Among poor women, 33 percent are currently married, compared with 59 percent of higher-income women. Differences in marital status exacerbate the differences by age and income status in levels of contraceptive use.

Data on contraceptive use by currently married women shown in chapter 4 revealed differences by income status among both younger (20–34 years old) and older (35–44 years old) currently married women. Among the younger women, the overall level of use is similar by poverty status, but lower-income women are more likely to use effective methods, especially sterilization. This may reflect the fact that a larger proportion of poorer married women want no more children. Of the younger married women who are poor, 90 percent have had at least one child, and 70 percent have had two or more. One-third have had at least three children. Married women in this age group with incomes greater than 150 percent of the poverty standard have had fewer children—only 74 percent have had any, and 46 percent have had two or more. Similarly, poor unmarried women are also more likely to rely on sterilization than higher-income women (10 versus 5 percent of those aged 20–34 and 27 versus 22 percent of older women). Some 37 percent of younger low-income women who are not currently married have had two or more children, compared with 10 percent of those above 150 percent of poverty, while 76 percent of older unmarried women earning less than 150 percent of the poverty standard have had at least two children, compared with 53 percent of higher-income women.

Differences in parity are narrowest for currently married women aged 35–44. Among the poor, 92 percent have had two or more children, while only 80 percent of higher-income women have. The lower levels of use of all three effective contraceptive methods, including sterilization, by older poor women probably reflects their greater difficulty in obtaining contraceptive services.

Barriers to Service
Family planning services in the United States are delivered like other health-care services. The normal expectation is that women who want a prescription method (pill, IUD, or diaphragm) or a man or woman seeking sterilization will go to a private physician for services. Because the health-care system is based primarily on specialists, it is likely that this physician will not be the doctor whom the patient would see for other types of health care. Obstetrician-gynecologists and general and family practitioners, who provide most of the reproductive health care, do not offer all services, but they usually refer their patients to a physician who offers what the patient needs.

The woman who cannot afford private physicians' fees, and the teenager who fears the doctor will tell her parents about her visit, however, rely primarily on clinics for medical contraceptive services. Family planning clinics are usually publicly supported and offer free or low-cost services based on a woman's family income. Because they were established primarily to serve poor women, clinics often carry the stigma of being second-rate services for the poor, even though they have expanded their focus to provide services to adolescents and to offer other reproductive health services besides contraceptives, and even though they usually operate under guidelines to ensure quality medical care.

Because of the need to maneuver through the health-care system to find an appropriate private physician or a lower-priced alternative, obtaining contraceptives can be difficult in the United States. Little effort is put into informing women about sources and costs of services. Those who are the main targets of publicly subsidized family planning services are not adequately served, since their rates of nonuse of contraception are much higher than those for women who can use private physicians. Rates of nonuse of contraception among women with incomes at or below 150 percent of poverty are 80 percent higher than they are among women with higher incomes. Nonuse among exposed adolescents is more than twice the level of women in their early twenties (Forrest 1987a).

Difficulties in obtaining services appear to be only one problem hindering contraceptive practice in the United States, even for poor women and teenagers, for the rate of nonuse is fairly high even among those who presumably can afford private physicians. Other basic factors underlying poor contraceptive use are probably the fear of side effects or health problems from the more effective contraceptives and the sense that even if contraceptives are used, the chance of pregnancy is fairly high. Experiences with oral contraceptives, the Dalkon Shield IUD, and sterilization have left a legacy of consumer fears and mistrust that has not yet been counterbalanced by the less sensational news disproving some of the fears and identifying the health benefits of some methods and of avoiding unintended pregnancy in general.

In addition, no consensus exists in the United States about sexuality. Exploitative use of sex in some of the entertainment media and in advertising lies at the opposite pole from the argument, made by some federal administration officials, that public information about AIDS should not include any reference to condoms. Americans are often confused and ambivalent about their sexual behavior. Many people, especially the young, have intercourse but do not prepare for it in advance by obtaining a contraceptive because they feel guilty about having sex.

Although most of those at risk of unintended pregnancy use contraceptives, a sizable minority, especially lower-income women and younger women, do not. They may be worried about method safety and effectiveness, and they may have a hard time finding someone to serve them. Clinic staff are often dedicated people working in poorly funded facilities with patients who bring with them the myriad problems that accompany poverty in this country. Besides just delivering medical services, clinics are often asked to counteract the strong societal influences of ambivalence regarding sexuality and fear and mistrust of contraceptive methods.

Relation of Services to Method Use
The differences in types of services used by poor and nonpoor women and by younger and older women in the United States do not have great impact on the type of method used, except that women whose most recent family planning visit was to a private physician are more likely than those who last went to a clinic to be relying on sterilization of themselves or their partner, primarily because women and men must usually obtain sterilization through a private physician. Otherwise, there are few differences in patterns of reversible-method use among women by whether they went to a clinic or private physician. Differences between lower- and higher-income women in methods used are more closely related to their age, marital status, and parity than to their source of service. Pill use is slightly higher among those using clinics (54 versus 48 percent), primarily because clinic users are on average younger than those seeing private physicians (Forrest 1987a). There are no significant differences in effectiveness of method use by source of contraceptive care (Zelnik, Koenig, and Kim 1984).

6

Ontario and Quebec

GENERAL DESCRIPTION

Overall Health System

In 1967, the Canadian federal government passed legislation providing generous federal subsidies for universal health insurance plans adopted by the provinces. Although the provinces were not required to provide health insurance, all did so in view of the federal support. The plans are administered by the provincial governments and differ from province to province. All, however, provide coverage for both hospital and physician care to almost all residents. No deductibles or copayments for medical services are required in Ontario or Quebec.

In Canada, 57 percent of public expenditures for health care is paid by the provinces, 42 percent by the federal government, and 1 percent by the municipalities (Statistics Canada 1985, table 6.17). Three provinces impose premiums to help finance their share of the cost. In

People interviewed: Francine Allard (M.D.), CLSC Laurentien; Rose Alper, Planned Parenthood of Ville-Marie; Normand Ayotte (M.D.), Centre Hospitalier Régional Mauricie; T. R. Balakrishnan, Faculty of Sociology, University of Western Ontario; Bonnie Bean, Department of Public Health, Toronto; France Beauchamp, Centre de Santé des Femmes; Charlene Berger, Montreal General Hospital; Gilles Bernier (M.D.), Corporation Professionelle des Médecins du Québec; Filimina Carvalho, Immigrant Women's Centre; Monique Châtillon, Clinique de Planification des Naissances, Centre Hospitalier de l'Université de Laval; Connie Clement, independent consultant; Rhoda Cohen, Planned Parenthood of Ville-Marie; Priscilla Cook, pharmacist; Roberta Cormier (M.D.), CLSC Hochelaga-Maisonneuve; André Côté (M.D.), Département de Santé Communautaire, Centre Hospitalier Ste.-Marie; Louise Desaulniers, Centre Hospitalier Régional Mauricie; Corinne Devlin (M.D.), Department of Obstetrics and Gynecology,

118

Ontario, for example, each family pays $400 a year for coverage.[1] The fee is often paid by employers and is waived for families on welfare and for residents aged sixty-five or more. Low-income families not on welfare can obtain a fee subsidy. Health insurance covers all residents except the few who fail to pay the necessary fees.

Ordinarily, no fee is paid at the time of a health-care visit. The patient shows his or her insurance card, and the provider is reimbursed directly. A patient who receives services outside his or her home province must pay and apply for reimbursement later. Physicians are reimbursed for each service rendered rather than by enrolled patient, as in England, and a fee schedule specifies the amount payable for each type of service, making it relatively easy for a patient to go to different physicians for different services or to change physicians.

McMaster University; Lucienne Ferrer, Centre Hospitalier Régional Mauricie; Peter G. Gillet (M.D.), Montreal General Hospital; Edith Guilbert (M.D.), Clinique de Planification des Naissances, Centre Hospitalier de l'Université de Laval; Claire Harting *Journal de Montréal*; Patricia Hayes, Immigrant Women's Centre; Debbie Honickman (M.D.), Parkdale Community Health Clinic; Alex Hukowich (M.D.), Porcupine Health Unit; Sue Johanson, sex educator; Ruth Groome Kurtz, Bay Centre for Birth Control; Mireille Lajoie, Département de Santé Communautaire, Centre Hospitalier Ste.-Marie; André Lalonde (M.D.), Hôpital Générale LaSalle; André Lapierre (M.D.), Corporation Professionelle des Médecins du Québec; Evelyne Lapierre-Adamcyk, Département de Démographie, Université de Montréal; François Laramée (M.D.), Corporation Professionelle des Médecins du Québec; Marie Leclerc, Service de la Condition Féminine, Ministère de la Santé et des Services Sociaux; Yves Lefebvre (M.D.), Clinique de Planification Familiale, Hôpital Notre-Dame; Francine Léger, Centre de Santé des Femmes; Sue McKenzie, Planned Parenthood of Ville-Marie; Helen McKilligin (M.D.), Public Health Branch, Ontario Ministry of Health; Michael McRae, Drug Benefits Program, Ontario Ministry of Health; Nicole Marcil-Gratton, Département de Démographie, Université de Montréal; Maresa Marini, Immigrant Women's Centre; Ann Moon, Department of Public Health, Toronto; Maureen Orton, School of Social Work, McMaster University; Ann Pappert, freelance journalist; R. Perkin (M.D.), College of Family Physicians of Canada; Dallas Petroff, Planned Parenthood of Toronto; Sylvie Pinsonneault, Département de Sexologie, Université de Québec à Montréal; France Poliquin, Département de Santé Communautaire, Centre Hospitalier Ste.-Marie; Marion G. Powell (M.D.), Bay Centre for Birth Control; Marcia Redmond, Family Planning Services, Waterloo; Cécile Richard, Service de la Condition Féminine, Ministère de la Santé et des Services Sociaux; Marthe Riopel, Clinique de Planification Familiale, Hôpital Notre-Dame; Jacques Rioux (M.D.), Clinique de Planification des Naissances, Centre Hospitalier de l'Université de Laval; Madeleine Rochon, Service de la Condition Féminine, Ministère de la Santé et des Services Sociaux; Lillian Romualdi, Porcupine Health Unit; Ellen Rosenblatt, School of Social Work, McMaster University; Janet Seale (M.D.), Porcupine Health Unit; Monique Séguin, Service de la Condition Féminine, Ministère de la Santé et des Services Sociaux; Percy Skuy, Orthopharmaceutical (Canada) Ltd.; Julia Tao, Immigrant Women's Centre; Martine Thornton, *Châtelaine*; Lillian Trombley, Porcupine Health Unit; Diane Villeneuve (M.D.), CLSC Hochelaga-Maisonneuve; Miriam Zeballos, Immigrant Women's Centre.

1. Unless otherwise specified, dollar figures are in U.S. dollars, converted at the rate of U.S. $0.75 equals Canadian $1.00.

In Ontario, during the period under study, some physicians charged fees in addition to the amount reimbursed by the insurance plan. This practice, called *extra billing*, appears to have been particularly common among specialists, including obstetrician-gynecologists, especially for abortion services. Physicians may legally charge patients for services not covered by the health plan, for example, referral. Since 1986 extra billing has been banned in Ontario, and it is not permitted in Quebec.

In Ontario, patients are randomly sent notices of the health services they have utilized in order to assure that physicians are not billing the insurance plan for services not rendered. This can pose a problem for teenagers who wish to keep physician visits confidential, but physicians can check "no verification" on insurance forms for family planning services. Some providers, such as the House, a comprehensive health program for teenagers in Toronto, have made special arrangements with the Ontario Health Insurance Program (OHIP) not to check their patients. Abortion services are not ordinarily subject to the random check.

Provincial insurance plans do not cover the cost of drugs used outside hospitals unless the patient is on welfare or is sixty-five or over.

Most primary care in both Ontario and Quebec is provided by general and family practitioners. In Ontario, about half of the primary-care physicians have had a residency in family practice, but for convenience they are all included below under the term *general practitioner*. Ontario and Quebec have tried to have general practitioners provide as many services as possible and to limit the number of specialists. Access to a specialist in Ontario usually requires referral from a general practitioner; in Quebec, patients may consult specialists directly but are usually referred.

In Ontario, besides private physicians, there is a public health system based on "health units," which are comparable to county health departments in the United States. Health units provide a variety of public health services, including screening tests for children, immunizations, home nursing visits, investigation of communicable diseases, parenting education, investigation and treatment of sexually transmitted diseases, health inspections, and other health education and promotion activities, as well as family planning education and services. The health units are financed in part by the provincial government and in part by the county or locality. A minor portion of the health care in Ontario comes from five community health centers, which may be financed by OHIP directly by contract or indirectly by fee-for-service reimbursement. Physicians in the community health centers are on salary.

Quebec has a system of local health centers, "centres locaux de services communautaires," or CLSCs, that perform the functions of public health units and also provide some primary health care. The province funds them directly. Hospital outpatient departments in Quebec also offer primary health care and family planning services.

Both Ontario and Quebec have youth centers that include birth control among the services provided. Health services for native peoples (primarily American Indians and Eskimos) in remote areas is the responsibility of the federal government.

Satisfaction with the health-care system appears to be extremely high, with the result that the attitude of officials could be characterized as complacent. Most people believe that the system provides satisfactory care and is easily accessible to all population groups, except perhaps those living in sparsely populated areas, where distance from a health-care provider may be a problem. Dissatisfaction among physicians surfaces from time to time, as, for example, in 1986 in Ontario, where strikes occurred when the ban on extra billing was proposed. Public and professionals both seem to believe that the supply of physicians is sufficient and that waiting times to obtain appointments are not excessive. The physician-population ratio, which in 1981 was 187 per 100,000 population in Canada, was almost as high as the U.S. ratio of 194 (OECD 1985). The physician-population ratio in Ontario and Quebec was slightly higher than that for the country as a whole: 196 in Ontario and the same in Quebec (Statistics Canada 1985, table 3.25, p. 114).

Family Planning Services
With a few exceptions, the contraceptive methods available in Canada are the same as those in the United States. The IUD has been available without interruption, although the publicity about its withdrawal from the U.S. market in 1985 and 1986 may have increased concerns among Canadians about using it. Morning-after pills, while not approved for use as a postcoital contraceptive, are widely available in clinics. The cervical cap, which is not regulated by the government and can be used without prescription, also appears to be offered in clinics in Canada more than in the United States. But the contraceptive sponge has not been approved for use, and the spermicidal suppositories Semicid and Encare are not sold. (A suppository not approved in the United States, the Ovule Pharmatex, is available.) The most commonly used oral contraceptives are triphasics.

The contraceptive method most frequently used in both Ontario and Quebec is sterilization, followed by the pill, the condom, the IUD, and other methods, in that order. In addition to their higher overall level of contraceptive use, the Canadian provinces differ somewhat from the United States in the distribution of methods. Canadians of all ages rely less on "other" methods (principally the diaphragm, spermicides, withdrawal, and periodic abstinence) than do Americans (see table 4.6 and figure 4.8). Married Canadian women aged 35–44 are much more likely to rely on sterilization than are their U.S. counterparts (59 percent in Ontario, 65 percent in Quebec, and 42 percent in the United States),[2] and among unmarried women aged 20–29, a larger proportion of Canadians use the pill (48 percent in Ontario, 39 percent in Quebec, and 25 percent in the United States). In short, Canadians appear to be more effective practitioners of contraception than their U.S. counterparts, and largely for this reason experience lower rates of unintended pregnancy and abortion.

The pill, which is the most commonly used reversible method of contraception in Canada, can be obtained only by prescription. In both Ontario and Quebec, the principal source by far of medical family planning services is the general practitioner. Family planning services are considered a component of general primary care, and women seeking oral contraceptives know to go directly to their family or personal physician for the prescription. The pills themselves are ordinarily purchased from a pharmacy. Today virtually all general practitioners are willing to prescribe the pill, although as recently as the early 1970s some of the more traditional and conservative physicians were reluctant to do so.

Obstetrician-gynecologists also provide contraceptive services, but generally they serve women wanting specialized services and those with special needs. Many general practitioners are not trained to insert IUDs, fit diaphragms, and perform surgical sterilizations, so they refer patients to specialists or to family planning clinics. Specialist services and male and female sterilization are completely free under the health insurance plans of Ontario and Quebec.[3] Sterilization reversal is also covered by the insurance plans.

Both Ontario and Quebec have systems of clinics that provide family planning services to complement the services provided by general practice physicians. In both provinces, the clinics serve several special functions. They provide intensive contraceptive counseling to women who are seeking a medical method of birth control for the first time, they serve teenagers and unmarried women who may be reluctant to go to their family physicians, they provide specialized care to women who desire a method not available from their private doctors or who have a problem with the method they are using, and they attempt

2. The U.S. figure excludes sterilization for noncontraceptive reasons. Adjusted to the Canadian definition, which includes all tubal ligations and vasectomies, the U.S. rate is about 46 percent.

3. Quebec has recently ruled that vasectomy is not covered; however, this policy may be reversed. Vasectomy was covered during the period under study.

to educate the public about contraception and reproductive health. As part of the last function, the clinics provide sex education in some schools.

In Ontario, the clinics are organized by health units. Of the forty-three health units in the province, thirty-one have family planning clinics. The provincial government gives high priority to the family planning functions and does not require local matching of funds.

Quebec's CLSCs are similar to Ontario's local health units but are more comprehensive in the services they extend. Many of the approximately one hundred CLSCs provide primary medical care as well as preventive health services and health education, and many have family planning clinics. Just as in Ontario, the family planning clinics in the CLSCs are funded primarily by the province.

The family planning clinics in Ontario are expected to try to refer their patients to private physicians when possible. For example, after a new pill user has been counseled and has demonstrated that she can use the method without problems, she is encouraged to go to a private physician for prescription renewals and continuing care. In some cases, the clinics provide counseling alone, referring patients to private physicians for their initial prescriptions. Clinics in Quebec also attempt to target their services to new users and women with special problems, but they seem more relaxed about providing contraceptive services for several years to women who prefer to come to them.

The Ontario clinics reported 81,000 patient visits for medical family planning services and an additional 62,000 visits for counseling in 1985 (Ontario Ministry of Health 1986). Assuming two visits per woman, this amounts to only 3.3 percent of the 2,189,000 women aged 15–44 in the province. But 54,000 patients were served for the first time, and since 70,000–80,000 women become sexually active each year in Ontario, the family planning program reaches a majority of the province's women during their early years of contraceptive use. The proportion of women served by clinics in Quebec is probably similar, though comparable statistics do not exist.

Overall Policies. Although contraceptive use was widespread, distribution of contraceptive methods and information on family planning were indictable offenses in Canada until 1969, when federal legislation legalized contraceptives and made abortion permissible under certain conditions. One response to these changes, motivated in part by a desire to keep down the number of abortions, was the establishment of a federal division of family planning to provide educational materials and support for contraceptive services. Under a demonstration program, federally subsidized family planning clinics were opened in most provinces. In some of the provinces clinics were created by private, nonprofit organizations, while in others, including Ontario and Quebec, they were mostly public. In Ontario, the first facilities were under the jurisdiction of municipalities in the Toronto area.

Because of financial cutbacks and changing priorities, the federal government began to reduce support for family planning programs in the late 1970s and discontinued its program completely in the 1980s. Federal officials say that their role was to provide money for demonstrations and start-up, not permanent support. As the federal role decreased, most of the provincial governments assumed some responsibility for the clinics. In some cases, private agencies turned their clinics over to public authorities for continuing administration and financial support. In other provinces, services diminished as federal support declined.

The Ontario provincial government began funding family planning programs in 1975 and assumed responsibility for the clinic system when federal support ended. Level of support and number of clinics and patients have continued to grow to the present, and current policy supports family planning services. No legislation requires parental consent for medical treatment of minors.

The Quebec government has also been active in promoting and funding family planning services. Money has been allocated to the CLSCs specifically for family planning services, and funds were also allocated to hospitals to provide reproductive health services, including family planning and abortion.

Abortion policy and services. The 1969 abortion law (Criminal Code, Revised Statutes of Canada 1970, chapter C34, section 25) allowed a physician to perform abortions in an accredited or approved hospital provided that a majority of the members of the hospital's therapeutic abortion committee certified in writing that continuation of the pregnancy would be likely to endanger the life or health of the woman. The therapeutic abortion committee had to include at least three physicians other than the physician performing the abortion. Like all medical care, abortion services provided under this law were covered by health insurance.

In January 1988, the Supreme Court of Canada ruled that the law restricting abortions to those approved by a hospital therapeutic abortion committee was unconstitutional (*Morgentaler* v. *Attorney General of Canada*). Pending new legislation, the ruling has made all abortions legal, subject only to the restrictions that govern other surgical procedures.

Until the court's ruling, a woman who sought legal hospital abortion services in Ontario faced a number of barriers. First, she usually had to obtain a referral from a general practitioner, either her family physician or the physician in a family planning clinic, to a gynecologist who would agree to present her case to a hospital's therapeutic abortion committee. In many areas outside the largest cities, these referrals were hard to get. Second, even though legal abortions were covered by health insurance, physicians received no insurance reimbursement for referrals and other efforts they made in seeking approval of the abortion. Women sometimes had to pay. They could go directly for services to a small number of hospital abortion clinics, but it was not easy to get appointments (Powell 1987). Third, in most hospitals there was no assurance that an application for abortion would be approved. Fourth, the great distances involved made it difficult for many women to obtain both referral and abortion services. Nationally, only about three hospitals in eight perform any abortions (Statistics Canada 1986), and the hospitals most likely to provide services are in the large cities. Until recently, many abortion patients had to pay the physician a fee in addition to the reimbursement that the provider received from the provincial health plan. These obstacles caused significant delays for women seeking abortions.

Abortion services are relatively easily available in Ontario's large cities. In a few hospitals in the province abortions are routinely approved. Starting in 1985, two clinics provided abortion services in Toronto while the abortion law was still being tested in the courts. Although women had to pay for abortions in the clinics, which were not recognized as legal by OHIP, an estimated five thousand women a year were served.

In Quebec, the 1969 abortion law was challenged by Dr. Henry Morgentaler, a physician who opened an abortion clinic in which he performed abortions without the approval of a therapeutic abortion committee. He was prosecuted three times during the 1970s and each time was acquitted by a jury. Deciding that the federal abortion law was unenforceable, the provincial government discontinued the prosecution of violations and began reimbursement of nonhospital abortions through the provincial health plan. There are now several abortion clinics in Quebec, most in the Montreal area.

In Quebec, the presence of clinics makes abortion services relatively easily available, although distance from a provider can present a problem for women living in rural areas. The province is extremely large, and most of its territory is far from the St. Lawrence River, where the cities with abortion clinics are located.

In other provinces, abortion services are readily available in most of the large cities but rare elsewhere. Newfoundland and Prince Edward Island have no services (Sabia 1986; Statistics Canada 1986).

Target Groups for Family Planning
Canadians believe their system of primary physician care meets the health-care needs of the great majority of people. The family planning

clinic programs in both Ontario and Quebec are intended to extend services to certain groups with special needs: women who are beginning to use a medical contraceptive method for the first time and who may need special counseling—teenagers, unmarried women, and women using methods that their physicians are unable to provide, especially the IUD and the diaphragm. In addition, special efforts are made in Ontario to reach women in remote areas poorly served by private physicians. With one exception in Toronto (a clinic for immigrant women), programs are not designed specifically for low-income women or women of disadvantaged racial or ethnic groups, nor is there evidence of a need for such programs.

These observations do not include the native peoples, who represent only 2 percent of the population of the country as a whole and 1.3 percent in Ontario and 0.7 percent in Quebec (Statistics Canada 1985). Health care for native peoples is provided by a federal agency similar to the Indian Health Service in the United States. Because of the remoteness of the areas where the indigenous people live and the fact that the services are a federal rather than provincial responsibility, no information was obtained about those family planning services.

PRIVATE PHYSICIANS

Private general practitioners (including family practice specialists), the principal source of medical family planning services, are said to be widely distributed in both Ontario and Quebec. The number of physicians per capita is almost as high as that in the United States, as the introduction to this chapter noted. About half of Canadian physicians, however, are general or family practitioners (Statistics Canada 1985, 94), compared to only 16 percent in the United States (see chapter 5). Therefore, the availability of general practitioners is much higher in Canada than in the United States.

Few barriers stand in the way of going to family physicians for contraceptive services. Because payment in Ontario and Quebec is by fee for service, it is relatively easy for a woman to go to a physician other than her own family doctor for contraception. Although a physician visit typically requires an appointment, one can usually be obtained within a few days. Non-English-speaking immigrants are generally able to find physicians who speak their language, since many Canadian physicians are foreign-born.

Although the supply of physicians is considered adequate in Canada, there is some concern that areas with sparse populations are underserved (Boulard and DuFour 1983). In Quebec, new physicians are reimbursed on a higher fee schedule for the first three years if they locate in a rural area than if they locate in Montreal, where it is said that physicians want more patients. In Ontario, the Underserviced Area Program recruits physicians and provides a monthly living bonus.

Women comprise 17 percent of physicians, and this proportion is likely to increase, as about half the present medical students are female. In both Ontario and Quebec, physician fees for family planning services are paid by the provincial insurance plans. In Ontario, physician office visits are divided into three levels, from simple to complex, and reimbursement is adjusted accordingly. If a patient requires extra counseling, however, in neither province would a physician feel he or she could charge for the extra time. Although it is theoretically possible to charge an additional amount, physicians believe that questions could be raised by OHIP or the Régie de l'Assurance-Maladie du Québec (the Quebec health insurance administration), and reimbursement could be jeopardized. Reimbursement for thirty minutes' counseling is significantly less than for three regular ten-minute visits, giving physicians a financial incentive to minimize counseling time. Otherwise, there is no particular financial incentive to serve or not to serve contraceptive patients. Visits to nurse-practitioners are not reimbursed by the health plans, and private physicians see all patients instead of delegating family planning patients to a nurse.

Contraceptive supplies and devices are not covered by the provincial health plans. A cycle of birth control pills costs between $7 and $11, and there is a small charge, usually $15–20, for an IUD inserted by a physician. Pill supplies are available without charge to patients receiving welfare benefits, and many employers provide supplementary insurance plans that cover drugs, including oral contraceptives.

Private physicians give medical contraceptive care to the great majority of women who obtain such care—all except those who attend family planning clinics or other special programs. They do little if any outreach to new patients needing contraceptive services, although they may on occasion raise the subject of contraception with patients they are seeing for other reasons.

Parental consent is not legally required in either Ontario or Quebec for anyone over thirteen, and most but not all physicians will serve unmarried minors without parental consent (Boldt, Roberts, and Latif 1982). Teenagers are said to learn from each other which physicians are willing to serve them. In Quebec, each teenager has her or his own health insurance card, so they have no difficulty in obtaining confidential services once they locate a provider. In Ontario, however, teenagers have to use the family insurance card, which means they may have to explain to their parents why they need it.

When considering contraception, physicians tend to think first of the pill and sterilization, the methods used by most women. A woman who asks for the pill is unlikely to be counseled about other methods unless the pill is contraindicated. Other methods will be discussed with a woman who does not know what method she wants, but it tends to be assumed that a woman seeking reversible contraception will use the pill.

Many physicians do not insert IUDs or fit diaphragms (Springate, Danaher, and Morrison 1987). Women choosing these methods are often referred to a specialist or to a family planning clinic. Similarly, women seeking sterilization are referred to specialists. Sterilization is approved of by most physicians, and almost all general practitioners are willing to refer women seeking it. Few physicians feel that sterilization regret is a problem.

More detailed information about the attitudes and practices of physicians in Quebec is available from a survey of 215 obstetrician-gynecologists conducted in 1981 (Marcil-Gratton, Lapierre-Adamcyk, and Duchesne 1985). Tubal ligations were performed by 88 percent of the respondents, and services could be had even in less populated areas far from Montreal and Quebec City. In areas outside of Montreal where there were fewer obstetrician-gynecologists, general surgeons performed one-third of female sterilizations. Although sterilization on demand did not exist as such in Quebec, few patients were refused, as the great majority of respondents said they refused fewer than 10 percent of applicants. One-fourth of the obstetrician-gynecologists had no fixed requirements based on age, number of children, or marital status. Half would perform a tubal ligation for a woman aged 25–29 with only two children, 40 percent would serve women under thirty-five who had never been married, and 65 percent would serve women younger than twenty-five under some circumstances. The physicians believed that vasectomy was less common than tubal ligation because of fear of reduced virility, fear of other secondary effects, and the tradition of leaving the responsibility for birth control to women. Almost all said the subject of sterilization was usually raised first by the patient, not the physician.

The Quebec respondents perceived little sterilization regret: 80 percent say that fewer than 10 percent of sterilized women regret the decision, and of those who express regret, few are reported to go so far as to request reversal. (Somewhat higher levels of regret have been found in surveys of sterilized women in Quebec, described below.) When faced with patients who regret having been sterilized, most physicians warn patients about the complexity of the reversal operation and tend not to encourage women to request it, but 35 percent did say that more facilities for reversal surgery were needed.

With so many physicians willing to perform the procedure, barriers to sterilization are minimal. Although in the past many hospitals in Quebec required each case to be approved by tubal ligation committees, in recent years most committees have been discontinued. Two-thirds of the physicians responding to the Quebec survey reported that the average delay for hospital admission for sterilization was less than three months (Marcil-Gratton, Lapierre-Adamcyk, and Duschesne 1985, 51). It is still difficult to have sterilization performed in Catholic hospitals in Ontario, but since other hospitals are available, this presents little problem. Vasectomies are frequently performed by general practitioners, and here again, barriers are minimal.

When the pill is prescribed, a pelvic examination is usually but not always performed. The first return visit for a new pill patient is usually scheduled for three or six months. Subsequent visits may be scheduled at one-year intervals.

Counseling of pill patients centers on how to use the method and what side effects to expect. All physicians mention the possibility of short-term side effects, but they vary in how much they feel the patient should be told. Some think that the more side effects patients are told about, the more they will notice. Others believe that telling patients in advance about all the possible side effects tends to prevent patients from calling or coming back later with questions and complaints. In either case, the physician's goal is to minimize the number of calls from patients.

The extent of counseling patients about possible dangers to health caused by the pill underwent a change as a result of a Canadian court decision in 1984 that found that Orthopharmaceutical (Canada) Ltd., a maker of oral contraceptives, had not adequately warned doctors about possible adverse effects of the pill. In 1985, the federal government released instructions for a new informational pamphlet about the pill, to be used as a supplement to the patient package insert. The pamphlet describes contraindications, risks, failure rates, and mortality rates involving the pill compared with other methods and no method, as well as its noncontraceptive benefits. Most physicians now give this pamphlet to their pill patients and tend to rely on it to inform them about the possible dangers of the pill. Although physicians mention the specific symptoms that a patient should immediately report to her doctor, most do not mention such serious illnesses as heart attacks, which could result. Many physicians believe that calling attention to serious problems unnecessarily frightens patients. Some tell patients that the risk of side effects is ten times as great for childbirth as it is for the pill.

Although concern about lawsuits is increasing in Canada, the problem is less acute than in the United States. Malpractice insurance for obstetrician-gynecologists who perform surgery in Montreal is going up to $6,000 per year from about $4,000. Insurance for family physicians in Quebec is about $1,200. In contrast, malpractice insurance costs U.S. obstetrician-gynecologists anywhere from $20,000 to $100,000, depending on the state and the insurance company (ACOG 1987a).

The amount of time physicians spend with new contraceptive patients is difficult to estimate. Physicians say they spend fifteen to thirty minutes, while other observers say that five to ten minutes would be a more accurate figure. In some practices, a nurse or assistant provides some of the contraceptive counseling, particularly about how to use a method. Physicians take no active steps to follow up patients who fail to return for appointments.

FAMILY PLANNING CLINICS

Ontario

Ontario has forty-three health units, each of which serves a catchment area, usually corresponding to a county. Some catchment areas are very large and sparsely populated. For example, the Porcupine Health Unit, which the study team visited, serves an area in northeastern Ontario the size of East and West Germany combined. In large districts like this, there are satellite clinics served by personnel who divide their time among several different locations.

Most of a health unit's family planning services are provided in clinics organized for this purpose, but some are also provided in multi-purpose clinics along with immunizations, sexually transmitted disease treatment, and other services. Of the forty-three health units in the province, all have family planning coordinators who provide outreach, and thirty-one also provide family planning services in a total of forty-seven clinics. In a few locations, the health units have subcontracted with affiliates of the Planned Parenthood Federation of Canada to provide family planning services.

Funding for the health units is provided by the province and by municipalities. Some of the provincial money is targeted for specific purposes, one of which is family planning. Provincial grants cover most of the cost of family planning programs, and no local matching funds are required. Family planning patients are never charged a fee, and pills are provided without charge to new users and to low-income women who cannot afford to purchase them from a pharmacy. A few clinics sell pills to patients who can pay, using the profits to help support the clinic. This practice has been controversial, since it may violate laws governing the dispensing of pharmaceuticals.

The family planning clinics engage in a number of education and outreach activities, including education on sexuality and contraception in schools, sessions with interested community groups, participation in health fairs, setting up booths in malls, and occasional advertising using posters or other media. When the case load is low, outreach activities are stepped up to increase the number of patients; when it is high, more time is spent on patient care and less on outreach. A factor limiting the case load is the practice of encouraging patients to switch to private physicians for ongoing care unless they have special reasons for needing clinic services. In general, the demand for services is small enough that a generous amount of time can be spent with each patient without creating long waiting times for services.

Clinics serve primarily young and unmarried women. In 1985, 52 percent of patients were under twenty, and 84 percent had never been married. Sources of referral to the clinic were as follows: 63 percent were self-referred, 15 percent by friends, 10 percent by other personnel within the health unit, 4 percent by physicians, 1 percent by schools, 1 percent by hospitals, and 6 percent by other sources. Of those who received services other than counseling, 13 percent came for pregnancy tests (Ontario Ministry of Health 1986). One study of teenage clinic patients found that 16 to 18 percent of new patients had never had intercourse (Conway and Ridley 1984).

The family planning coordinators, whose responsibilities include outreach, are public health nurses in all health units except those in Toronto, where outreach workers have social work or other types of training. Coordinators periodically approach the public and parochial schools with an offer to provide sex education and information about contraceptive methods and services to students. The schools are under no obligation to accept the offer, and many or most do not. In the Porcupine Health Unit, most schools are contacted each year with information about the family planning and sex education services available. Several public schools invite the family planning coordinator to provide information to students. Catholic schools occasionally allow the family planning coordinator to make presentations to students but usually do not.

Most nurses in public schools and some in Catholic ones will refer students to the clinics or to private physicians for contraceptive services. Schools commonly give students passes to attend the clinic during school hours. Some school nurses perform pregnancy tests for students.

The province requires clinics to provide whatever method a woman chooses, either at the facility or by referral; to offer nonjudgmental comprehensive counseling; and to accept all patients. There is no age limit for patients.

Medical services are provided by physicians, usually local general practitioners hired by the session. The doctors tend to be young, and many are women. Patients may not see the same physician at each visit, but they usually see the same nurse. Satellite clinics often have no physician, even part-time, so patients are referred to an outside physician or to another clinic after being counseled.

Clinics emphasize counseling, which is most usually done by nurses. (Overall, there are two nurses for every physician.) The major purpose is seen as motivating new contraceptive users (frequently teenagers) to prevent pregnancy and helping them to use their method effectively. At the first visit a new patient may have three counseling sessions before receiving a pill prescription: a brief initial interview with a nurse, a one-hour group teaching session, and an individual counseling session in which the patient's history is taken. A second visit is often necessary to see the physician and obtain a prescription, which some health units will not write until the patient has attended the teaching session. A temporary nonprescription method is sometimes provided.

The counseling usually covers foam, condom, and postcoital contraception as well as the pill. The diaphragm may also be mentioned. Periodic abstinence, the IUD, and sterilization are not necessarily mentioned to the average patient, who is young and nulliparous. In some instances, counseling includes discussion of the disadvantages of childbearing at a young age. The purpose is to increase the motivation of unmarried teenagers to prevent pregnancy and childbearing. Those who come for pregnancy tests that prove to be negative are the special target of this counseling.

Although not required, a pelvic examination is normally performed before oral contraceptives are prescribed. Each patient receives a pamphlet describing possible side effects of the pill, but the dangers of heart trouble and other rare consequences of pill use are not emphasized or necessarily even mentioned. Neither private nor clinic physicians seem to feel that they need to inform patients of the worst possible potential effects of the pill in order to protect themselves from litigation, which rarely occurs.

The first follow-up visit for a new pill user is usually scheduled for three months and sometimes after only one month. Thereafter visits are scheduled half-yearly or yearly, depending on the age and circumstances of the patient. Clinics generally do not try to reach a patient who does not return as scheduled, and it is common for patients not to return for follow-up visits.

Unlike many general practitioners, the clinics insert IUDs, fit diaphragms, and train patients in periodic abstinence, and some patients are referred to clinics by private physicians for these services. As with general practitioners, however, the prevailing attitude at the clinics seems to be that these methods are only for women who have a problem with the pill. Especially for teenagers, the pill is considered preferable to other methods. Patients desiring sterilization are referred to specialists. Clinics offer postcoital contraception, which many physicians refuse to provide. In a major clinic in Toronto, 7 to 8 percent of first visits are for postcoital contraception.

One clinic in Toronto is devoted to serving the women of six immigrant communities: Chinese, Italian, Portuguese, Spanish, Vietnamese, and West Indian. The facility employs counselors from these communities who speak the appropriate languages. Although almost all of the clinic's clients have family doctors, most of whom speak their language, clinic personnel believe the doctors usually do not provide adequate information and counseling about contraception, a gap that the clinic fills. Many of the women come from cultural backgrounds where women receive little information about contraception. In addition to serving individual clients, the clinic is active in disseminating information in the various communities and at workplaces with large numbers of immigrant women. A majority of the clients are over twenty-five; younger women, who get information from school and speak English, are less likely to attend the immigrant clinic.

The Ontario family planning program concentrates its resources on counseling women who are new users of contraception, especially teenagers, and on serving women with special problems. Medical services are provided, but most women who need only medical services rely on private physicians, to whom they are expected to switch once they no longer need the special counseling and expertise the clinics offer. Officials credit the targeting of teenagers by the family planning program, together with increased sex education, with having caused a sharp reduction in teenage pregnancy in the province between 1977 and 1984.

Quebec

CLSCs. Two types of organizations provide the great majority of family planning clinic services in Quebec, CLSCs (*centres locaux de services communautaires*) and hospital outpatient clinics. In addition, there are a handful of specialized services for women or teenagers that provide family planning counseling or services.

The CLSCs are community health and social service centers controlled by local boards and funded by the province to serve a specified geographic area. The CLSC program was started in 1974 and has grown over the years so that about a hundred CLSCs now cover most— but not all—of the more populated sections of the province. The CLSCs tend to be ideological in inclination, sometimes socialist and sometimes antiphysician. They vary widely in their focus, with some concentrating on mental illness, aging, or preventive services rather than primary health care. Some do not have physicians. Many, however, provide general medical care, and most have family planning clinics. About 10 percent of the population of the province received health care from the CLSCs in 1980.

In the past, the province specified a minimum amount of money to be spent on family planning. Now, however, the CLSC boards have discretion to decide how most funds are used, and the emphasis given to family planning has declined, in part because of antiabortion pressure. Nevertheless, accessibility to CLSC family planning clinics is good, and a nurse can almost always be seen on short notice, although an appointment several weeks in advance is sometimes needed to see a physician.

Patients incur no charges for family planning services except for a $12 charge for the IUD to patients who can afford to pay. Pill patients are given their first supply of pills without charge, and additional supplies may be given to those who cannot afford to buy them from a pharmacy. Some women's insurance coverage through their employers pays for oral contraceptives.

Patients who use the CLSCs do so for a number of reasons: they are teenagers who heard about the service at school or from friends, they have problems with their contraceptive method or want a method not available from their physicians, they are concerned about confidentiality and prefer not to go to their family physician, they want the supply of free pills, they prefer a female physician, they like the greater amount of professional time they receive at a clinic, or they came as abortion patients and have continued to use the clinic's family planning service. One-fourth to one-half the family planning patients are teenagers. Low-income women are considered to have access to private physicians and are not a particular target group for the CLSCs.

The extent and type of outreach varies among CLSCs. Many patients hear about the family planning services through the clinics' sex education activities in the schools and their work with community groups. The public school nurses, who are under the jurisdiction of the CLSCs, are a natural source of referral. To make their services better known, clinics may occasionally advertise in newspapers or on the radio.

CLSC physicians are usually private general or family practitioners who are paid by the clinic session. A much larger proportion of CLSC physicians is women than is the case among all general practitioners. The clinics also employ nurse-practitioners, who sometimes perform pelvic examinations and give out the pill when a physician is not present. Medical services are usually provided by a physician.

CLSCs generally have one or two family planning sessions a week with a physician present and additional sessions when other personnel may be seen. An appointment is usually necessary to see a physician, but walk-in patients may be accepted for visits with a nurse or counselor. In some centers, appointments must be scheduled several weeks in advance. The pill is the most frequent method, although IUDs, diaphragms, and morning-after pills are also available. Patients are usually referred to specialists for sterilization. Training in periodic abstinence is offered in some locations, but many providers refer patients desiring this method to the Service de Régulation des Naissances (SERENA), an organization devoted to its promotion.

Patients requesting the pill generally receive a pelvic examination at the time of the prescription, but the pelvic is not legally required, and practice varies. One CLSC allows a nurse to dispense the pill without a pelvic exam if neither nurse nor doctor has time for the examination. The patient is then scheduled to return in one to three months for the physical. Another CLSC has a policy of not performing the pelvic exam on a woman who has never had intercourse, although it will supply her with pills. Practice regarding the scheduling of return visits varies. One CLSC usually schedules the first return visit for a new pill user for three months and thereafter schedules revisits at six- or twelve-month intervals, depending on the patient.

Most providers believe that the pill is the best method, especially for teenagers. After a woman has had two children, sterilization is considered appropriate by many providers if a woman wants to terminate childbearing. For a woman over thirty-five who smokes but is not ready for sterilization, the IUD would probably be recommended. The IUD is also used by many women aged 25–35, in some cases because of concern about the adverse synergistic effect of smoking and pill use. Other methods are sometimes mentioned by providers, but these three get the most serious attention.

Clinic physicians spend fifteen to thirty minutes or more with family planning patients, which is more than the time spent by physicians in private practice. The fact that clinic physicians are paid by the length of time spent (the clinic session) rather than by the service provided may help to account for the difference. A pill patient sees a nurse as well as a physician; the nurse spends between thirty minutes and an hour with the patient. No standard procedure for follow-up of patients who fail to return for appointments exists, although individual providers may follow up particular patients where they believe it is necessary.

During the time spent with the patient, the nurse takes her history and discusses methods, sexuality, the risk of sexually transmitted diseases, the patient's menstrual cycle, and her general health. The nurse also takes the patient's blood pressure and records her weight. The information provided by doctors and nurses about the side effects of the pill covers spotting and other minor side effects. The patient is instructed to contact the provider immediately if specific signs of a major problem occur, but little else is said about these problems or the likelihood of their occurring. Before the government issued recommendations in 1985 regarding the distribution of an informational pamphlet about the pill, apparently even less was said. Both doctors and clinics rely on the pill pamphlet to inform patients about possible major health consequences of pill use. Generally, it is considered undesirable to provide information that might make patients fearful of the pill.

Life-options counseling to discourage women from early childbearing is uncommon, because the desire to have children is rare among unmarried teenagers in Quebec. Most young women with low incomes want employment, money, and independence rather than children. The few who want children often have personal problems, and these may be counseled about the responsibilities of parenthood.

Other fertility-related services offered by the CLSCs include free pregnancy tests, STD (sexually transmitted disease) treatment, and abortion services or referral. Each of these services can be a source of family planning patients.

Hospital clinics. A number of the hospitals in Quebec, including eight in Montreal and several in other cities, have clinics that provide family planning services. Several of the clinics were established under a provincial program begun in 1977 to improve reproductive health care. These "Lazure clinics," named after the cabinet minister who proposed their creation, were intended to provide specialized reproductive services including infertility care, abortion, and sterilization as well as contraception. While hospital clinics are fewer than CLSCs, they serve more family planning patients per clinic and appear to be of almost equal importance.

Hospital family planning services are funded in part by special provincial grants and in part out of the hospitals' budgets. As with private physicians and CLSCs, hospital clinics do not charge patients, except for IUDs, which cost $14 to $17.

Hospitals see it as their mission to provide services not available from general practitioners, including counseling for new contraceptive users and women with special problems, so that the role of the hospital clinic is very similar to that of the CLSC. They do little active outreach; most patients come to the programs by referral from physicians, school nurses, or others, or come for reproductive health care like abortion or delivery and stay for contraceptive care. Activities that may increase a program's visibility in the community include continuing education activities for physicians, presentations to community organizations, and presentations in schools. Although many patients come by referral, a referral is not necessary to obtain an appointment.

Some of the hospitals serve primarily poor or working-class clients, in part because these groups traditionally used hospitals for health care before universal health insurance was initiated. Others use the hospitals because they want the extra counseling provided, they do not want to go to their family doctor for certain sensitive services such as treatment for STDs, or they need care not available from their private physician. Parental involvement is not required for patients aged fourteen and over, and some hospitals report that a large proportion of their patients is teenagers. The hospital clinics provide most of the same advantages as the CLSCs, and the province has attempted to avoid duplication of services. Women are in theory expected to return to their family physicians once their special need for the hospital clinic has been met, but in practice hospitals appear to be generally willing to continue to serve patients who prefer their care.

Medical care is provided by physicians, and nurse-practitioners do not usually perform physical examinations. As in the CLSCs, the physicians are usually private practitioners paid by the session. In some hospitals, however, they are paid according to the service provided, as in private practice. The physicians tend to be young, a feature that may be attractive to teenagers. Nurses provide much of the counseling.

Hospital clinics normally have several family planning sessions a week. Most expect patients to make appointments, for which there may be a wait, but some accept patients the same day. Patients see a nurse for counseling and history-taking and a physician for physical examination and prescription. Counseling tends to be extensive, and a visit may take as long as one and one-half hours, not including waiting time. In most but not all hospitals, the physician probably takes more time with the patients than is usual in private practice.

Pill patients must undergo a physical examination before the pills are prescribed. The first follow-up visit for a new pill patient is scheduled for three or six months. Thereafter return visits are expected each twelve months if there are no problems. Attempts to contact a patient who fails to return at the expected time are rare.

Counselors mention contraceptive methods they think appropriate for a particular patient but do not systematically describe all methods. Providers see the pill as the best method for most patients. One counselor said that if a patient complains about weight gain, she tells her that pregnancy also causes weight gain. As in other facilities, patients are warned about minor side effects and are instructed about symptoms that necessitate a call to the physician. Little emphasis is given to possible health dangers associated with the pill; the pill pamphlet serves as the only warning of these risks.

The hospitals visited shared with the CLSCs the philosophy that the patient has a right and responsibility to select and use an appropriate birth control method. This view extends to teenagers, and hospitals make no recommendation to minors that they discuss contraception with their parents.

OTHER FACILITIES

Pharmacies. Pharmacies are the principal source of contraceptive supplies, both prescription and nonprescription. Their role is similar to that of pharmacies in the United States. Nonprescription methods, including condoms, are almost always stocked, even in rural areas, and are frequently displayed where they can be easily found and examined by customers, although the displays tend to be located at the back of the store near the pharmacist. While they are not featured in prominent displays, they increasingly have erotic pictures on the packages and other attention-getting devices.

Pharmacists frequently serve as a source of information about methods, especially the pill, to women already using a method. For example, women often ask about the long-term safety of pill use. Some pharmacists make special efforts to assure that new pill patients are adequately informed. Pharmacies also serve as a referral source for clinics.

University health centers. All or almost all university health centers provide prescription contraceptives to students. Colleges in Quebec, which are between high schools and universities in academic level, do not generally provide family planning services but will refer students to other sources. Condoms are sometimes available from vending machines on university campuses.

Centres de Santé des Femmes. There are about six feminist women's health centers in Quebec. These were originally funded by the province but now must rely in part on fee-for-service insurance payments and other miscellaneous income because of cuts in provincial support. The centers organize workshops and discussion groups and provide reproductive health care. The center visited for this study, in addition to providing contraceptive care, including the cervical cap, performs abortions, provides childbirth training, and has a health clinic for lesbians. Because of financial limitations, it has not been able to accept new contraceptive patients in three years.

Youth centers. Both Toronto (The House, operated by Planned Parenthood of Toronto) and Montreal (Centre de Jeunesse) have multiservice youth centers that provide contraceptive care to many teenagers. These centers attempt to reach students on local high school and college campuses with information and family planning services as well as other health and counseling services. The special attraction for teenagers appears to be the emphasis on counseling and confidentiality and the assurance of a sympathetic caregiver.

The Toronto facility is funded largely by fee-for-service insurance payments. The physicians are on salary, and most of the counseling is done by volunteers. There is no charge to patients, who are given the choice of a male or female physician. The initial visit begins with a session with a counselor during which the patient chooses a contraceptive method; she is then seen by a physician and may be seen again by the counselor. The process can take two and one-half hours. The time spent per patient by the physician is greater than that spent by a private physician. For pill patients, a physical examination is ordinarily required before a prescription is provided.

Pill patients are scheduled to return after one month, at which time they are counseled again, and again seen by a physician. Further visits are scheduled after two or six months, depending on the circumstances. No routine procedure is in place for contacting patients who fail to return for follow-up appointments. Counseling covers the general subject of sexuality as well as the specific issues of contraception. Several birth control methods are mentioned, but the focus is on those considered most appropriate for teenagers. Fertility awareness is one of the methods always mentioned but not emphasized; it is rarely selected by patients. Information about the short-term and long-term effects of the pill is provided.

Hospital clinics for children. In both Toronto and Montreal, at least one hospital clinic for children and young people offers family planning services in addition to other medical care.

School clinics. Four schools in the Toronto area have family planning clinics, and condoms are distributed in some schools in Quebec. These programs have remained in effect in spite of some public opposition.

SERENA. The Service de Régulation des Naissances (SERENA) is a private organization in Quebec that promotes periodic abstinence, in conformity with Catholic doctrine. It has a number of locations in the province (as well as branches in Ontario) where instruction in the symptothermal method is given.

CLIENT PREFERENCES

No survey data are available documenting women's satisfaction with family planning services or their preferences among providers. The pattern of utilization of providers, however, probably reflects women's preferences. The fact that both physicians and clinics are able to meet the demand for services without excessive waiting times indicates that women are obtaining the services they prefer, within the limits of geographic availability. Most clinics can schedule appointments for a medical method of contraception within two weeks.

A principal reason for seeking clinic services appears to be the desire for confidentiality, that is, a desire (often of unmarried women and teenagers) to discuss the sensitive topic of contraception with a sympathetic person other than their family physician. The response to this need is usually to seek services from a clinic, although another option is to go to a different private physician. Most new clinic patients have probably selected the clinic for reasons of confidentiality rather than a perceived need for the extensive counseling they receive, although some women go to clinics because of the desire for counseling and the availability of free pills. Clinic or specialist services may also be preferred by women seeking methods other than the pill and by women who have experienced a problem with their contraceptive method.

The pill is the contraceptive method most younger women prefer, and sterilization is chosen by most women who do not want more children. The preference for oral contraceptives appears to be based on their effectiveness and on their independence from the sex act. Several providers described women as being grateful to have a method of birth control as easy to use as the pill. The preference for the pill is reinforced by the support of health-care providers, who regard it as the preferred method for most women. Widespread publicity during the early 1980s made Canadian women aware of possible adverse health effects of the pill, but increased concern did not result in a noticeable shift to less effective methods, although it may in part account for the high rate of sterilization. Continued use of the pill may have been due to women's trust in the recommendations of their physicians, and little change reportedly occurred in providers' preference for oral contraceptives. In recent years, women have become more aware of the reported noncontraceptive health benefits of the pill and have regained confidence in it, although it is not usually recommended for use by women past thirty-five. The pamphlet that accompanies oral contraceptive packages states, "After the age of 35 years, it is generally inadvisable to use oral contraceptives. Your doctor should be consulted in this regard" (Ortho 1985, 18).

Women who want no more children are said to choose sterilization because of its effectiveness, the inconvenience of taking the pill every day, and the increasing health risk associated with pill use as they grow older. A study of a random sample of 497 sterilized women interviewed by telephone in the Montreal area in 1985 reported that a major reason for choosing sterilization was the desire for a method that is completely effective (cited by 90 percent of the respondents) and the desire not to have to worry about contraception any more (cited by 80 percent). Health problems that could result from pregnancy were named by four in ten, fear of the pill's side effects by one-fourth, and problems with other contraceptive methods by one-fifth (Marcil-Gratton and Lapierre-Adamcyk 1987, 33). These results suggest that Canadian women place a high value on efficacy, and that health concerns in relation to the pill are of secondary importance in the sterilization decision. That pill use is discouraged after age thirty-five does not explain the high rate of sterilization before age thirty, which is characteristic of both Canada and the United States. The cost of pill supplies may also be a factor, although it is impossible to know how important a role it plays (sterilization is free).

Sterilization regret occurs in Quebec at about the same rate as in the United States. The study cited above found that 25 percent of the respondents said that they had felt regret at some time since the operation because they might have liked to have another child, and that 13 percent would have "really tried" to have another child (Marcil-Gratton and Lapierre-Adamcyk 1987, 15). In the United States, according to the 1982 National Survey of Family Growth, 26 percent of women who were sterilized or whose partners were sterilized said they would like to have another child, and 10 percent said they would like to have the sterilization reversed (Henshaw and Singh 1986, 239). But these statistics may exaggerate the importance of the regret. In response to additional questions, only 5 percent of the Quebec women said that they thought they should never have been sterilized or should have had the procedure later and that they would really have tried to have another child. Only 4 percent said they had discussed a reversal procedure with their doctor, and 1 percent had asked to have the operation.

The respondents in the Quebec study were generally satisfied with sterilization: 95 percent were very satisfied or fairly satisfied with having had the tubal ligation. Thirty percent said that their sex life had improved after the sterilization (compared with 2 percent for whom it had deteriorated), and 54 percent said they felt better mentally; 4 percent said they felt less feminine. Regret was most common among women who had been sterilized in their twenties, women whose marital status had changed or who were unmarried, women with less education, and women who had been sterilized because of a health problem. The number of children bore little relation to the probability of regret.

Women for whom oral contraceptives are contraindicated because of smoking, age, or side effects and who are not ready for sterilization tend to use the IUD. For such women, the IUD is preferred over barrier methods because of its effectiveness. Some physicians in Quebec regard as optimal a progression from use of the pill before a woman has children, to the IUD during the childbearing period, to sterilization when childbearing is completed.

INFORMATION AND EDUCATION

Organized Communication Efforts
During the 1970s, the federal government's Family Planning Division was an important source of materials and information about birth control. Although the division launched no national education campaigns, it served as a resource for local and provincial groups seeking to educate the public. During the 1980s, the federal government gradually withdrew from this activity.

The provincial governments provide support for the creation of new materials but do not themselves engage in public education campaigns. For example, the Ontario Ministry of Health has produced a very explicit sex-education package called "Changing Me" that is now used in some schools; the Quebec education ministry financed the creation of a sex education curriculum and has recently adopted it.

Campaigns to educate the public about family planning services occur from time to time at the initiative of local authorities. One example is "birth control week" in Toronto, which took place each year from the mid-1970s to 1985. In 1984, the activity included a condom giveaway, which attracted a great deal of attention but ultimately led to the campaign's discontinuation. The health department has tried to place posters in the Toronto subway, but prohibitions against using the words *sex*, *birth control*, and *family planning* have made the attempts futile.

Planned Parenthood serves as a source of information in both Ontario and Quebec. The Toronto office handles five hundred information calls a week and has installed automated equipment to provide recorded information over the telephone. The Planned Parenthood youth clinic, The House, produces a newsletter four to six times a year that the board of education distributes free to students.

Sex education. In Ontario local school boards largely control sex education, which varies widely from district to district. Within education districts, the Catholic schools have education boards and policies that are completely separate from public schools'. Overall, surveys suggest that the amount and type of sex education in Ontario is similar to that in the United States (Nolte 1984).

One difference from the United States is the involvement of school nurses in family planning education and referral. School nurses are under the jurisdiction of the health units rather than the boards of education, and it is usual practice for them to refer students for contraceptive services. School nurses or family planning clinic staff members may also participate in sex-education programs or make presentations to students. In some schools the nurses perform pregnancy tests. These activities, however, are controlled by school administrators and are often not permitted. Catholic schools are less likely than others to let nurses or clinic staff provide sex education.

Until recently, Quebec has also had sex education programs in some districts but not others. Within the last two years, after over ten years of delay by opponents, the provincial department of education has adopted a sex-education curriculum. This program is too new to have had any impact on birth control or fertility statistics, but it indicates a resolve to provide education about sexuality and contraception.

As in Ontario, school nurses function under the jurisdiction of health officials, usually the CLSCs, and they often play a role in birth control education and referral. CLSCs assist in providing sex education in some schools but are not accepted in others. Starting in 1973 and continuing into the early 1980s, CLSCs received special funds from the province to provide basic information regarding contraception and sex. The program was aimed at high school students who were leaving school and not seeking higher education, because it was believed that these students were most likely to have problems with unintended fertility leading to poverty. Nurses and social workers acted as instructors. At its height, the program reached a large proportion of students leaving school.

Advertising of Methods and Services
Advertising of contraceptive methods is similar to that in the United States. Advertising the brand names of prescription drugs to the general public is prohibited, and pharmaceutical companies advertise their oral contraceptives only to professionals. Advertising of nonprescription methods is legal but not widespread. Small ads for foam have appeared recently in print. Condoms have been advertised—for example, a large ad was run in *Châtelaine*, a magazine, in 1969—but there is little or no advertising now, reportedly because the market is too small. In Toronto, a birth control hot line is advertised in the classified section of a newspaper, the classified telephone directory, and a handbook that is sent each year to all high school students.

Media Treatment of Contraception
Most of the television programming watched by Canadians is produced in the United States and rarely contains references to contraception. The Canadian-produced dramas in English similarly do not men-

tion contraception. Occasional news items and documentaries do contain information about it.

As in the United States, organizations in Canada have tried to place spot television ads encouraging birth control. In Manitoba, three such ads directed at teenagers have been created by the Committee on Unplanned Pregnancy and accepted as paid commercials by private television stations in the province. The ads show vignettes of teenagers talking about such subjects as their desire to finish school before having a baby and the importance of using birth control. The theme of the ads is "take control," and viewers are shown a toll-free number to call for information. Although the ads generated few complaints from the public, publicly owned Canadian Broadcasting Corporation has refused to broadcast them.

Television programming in Quebec, much of which is locally produced, contains somewhat more information about birth control and sexuality than do programs in other provinces. During the 1970s, the rapidly increasing rate of sexual activity among teenagers was a frequent topic on Quebec television, both in discussion programs and in dramas. Although teenage sexual activity was frequently disapproved of on these programs, a dominant theme was the importance attached to sexually active teenagers using contraception. A popular serial drama about a family with four adolescents contained frequent references to contraception.

Radio "open line" shows are open to questions about sex. Sue Johanson, the Toronto counterpart of Dr. Ruth Westheimer ("Dr. Ruth") in the United States, has a show called the *Sunday Night Sex Show* on the main rock station as well as a talk show about sexuality on a cable television channel. These shows feature phone-in questions about sex.

As in the United States, the print media, particularly magazines, are frequent sources of information about methods of contraception. Major articles appear periodically and present both favorable and unfavorable information about methods. Newspaper columns related to health, personal relations (including the Ann Landers advice column), and youth sometimes discuss contraception.

Climate of Opinion Concerning Sex
An earlier study concluded that Canadian attitudes about sexuality display the same tendencies and contradictions as those in the United States, although they may be slightly more accepting of sexuality (Jones 1986). In Canada as in the United States, a traditionalist movement supported by religious fundamentalists opposes the liberalizing of sexual mores and the legality of abortion. While these views are strongest in the Prairie and Maritime provinces, they also exist in Ontario and Quebec.

The proportion of the population with traditional views about sex, however, is lower in Canada than in the United States. In 1977, Gallup polls found that more Canadians than Americans believed that having sexual relations with someone other than the marriage partner was not always wrong; the difference was 12 percentage points (Jones et al. 1986, 86). In 1985, other Gallup polls showed similar results: 39 percent of Americans said it was wrong for a couple to have sexual relations before marriage, as compared with 30 percent in Ontario, 18 percent in Quebec, and 28 percent in Canada overall (Brodie 1987; Gallup 1985). Other evidence of more liberal attitudes is the higher rate of cohabitation among Canadian women (Bachrach 1987; Norland, 1983), and a widespread acceptance of extramarital childbearing.

Canadian television is little different from U.S. television in its policies regarding the portrayal of nudity or explicit sex. However, Sue Johanson said that she could discuss subjects on her Canadian cable television program, *Talking Sex with Sue*, that would be proscribed in the United States. Canadian magazines appear to exploit sex less in ads and to have fewer sexually titillating articles than do U.S. magazines.

In Quebec, while there is still a body of conservative opinion, advocates of liberal sexual attitudes are more outspoken and visible, for example, in the department of sexology at the University of Quebec at Montreal. In 1980, Denis Lazure, who was then the Quebec minister of social affairs, delivered a paper advocating the right of children to full sexual development and suggesting that schools should assist in this development. As indicated in the poll cited above, Quebec public opinion seems more liberal than that in Ontario.

The reports of several family planning service providers that a surprising number of mothers bring their virgin daughters to clinics for birth control before the daughters even have plans to have sex may reflect attitudes in Quebec. Estimates of the proportion of new teenage patients who have never had intercourse range from "few" to 25–33 percent, 30 percent, and 50 percent. A study in the United States found that 12 percent of teenagers had never had intercourse when they first visited a clinic (Kisker 1984b).

ASSESSMENT

Proportion of Overall Need That Is Met

Family physicians meet most of the need for family planning services efficiently, and they are easily accessible both because of their numbers and because provincial health insurance covers their services without charging the patient. Immigrants are usually able to find a physician who speaks their language.

The majority of women whose family physicians do not meet their needs are those who prefer not to confide in them about sexual behavior. Many of these women are unmarried, and many are teenagers. Such women have easy access to other general practitioners, since the insurance reimburses physicians by fee for service and the majority of physicians are willing to accept new patients. (A survey of 80 family physicians in an urban area of Ontario found that 62 percent were willing to provide family planning services to women who were not established patients, and 64 percent would serve minors without parental consent [Springate, Danaher, and Morrison 1987].) Although some general practitioners (a minority) do not want to serve unmarried minors (Boldt, Roberts, and Latif 1982), young women can often get the names of ones who will. Alternatively, women can go to family planning clinics, which provide free confidential care to anyone over thirteen.

The clinics fill other gaps in services as well. First, they are able to give much more extensive counseling than private physicians usually do. This is especially important to women who are using a birth control method for the first time, and such women constitute a large proportion of clinic case loads. Second, they offer methods that many general practitioners cannot provide, including the IUD, postcoital contraception, the diaphragm, and sometimes periodic abstinence and the cervical cap. Third, they can serve women who have had problems with their method.

Most towns and cities have family planning clinics, and special facilities are available for teenagers in Toronto and Montreal. In Toronto, one family planning clinic is devoted to serving immigrant groups. The only obvious group whose needs may not be met is the rural population in remote areas, but because the population of both Ontario and Quebec is concentrated in cities and towns in the south, the actual number of rural couples unable to obtain services is relatively small. Women who obtain their first contraceptive care from a private physician and receive less than optimal counseling about how to use the methods, their other options, and sexual relationships comprise a second possible area of unmet need.

Vasectomy and female sterilization are readily available from physicians. Because insurance covers sterilization, there is no financial barrier.

Barriers to Service
Although the overall need for family planning services appears to be substantially met, the following barriers remain (not necessarily listed in order of importance):

- Some women undoubtedly find clinics somewhat inconvenient because of distance, waits to obtain appointments under certain circumstances, and the two visits some clinics require before dispensing a medical method. Some women may view the extensive counseling as an imposition making the service less attractive.

- Because most women go to local physicians for birth control, the fact that many physicians offer only the pill limits the ability of women to learn about and obtain other methods. The bias in favor of the pill may have the result of reducing the rate of unintended pregnancy, since the pill is more effective than other reversible methods. It means that women who would prefer a reversible method other than the pill or IUD, however, may not obtain it unless they make the effort to go to another source.

- Although referrals to clinics are easy to obtain from friends, hospitals, physicians, school nurses, and others, some women, especially immigrants, may remain unaware of the existence of these facilities. Unfortunately, no one has collected data to indicate whether lack of awareness of family planning clinics forms a significant barrier to use of services.

- The cost of the pill may be a barrier to some women whose income is not low enough to qualify for welfare benefits. Most Canadians, however, believe that their insurance systems make health services as accessible to low-income families as to more affluent ones, and no evidence to the contrary was found.

The system relies in part on a high level of motivation among women to avoid unintended pregnancy. There is little advertising of services or active outreach. Most health professionals expect women to use the most effective methods—the pill and sterilization—and to tolerate their side effects as a small price for avoiding pregnancy. The extensive counseling clinics give new contraceptive users can be viewed as an attempt to reinforce women's motivation. Regardless of the content of the counseling, it conveys the message that avoiding pregnancy until one wants to have children is extremely important.

Relation of Services to Method Use
The high rate of sterilization nationally—as well as in Ontario and Quebec—is a notable aspect of Canadian contraceptive use. In both provinces, about 60 percent of married women aged 35–44 rely on their own or their partners' sterilization. On the one hand, the method's availability, the favorable attitudes of providers, and the absence of any financial barrier are important factors in explaining this phenomenon. There are few barriers such as age or parity requirements, and concern about sterilization regret is not high among providers. On the other hand, the structure of the system does not promote sterilization over other methods. Sterilization is usually performed by specialists, so

general practitioners have no economic incentive to encourage it. On the contrary, they lose revenue from visits for pill prescription renewals when patients choose sterilization. The reason for the popularity of sterilization appears to be desire for high effectiveness combined with the perceived disadvantages of other methods.

For women not dependent on sterilization, the pill is the most commonly used method. Even aside from the generally held view that the pill is the best reversible method for most women, several factors encourage choosing it. It is the easiest and most convenient method for physicians to provide, and because it is available from virtually all general practitioners, it is the most accessible medical method. For women on welfare and those who obtain free supplies from clinics, it is less expensive than nonprescription methods or the diaphragm, for which a spermicide must be purchased.

The IUD is used much less than the pill but slightly more than in the United States in 1982 (when it was still easy to get there). Of the two methods, practitioners generally prefer the pill because it has a low failure rate, less risk of complications, and is easier to provide. Among women who should not use the pill or sterilization, the IUD is encouraged because of its low failure rate compared to other methods. For the patient, the IUD is less expensive than nonprescription methods over time.

The diaphragm is unpopular among physicians, possibly in part because of the time needed to train women in its use, and is therefore not encouraged. Most general practitioners have not been trained to fit it. This may account in part for the greater use of condoms by unsterilized married couples in Canada, than in the United States.

COMPARISON WITH THE UNITED STATES

Contraceptive practice in Canada is clearly superior to that in the United States, with the expected result that the rate of unintended pregnancy is lower. In a case study like this one cannot pinpoint the exact reasons for the difference between the countries. Some of it may be attributable to differences in national character. For example, compared with Americans, Canadians are generally more law-abiding and respectful of authority, qualities that may be associated with less risk taking and more careful use of contraceptives. They seem to place a higher value on the avoidance of unintended pregnancy, which leads them to select the most effective contraceptive methods and to show greater tolerance for the problems in using them. In addition, their more relaxed attitudes toward sexuality, especially in Quebec, may promote more rational contraceptive behavior. Nevertheless, there are four striking differences between the family planning service delivery systems of Canada and the United States that probably contribute to Canadians' success in preventing unintended pregnancy.

1. Canadian women can get prescriptions for oral contraceptives from general practitioners easily and without cost or long waiting times for appointments or in waiting rooms. Similarly, sterilization services are free and readily available. In the United States, significant economic and other barriers to the use of private physicians cause many women who would prefer the services of their own doctor to seek an alternative provider or possibly to forgo a medical method of contraception.

2. The clinic systems in Ontario and Quebec devote extensive resources to counseling new contraceptive patients. Patients receive a minimum of one half hour of counseling and sometimes as much as one and one-half hours. Although some clinics teach groups, most education is individual, and all patients receive some individual counseling. In addition to focusing on how to use a particular method, counseling may also cover such subjects as sexuality and sexual relationships. Regardless of the content, the extensiveness of the counseling tells the patient that it is very important to avoid unintended pregnancy. The importance of avoiding early childbearing is also emphasized where appropriate.

   Although the family planning clinic systems in Ontario and Quebec are no more extensive than those in the United States, they are better able to focus their efforts on counseling women of all social classes because they need not provide basic services to large numbers of low-income women. Poor women who have no special need for a clinic have ready access to private physicians. The public looks on clinics as resources for all who wish to use them rather than as facilities for the poor. A majority of young women in Ontario and probably also in Quebec utilize clinics and receive the extensive counseling they provide. Clinics can also serve women whose needs are not met by private doctors but who, were they in the United States, might feel stigmatized by attending a clinic.

3. The family planning service system promotes use of the pill, the most effective reversible method. Although other methods are available, both clinics and private physicians encourage women to use oral contraceptives, which providers feel are safe and effective and are therefore the best method for most women under thirty-five.

4. School nurses in almost all public schools and in many Catholic schools refer students for contraceptive services. School

nurses are under the authority of health departments, whose
policy is to promote family planning, rather than under the
boards of education, which tend to view family planning for
students as controversial and beyond their educational mission. The school nurses are required to offer sex-education
services to the schools (which do not always accept the offer,
however), and students recognize them as a source of information about family planning.

The outstanding service-related differences between Canada and
the United States are lower economic barriers to contraceptive services,
more counseling for women when they become sexually active, more
positive attitudes toward the pill, and more frequent referrals of high
school students for birth control. It seems likely that these differences
play a significant role in Canada's lower unintended pregnancy rate.

7

The Netherlands

GENERAL DESCRIPTION

Overall Health System

The Dutch people rely heavily on a national health insurance system for their medical needs. The health system in the Netherlands emphasizes preventive care, with the family physician (*huisarts*), who is a general practitioner, acting as the entry point into the system (Biesta 1982). Almost all residents in the Netherlands are registered with a general practitioner, the choice of physician being left to the individual. Patients consult these physicians, most of whom are men, for all medical problems; the physicians provide all routine medical services and refer their patients to specialists for services and treatment they are unable to provide for. They also arrange for their patients' hospital or institutional care. Medical supplies are dispensed at the physician's office or obtained from the pharmacy upon presentation of the physician's prescription.

People interviewed: W. J. Atsma (M.D.), Organon International; W. Beekhuizen (M.D.), Medisch Centrum voor Geboorteregeling; Gijs N. C. Beets, Centraal Bureau voor de Statistiek; Doortje Braeken-van Schaik (M.D.), Rutgers Stichting; B. Haberland, Schering Nederland BV; R. Haj Mohammed, Havinga Apotheek; A. J. B. N. Houba, Schering Nederland BV; Malou Kempers, Bureau Buitenland Nederlandse Organisatie voor Verloskundigen; Evert Ketting, Nederlands Centrum voor Geestelijke Volksgezonheid; Boudewijn Klap, Inter Kerkelijke Omroep Nederland (Televisie); Bert Lam, Rutgers Stichting; Astrid Limburg-van Vessem, Bureau Buitenland Nederlandse Organisatie voor Verloskundigen; Hein Moors, Nederlands Interuniversitair Demografisch Instituut; Jan P. C. Moors (M.D.), Royal Dutch College of General Practitioners; Mariette C. T. Moors-Mommers (M.D.), Royal Dutch College of General Practitioners; P. J. Nieman, Redactie *Libelle*; J. M. J. Palmen, Hoofd afdeling Verstrekkingen en Erkcn-

Medical specialists typically provide services either as members of hospital staff or in outpatient settings. Nurses are ordinarily involved in preventive care (for example, immunizations and medical services in schools), home nursing care, and dissemination of information from public health services and private nursing organizations.

Almost all family physicians participate in a government-sponsored insurance plan administered by the Sickness Fund Council, a quasi-governmental body that determines health-care standards and regulates insurance benefits, premiums, rates, and fees (Biesta 1982). Provincial and municipal authorities implement the council's policies and contract with local doctors, pharmacies, hospitals, and health-care providers for their services. The national insurance plan reimburses family physicians according to the number of covered patients they serve. Patients who do not subscribe to the plan pay the doctor for services and are eligible for full or partial reimbursement by private insurance (Biesta 1982). Specialists, if not salaried, are paid on a fee-for-service basis. Although some public health facilities exist, private organizations or foundations operate many hospitals and other health-care facilities, including an important network of infant health centers, that are supported by government funds. In order to obtain public funds, institutions must comply with regulations established by the council. Public financing of hospitals and other health-care facilities is based on the facilities' budget.

National health insurance plans financed by employer and employee contributions and by central government revenues cover every resident of the Netherlands to some extent. These plans differ according to the segment of the population included and the health services covered (Biesta 1982).

The broadest scheme, mandated by the Exceptional Medical Expenses Act, covers all residents regardless of income and the medical costs of extensive illness. To finance the Exceptional Medical Expenses plan, everybody pays a premium based on income. Employers assume

ningen, Somatische Gezondheidszorg; Anika Parent, Nederlands Instituut voor Sociaal Sexuologisch Onderzoek; Jany Rademakers (M.D.), Vereniging Stimezo Nederland; Hans Rekers (M.D.), Organon International; Jeanette Schoorl, Nederlands Interuniveritair Demografisch Instituut; Maria Schopman, MR'70; Jon Schraag, Boerhaavecommisie voor Postacademisch Onderwijs in de Geneeskunde; C. Straver, Nederlands Instituut voor Sociaal Sexuologisch Onderzoek; J. Tielens (M.D.), Royal Dutch College of General Practitioners; Mies van Dam, Aletta Jacobshuis; Gerda van Dijk (M.D.), VrouwenKliniek, Academisch Ziekenhuis; M. van Neerven, MR'70; N. van Nimwegen, Nederlands Interuniversitair Demografisch Instituut; Rob van Tergouw (M.D.), Rutgers Stichting; P. Vennix, Nederlands Instituut voor Sociaal Sexuologisch Onderzoek; Wil Verhoeven, Buro Voorlichting Gezondheidszorg Buitenlanders; Fritz Wafelbakker (M.D.), Ministerie voor Welzijn, Wolksgezondheid en Cultuur; Pieter Wibaut (M.D.), MR'70.

the costs for their employees, however, and people sixty-five or older do not pay for this insurance.

In addition to coverage for extensive illness, roughly two-thirds of the population currently have Sickness Fund insurance that covers such basic medical care as physician visits, medical supplies, and hospital care for illnesses of short or moderate duration. The Health Insurance Act legislated this plan. People with incomes below $19,600 (48,000 guilders),[1] which is roughly equivalent to the average family income, are enrolled in a Compulsory Health Insurance plan, except for civil servants, who are insured under a separate scheme (Office of the Ministry of Welfare, Health and Cultural Affairs 1987). A premium amounting to 9.7 percent of wages is paid by the employer, who deducts half the premium from the employee's earnings. Persons sixty-five or over whose incomes fall below $9,800 (24,000 guilders) are included in the Old Age Insurance plan. They pay premiums depending on their income, but the bulk of funding for their health care comes from compulsory insurance and government funds. The unemployed, including full-time students and the disabled, are covered by insurance without having to pay a premium. Those who do not qualify under any of these plans (for example, the self-employed) but whose incomes do not exceed the limit may take public insurance on a voluntary basis. People with incomes exceeding the limit are expected to obtain private insurance. The Sickness Fund gives the insured person a family card with the name and address of his or her doctor and pharmacy. Covered patients must show the card, which entitles family members to free services, at every visit to the doctor or the pharmacy.

In 1982, about one-fifth of the population had private insurance and roughly four-fifths public insurance (Biesta 1982). Since that time, the proportion of the population covered by public insurance has declined as a result of a lowering of the income threshold for compulsory insurance (Office of the Ministry of Welfare, Health and Cultural Affairs 1987).

In 1983, more than 70 percent of the cost of health care in the Netherlands came from national health insurance funds—27 percent from the Exceptional Medical Expenses Fund and over 43 percent from the Sickness Fund (CBS 1984, 178, table 11). Individuals and private insurance paid about 25 percent of health-care costs, and direct government subsidies to health service institutions financed 5 percent.

Family Planning Services
As recently as twenty years ago, contraception was considered appropriate mainly for couples wanting to plan their families. Since then,

---

1. Dutch guilders have been converted to U.S. dollars at the 1986 rate of 2.45 guilders to the dollar.

social attitudes towards sexuality and birth control have changed dramatically, and contraception has been accepted as a routine part of life.
Access to reliable methods of contraception has improved. Sickness
Fund insurance has covered the cost of prescriptions for the pill, the
IUD, and the diaphragm since 1971 and has financed sterilizations
since 1973 (Ketting 1983a). The morning-after pill is also offered
under the publicly financed scheme. A recent attempt to delete both
kinds of pill from expenses covered by the fund as an economy measure was rejected and the decision was made instead to reduce costs by
lowering the income threshold for compulsory insurance. Insurance
does not cover nonprescription contraceptives. Although the condom,
foam, jellies, cream, and suppositories are readily available, the sponge
is not.

In keeping with the national emphasis on preventive care, family
physicians play a central role in providing contraceptive services. They
offer medical contraceptive services and refer patients who seek sterilizations, abortions or, in some cases, the IUD to specialists. Hospital
involvement is limited to the majority of female sterilizations and to
contraceptive services provided in teaching facilities as part of training
programs for family doctors.

No law or public policy requires parental consent or notification as
a condition for adolescents' obtaining contraceptive services. Doctors
must respect all requests for confidentiality (Braam and Leemhuis
1983). There are no restrictions on sterilizations regarding the age of
the patient, the number of children, or the need for special consent
(see chapter 2).

In the Netherlands, abortion is regarded as a backup service, not a
method of birth control. Although abortion became legal in 1981,
regulations governing its practice were not formally adopted until
three years later. Even before the law was passed, however, abortion
had been widely available in private, nonprofit clinics, which many
women from neighboring countries also used, and in some hospitals
("Netherlands Liberalizes Abortion Law after Ten Years of Wide Availability, Low Abortion Rates" 1981). The law states that first-trimester
and second-trimester abortions may be performed in hospitals and
nonprofit clinics after a five-day waiting period. Menstrual extrac-
tions,[2] which have always been counted as abortions in the Netherlands, are not subject to the five-day waiting requirement.

Parental consent for abortions is theoretically required for women
under twenty-one, but in practice women sixteen or older can obtain
abortions without the consent of their parents. Since November 1984,

2. Menstrual extraction is a suction curretage procedure limited to the first two
weeks after a missed menstrual period (Tietze and Henshaw 1986).

residents have been able to obtain abortions free of charge under the government-sponsored national health insurance system. The Exceptional Medical Expenses Fund (also known as the General Fund for Special Health Cost) covers the cost of abortions performed in clinics (Ketting and Leseman 1986), and the Sickness Fund or private insurance companies cover those performed in hospitals (Ketting 1987). Payment by the Exceptional Medical Expenses Fund for clinic abortions has not caused a rise in abortion rates, but it has caused a shift in the balance of providers from hospitals to clinics.

In addition to the inclusion of contraceptive services in the Sickness Fund insurance, the government provides subsidies to private institutions for the development of family planning information and services for groups with special needs. An interdepartmental committee set up to study and recommend ways of improving contraceptive behavior identified adolescents and immigrants as the groups most in need of special attention.

Target Groups for Family Planning
Despite the overall high use of effective birth control methods and the low rates of abortion, compared to other industrialized countries (see chapter 2), the Dutch themselves consider their situation far from ideal. Many adolescents do not use reliable methods, particularly at first intercourse (Rutgers Stichting 1987), and women under twenty compose a significant proportion of abortion patients (Ketting and Leseman 1986). Some of the reasons cited suggest a substantial need for greater availability of information about sexuality, contraception, and contraceptive services among Dutch adolescents. Although attitudes toward sexuality have become more open, some parents still find it difficult to talk with their children about sex. Sex education in schools is not integrated in the system and, for the most part, is confined to the biological aspects of reproduction. Although family doctors are the most important source of contraceptive services among young and older women, some adolescents still find it difficult to confide in them for fear that their parents will find out. One of the hundred most frequently asked questions about contraception in a popular women's weekly magazine is whether the family doctor can tell parents that their daughters are using the pill (Braam and Leemhuis 1983).

About six percent of the Dutch population are immigrants. Contraceptive use among Surinam women, after the women's prolonged residence in the Netherlands, has become much like that of Dutch women (Rutgers Stichting 1987). A study comparing data for migrant women from Turkey and Morocco who now live in the Netherlands and data for their counterparts in their country of origin also indicates that, in the relatively short period since migrating to the Netherlands, contraceptive use among these immigrants has increased remarkably (Schoorl 1985a, 1985b). Data for married women aged 15–49 in these ethnic groups living in the Netherlands show high levels of current contraceptive use (72 percent among the Turkish women and 67 percent among Moroccan women) (Schoorl 1987a). Turkish women under forty are just as likely as all women in the Netherlands to use some method of contraception. The vast majority of Turkish and Moroccan women aged 15–44 who were currently practicing contraception were using effective methods, particularly the pill—61 and 85 percent, respectively, substantially more than the corresponding percentage of all women in the Netherlands. Moroccan and Turkish women, however, are much less likely than Dutch women in general to rely on sterilization. Only 11 percent of Turkish women and 8 percent of Moroccan women (or their husbands) had been sterilized (Schoorl 1987a).

Despite the high levels of contraceptive use among immigrant women, most of those not currently using a method have never used one. Yet, two-fifths of never-users and their husbands—50 percent of Turkish and 28 percent of Moroccan immigrants—approve of contraception (Schoorl, 1987b). Some immigrant couples still want large families, but these data on nonuse, and findings from other studies indicating high levels of abortion among immigrant women suggest that current contraceptive needs among ethnic minorities are not being fully met. Besides communication problems, cultural barriers may inhibit them from moving about freely outside the home or obtaining contraceptive services from a male doctor.

FAMILY DOCTORS AND SPECIALISTS

Most family planning patients obtain contraceptive services from their family physicians. The available data indicate that geographic access to medical services provided by family doctors is not a barrier for most Dutch people. Nationally, forty family physicians are in active practice per 100,000 residents (or one doctor per 2,500 residents) (CBS 1984, 168, table 10.5), compared with thirty-one per 100,000 in the United States. Family physicians are fairly equally distributed among the population of the twelve Dutch provinces, ranging from thirty-six to forty-two physicians for every 100,000 residents in each province. About 62 percent of the doctors are in solo practice, and 31 percent are in a partnership or group practice. The remaining 7 percent work in health centers (CBS 1984, 146, 162, and tables 9 and 9.18).

There are fewer specialists who might be involved in the provision of contraceptive services than family doctors. For example, there are only 4.5 obstetrician-gynecologists per 100,000 residents (CBS 1984, calculated from pp. 30 and 169, tables 1.5 and 10.6).

Just as most family doctors participate in Sickness Fund insurance, most of their patients are covered by it. Family physicians are paid by the number of covered patients they serve, not by services. Contraceptive services are free to all patients enrolled in the Sickness Fund; some, but not all, private insurance plans also cover the costs of contraceptive services (Dersjant et al. 1986). With a written reference from the family doctor, patients covered by the Fund can obtain services at family planning clinics or from specialists without charge. Otherwise they pay the doctor and are eligible for reimbursement under private insurance.

Doctors wrote a total of 2.3 million pill prescriptions in 1986 (Atsma 1987), with family physicians accounting for about 90 percent of them, physicians working in family planning clinics for 5 percent, and specialists (gynecologists) for the remaining 5 percent (Sips 1986). As the average prescription covers six months, it is estimated that about 1,150,000 Dutch women were using oral contraceptives in 1986. Among women who were using the pill, 18 percent were under 20, 53 percent were aged 20–29, 22 percent were aged 30–39, and 8 percent were 40 and older (Atsma 1987). About 75 percent of pill users were getting refills; 16 percent were new users and the remaining 9 percent had switched from another method. Seventy-five percent belonged to the Sickness Fund and were entitled to free services and prescriptions.

Although the number of family doctors who provide the IUD is increasing, it is generally believed that more than 50 percent still refer patients who want an IUD to a gynecologist. Family physicians who do offer IUDs are likely to perform fewer than ten insertions a year. They refer patients who want sterilizations to specialists, most of them affiliated with hospitals or outpatient clinics. Estimates of the number of IUD patients family doctors served and the number of IUD insertions and contraceptive sterilizations referred to a specialist or a hospital are not available. Other forms of contraception are far less popular among family doctors' patients.

Family physicians do little if any family planning outreach. Although the consent or notification of parents is not required for adolescents to obtain contraceptive services, and although services are confidential, some adolescents prefer not to go to their own doctor for fear that their parents will find out. Although physicians send bills for patients covered by private insurance to the home, teenage patients who do not want their parents billed for a visit can pay directly for the contraceptive services or supplies they receive. Patients who wanted to see another general practitioner for contraception would have considerable difficulty finding a physician willing to take them unless their situation was urgent.

Patients must generally make appointments, but they are easy to get. One can usually obtain an appointment for the same day. Some doctors set aside at least an hour for unscheduled visits. Doctors in big cities are less likely to make an appointment to see a patient on the same day, however. Family doctors usually offer daily services, but few have services during evening hours or weekends. They all provide patient counseling and medical services themselves. Most employ a doctor's assistant, who does most of the oral contraceptive follow-up work. On average, a visit for contraceptive services to a family physician takes seven to ten minutes.

The law does not require doctors to raise the subject of birth control with their patients, but they must provide information, services, or referrals upon request. Because the Dutch public is quite sophisticated about birth control, most doctors assume that women who seek family planning services are well-informed about their contraceptive options.

When a patient requests the pill, her doctor is likely to discuss its possible short-term side effects rather than its long-term effects. Doctors are not required to discuss the latter, nor is a pelvic examination necessary before prescription of the pill. A protocol for family doctors reviewed by the Royal Dutch College of General Practitioners states that unwarranted medical advice or examination results in inefficient use of the doctor's time and causes undue anxiety and insecurity among patients, particularly among young people (Sips 1986). The protocol suggests that it is preferable for doctors to spend their time assessing and monitoring the suitability of the pill for the patient instead of discussing its possible long-term health effects.

Women who request the pill are usually given a six-month prescription and counseled about use. Patients are asked to come back for renewal of the prescription, and the doctor's assistant usually handles return visits (de Haan 1986). At return visits, before the doctor prescribes another six-month supply, the doctor's assistant will generally ask the patient if she has noticed any side effects related to pill use, but the assistant need not review all the possible side effects.

Family doctors tend to refer women who want an IUD to specialists, presumably because they have little training or experience in IUD insertion. The physicians who offer IUDs generally assess the patient's health, perform a medical examination, and counsel the patient on use. The doctor handles return visits for IUD checkups. (Patients referred to a specialist for IUD insertions return to the family doctor for follow-up visits.)

Family doctors appear to be willing to refer men and women for voluntary sterilization, but there is some concern about sterilization regret. They will provide counseling on reversibility if the question is raised by persons who have not yet firmly decided on sterilization, but they do not try to influence the patient's decision.

Family physicians most commonly prescribe the low-dose pill (less than 50 mcg of estrogen) because it is considered effective, reliable, and useful for maintaining cycle control. Doctors seem to agree that the long-term health risks associated with low-dose oral contraceptives are small. Currently there is growing support among doctors both for making the pill available without prescription and for changing the duration of pill prescriptions from six months to a year. There is also increasing support for the delegation of some of the routine medical supervision to doctor's assistants.

Doctors more or less actively discourage the use of reversible methods other than the pill or the IUD because they consider them as much less effective. The diaphragm is rarely prescribed, condoms are advocated mainly for prevention of sexually transmitted diseases, and spermicides are usually prescribed only in conjunction with other methods such as the condom, or with initial use of IUD.

Divergent opinions about the risks and benefits of certain methods of contraception and who should use them came to light during conversations with two physicians. They represent to some extent opposite ends of the spectrum of contraceptive service provision by family doctors in the Netherlands. The point of view of the first physician is evidently the more common one. But even physicians who may disagree usually conform in some way to the standard set by the medical profession.

The first physician initiates discussion with all new patients about general health, usually brings up contraception himself, and believes in investing more time in counseling in order to instill "good pill practice." He feels the pill should be available without prescription because the health risk involved is so small, and he interprets contraindications liberally. The low-dose pill is a safe method until after age thirty-five, provided there is ongoing discussion about choices after age thirty. He believes the IUD is highly effective and provides it himself, and thinks abortion backup important. The diaphragm is not reliable except for some highly motivated couples; he prescribes it only when the woman insists. He mentions other female methods but stresses their general ineffectiveness. He offers contraceptives to patients regardless of marital status and provides the morning-after pill on request.

The other physician does not prescribe oral contraceptives routinely. The pill is not "everyday, common" medicine because it affects the body. He is concerned not so much about the pill's long-term negative effects, but believes it is not good for mental health to take sex for granted. He prescribes the pill only to married women with a stable relationship, including those whose reason for practicing contraception is to delay childbearing. He works primarily with married women. He usually discusses natural family planning. In his opinion, natural family planning is difficult to teach, and he does not bring it up with couples he feels would not understand. The IUD results in abortion. He does not prescribe it but would refer a request to the hospital. He also refers for sterilization when requested. He never prescribes the morning-after pill and never discusses abortion. He indicates that patients may obtain contraceptive services from another doctor who works at different hours in the same office. He also believes that most Dutch women, including teenagers, know that they can go to family planning clinics for birth control assistance.

RUTGERS STICHTING FAMILY PLANNING CLINICS

Although most family planning patients get contraceptives from their own physicians, private family planning clinics remain a small but important network for providing of contraceptive information and services. Clinics extend services otherwise difficult to obtain, especially by teenagers and members of cultural minorities. Unlike the offices of family physicians, whose visiting hours are usually limited to weekdays, many clinics are open in the evenings and on weekends. Although appointments are preferred, clinics accept walk-in visits from women seeking the morning-after pill, abortion referrals, or other emergency services.

The largest network of family planning clinics in the Netherlands is run by the Rutgers Foundation (Rutgers Stichting), a private, non-profit organization that has thirty-six clinics throughout the country. These clinics account for most contraceptive visits made to private family planning clinics. Rutgers Stichting clinics provide a broad array of family planning services, but their primary focus is on the delivery of contraceptive services to immigrants (who make up 6 percent of the population) and young people—two groups that the government has singled out as needing special attention. The clinics are among some eighty "counseling bureaus" across the country that provide information and counseling related to sexuality and birth control. The organization considers itself an alternative service provider and not in competition with family doctors.

The Rutgers Stichting has received considerable support from the central government (the Ministry of Welfare, Health and Cultural Affairs) since 1971. Government subsidies accounted for 70 percent of its total budget in 1986; patient fees cover the rest of the clinics' expenses (Rutgers Stichting 1987). The standard fee for a contraceptive visit is $11 (26 guilders). Patients who have a written reference from their family physician are entitled to free services, and government subsidies partially cover the cost of visits made by adolescents under eighteen, who need pay only $5 (12.50 guilders). Small municipal grants also help to subsidize visits made by women aged 18–20, and student insurance often covers the service fee. Although the cost of all prescription contraceptives dispensed at the clinics is covered by the Sickness Fund, women under twenty who the fund does not cover and who cannot afford to pay are given supplies free. Free family planning education and services for immigrant women provided by the organization at infant health centers in Amsterdam are partly subsidized by municipal and community grants.

About 90,000 patient visits were made to the Rutgers Stichting clinics in 1986. A majority of visits (about 60 percent) were made by women aged 18–25, and 12 percent by young teenagers. Oral contraceptives, particularly the low-dose pills, were the most popular method. Sixty-six percent of patient visits were for the pill (including the morning-after pill), 7 percent for the IUD, 6 percent for the diaphragm, and 1 percent were for contraceptive injections. The remaining 20 percent were for other purposes, such as screening for sexually transmitted diseases, pregnancy testing, and counseling and referral for sterilization and abortion (Rutgers Stichting 1986a).

The clinics do not do any paid advertising but rely on outreach efforts to inform the public of their services. In 1986, the foundation launched a highly successful campaign that increased the clinic case load about 10 percent in two months. The campaign consisted of displaying posters and distributing brochures about birth control, abortion, and "safe sex" (condom use to prevent sexually transmitted diseases) in subway and railroad stations, at libraries, family doctors' offices, and all branch clinics. The brochures also included information about services or referrals obtained through the family doctor free of charge under the Sickness Fund, and a list of alternative clinics (Rutgers Stichting and others) where services were available and how much they cost. In addition to their outreach activities, clinic staff are often consulted by the media on various questions related to sexuality and contraception.

Contraceptive Services

Appointments are preferred, and the waiting time for an appointment at a Rutgers Stichting clinic usually is one or 2 days, but walk-ins are accepted for urgent medical treatment or referral. Clinics in big cities are open all day and evenings, and medical sessions are held in mornings, afternoons, and evenings. Emergency-care services are available on weekends and holidays as well. Regular appointments for contraceptive services are staggered at fifteen-minute intervals during session hours.

About 80 percent of the clinics' staff are women. Receptionists are present at all hours, answering information requests, making clinic appointments, and receiving patient fees. One doctor and one nurse staff a medical session. Both do routine checkups. The first visit takes at least fifteen minutes, but the patient may have to wait longer to see the doctor. A return visit typically lasts around seven minutes. The time to complete a visit can range from ten minutes to an hour.

The woman who comes for services pays the fee before she sees the clinician. She is given literature to read while waiting. Counseling is not routinely provided but is offered where there are special problems, and a physical examination is no longer routinely provided for pill patients. First-visit patients who request the pill are routinely asked if they have considered other methods. The pill is explained, including its possible adverse effects for women over thirty-five and for smokers. Because of the risk of infection associated with IUD use, clinics do not recommend it for the young. Most women who want a diaphragm get it from the clinic instead of from the family doctor.

At fifteen of the clinics, individuals who request psychological and sexual counseling can receive it. Six centers send teams of nurses and social workers to conduct informal sex-education sessions and discussion groups at schools and in community centers. The main job of these teams is to train teachers, nurses, and counselors in matters related to sexuality and birth control. Because educational and counseling services receive little government funding, the foundation charges small fees for such programs.

The foundation also provides free family planning services to immigrant women who bring their infants and young children for medical checkups to the publicly funded infant health centers in Amsterdam (Aletta Jacobshuis 1986). (In the Netherlands, well-baby care is widely available and parents are expected to utilize primary health services for their children—over 90 percent of all infants attend infant health clinics [CBS 1984].) Translators from the Amsterdam City Council's Interpreter Center participate in this program. The program began when workers at a health station affiliated with the Community Department of Youth Health Care invited the Rutgers Stichting clinic to provide family planning services, because mothers who accompanied their children to the center often raised questions and problems about birth control (Aletta Jacobshuis 1986). These health sessions drew large audiences but there were not enough family planning and birth control specialists to respond to the need. Services began on an experimental basis late in 1980; the family planning sessions were very well attended from the beginning. By 1986, Rutgers Stichting staff held weekly sessions during visiting hours at six community health stations. Another private organization (MR'70; see below) provided services at two additional health stations.

Funding came initially from the development and information

budget of the Rutgers Stichting, supported by funds from the central government. Additional support since has come from community funds for ethnic minorities and for emancipation affairs, as well as from municipal government subsidies. Currently, about 450 Moroccan and 270 Turkish women obtain family planning services at infant health clinics in Amsterdam (Aletta Jacobshuis 1986, 15).

Sessions take place at offices adjacent to the well-baby clinics, and no appointment is needed to attend. Before visiting the infant health center, the mother has most likely heard about family planning from the midwife who delivered her baby or from a visiting nurse. At the center, the interpreter approaches the women to ask if they wish to attend, or the doctor brings it up. The family planning doctor and nurse and the translator are always women. During the family planning session, a Pap smear is taken (usually every two years) and various methods of contraception are discussed. Great emphasis is placed on successful communication with the immigrant women through the translator, so that the information provided can be repeated back by the women. Immigrant women are most likely to choose the low-dose pill, in which case they are given a six-month supply and asked to return to the clinic or to a general practitioner in six months. Those who request an IUD can have it inserted at the foundation's clinic in Amsterdam or be referred to a hospital. Rarely do immigrant women request the diaphragm or condoms. For all their other medical needs, clinic staff refer immigrant women to the family physician, whom they contact by phone or by mail.

INDEPENDENT FAMILY PLANNING CLINICS

In addition to Rutgers Stichting clinics, several smaller organizations offer family planning services. MR'70 is an independent clinic in Amsterdam that provides birth control and abortion services. The organization receives municipal grants for family planning services it provides immigrant women at two infant health centers in cooperation with the Rutgers Stichting, but it relies on insurance reimbursements for abortions and fees from private family planning patients to support its other clinic operations. The organization provides all contraceptive methods. The full fee for a contraceptive visit is $10 (25 guilders), but high school students are charged only $2 (five guilders). The standard rates for IUD and diaphragm fittings are $37 (90 guilders) and $25 (60 guilders), respectively.

The Academic Hospital (Academisch Ziekenhuis) in Leiden operates a variety of outpatient clinics, including a family planning clinic, the Women's Clinic, that serves about 2,000 patients a year (Dersjant et al. 1986). The hospital is the only teaching facility in the Netherlands that trains postdoctoral medical students and nurse-midwives in family planning care regardless of their specialty. As an affiliate of the University of Leiden it receives government support and also does research for pharmaceutical companies. The clinic charges family planning patients a flat fee of $10 (25 guilders) a year (Dersjant et al. 1986).

Clinic sessions are held one evening and one afternoon a week. Once a week, staff visit the maternity ward to give information about contraception to mothers interested in family planning. No appointment is required to attend a clinic session. The regular clinic staff consist of a doctor, a midwife, and a nurse. Trainees, during their own visiting hours, assist the staff in all procedures. Services last twenty to thirty minutes per patient, and patients usually complete the visit in seventy-five minutes.

During a woman's first visit to the Women's Clinic, she is counseled about various contraceptive methods and receives a complete checkup, including gynecological examination, Pap smear, and breast examination—a standard practice that may have been dispensed with under new policy guidelines that were being formulated at the time of the site visit in February 1987. The initial visit concludes with instructions on use and scheduling for follow-up visits, starting with a three-month checkup for the pill, a six-week follow-up visit for the IUD, and a seven-week visit for the diaphragm. A Pap smear is required once for women under 25, every two years for those aged 25–40, and once a year for older women. Psychological problems are referred to hospital staff providing counseling in an adjacent clinic. Medical problems not related to contraception are referred to the patient's own doctor.

SPECIALIZED SERVICES

Patients who seek sterilizations, abortions or, in some cases, the IUD are referred by their family doctor to such specialists as obstetrician-gynecologists. Geographic access to services provided by specialists appears not to be a problem. The law makes no legal requirements for obtaining sterilization, although young women may have to give written informed consent, and sterilizations are free for patients covered by Sickness Fund insurance. In 1984, specialists performed about 32,500 vasectomies and 28,500 female sterilizations in outpatient clinics, hospitals, and private family planning clinics that specialize in sterilizations (Ketting and Leseman 1986, 73, table 3.4). Although vasectomies are always done on an outpatient basis, three-quarters of publicly financed female sterilizations take place in hospitals, and patients usually require overnight inpatient care (Landelijk Informatie Systeem Ziekenfondsen 1984, 122–23, table 7.1.7).

No advertising or outreach is done for specialized birth control services, sterilization or abortion. Patients hear about these services by word of mouth or are referred by their family doctor. The Dutch are not used to looking for ads in this field, and family doctors expect medical service providers to keep them informed about what services are available and where to get them.

Eight private family planning clinics in five major cities specialize in sterilizations; five perform both male and female sterilization, and three do only vasectomies. These clinics, however, account for only a very small proportion of sterilizations obtained by residents of the Netherlands. As more physicians affiliated with outpatient clinics or hospitals have begun offering sterilization, specialized clinics have come to serve a smaller proportion of the national case load. The full fee charged by specialized clinics to paying patients ranges from $123–$163 (300–400 guilders) for a vasectomy and from $204–$327 (500–800 guilders) for a laparoscopy (Rutgers Stichting 1986b; SMCG 1986).

Unique among clinic service providers in this field is the Stichting Medisch Centrum voor Geboorteregeling (SMCG) in Leiden, a private clinic that has led the field into new areas in reproductive health care. The SMCG provides counseling and guidance in fertility and contraception problems, does male and female sterilizations and reversals of sterilization, has a sperm bank, and provides birth control and first- and second-trimester abortions. Office hours are all day, Monday through Saturday. Emergency calls outside visiting hours are answered. The clinic is staffed by a team of specialists, nurses, a biologist-pharmacist, technicians, and administrative staff. Most of the doctors are men, and almost all other staff are women. Clinic staff, including the specialists, are salaried. The clientele is mainly from Spain, Belgium, and other European countries.

Male sterilizations can be obtained the same day, unless there are special problems. Total visit time at the center is one to two hours, with a maximum one-hour waiting time. The treatment usually takes about an hour. No follow-up visit is necessary, but the patient is told to send in a sperm sample after six to eight weeks for testing. Female sterilization, using the laparoscopic procedure, takes fifteen minutes, plus a two-hour bed rest. A mail follow-up is done after one year.

A doctor counsels every patient. Research about the possibility or impossibility of further examination or treatment (that is, reversibility of sterilization) is discussed in the form of advice or guidance. Doctors do not participate in the decisionmaking because they consider contraception a social rather than a medical issue.

In addition to MR'70 and the SMCG, which are members of a voluntary nonprofit group called Vereniging Stimezo Nederland (National abortion federation of the Netherlands), six other Stimezo-affiliated clinics provide abortion and contraceptive services.

PHARMACIES

Pharmacies also play an important role in the distribution of contraceptive supplies and the dissemination of birth control information. Nationally, there are nearly fifteen pharmacies per 100,000 in the population, eight operated by pharmacists and seven by physicians (CBS 1984, 160, table 9.16). Pharmacies are open Monday through Friday. National policy is to have one pharmacy in a city (in rotation) open on evenings and weekends.

Clients can get pills and diaphragms from pharmacies on presentation of a doctor's prescription. IUD users obtain the device from a pharmacy and bring it back to the doctor for insertion; the same is true for patients who get injectable contraceptives. Pharmacies maintain a file of names of patients with Sickness Fund insurance. They keep prescriptions filled out for covered patients and send them directly to the fund for reimbursement of the initial costs of supplies. Reimbursements may take as much as nine months.

Clients insured by the Sickness Fund pay a basic prescription fee of $1 (2.50 guilders) for prescription drugs; those who are not insured pay $17–$21 (42–52 guilders) for a six-month supply of pills. Condoms cost $2 (five guilders) for a packet of three, and spermicidal creams, jellies, or foams cost $6–$9 (15–22 guilders).

One pharmacist in The Hague said that the pill is the most widely used method, particularly the low-dose pill (under 50 mcg of estrogen), an observation borne out by accounts from family planning providers. He believes that early, easy access to contraception is crucial to high-quality contraceptive use generally. He serves teenagers as he does adults. He says immigrant women mainly use the pill (though it is difficult for illiterates to use it correctly), as well as injectables and the IUD. Few use other methods, because most prefer those covered by the Sickness Fund. For problems with a prescription, he calls the family doctor (the family insurance card includes the doctor's name), through the interpreter center if necessary.

Pharmacists are required to tell patients how to use the contraceptives they dispense, but information about possible health risks is routinely included in the package insert. For example, the insert that accompanies the high-dose pill (50 mcg of estrogen) includes a list of medical conditions that contraindicate its use and warnings about reported adverse reactions related to taking hormonal contraceptives, ranging from such minor side effects as headaches, weight changes, and breakthrough bleeding to more serious complications, like liver dysfunction and cardiovascular disease. Instructions about how to take the pill are given along with assurance of the pill's effectiveness if taken as instructed. The insert also details conditions that affect the reliability of the pill, for example, vomiting or diarrhea. It advises, the patient to tell the doctor about migraine headaches, vision trouble, leg pain, or swelling or other symptoms, also cautioning users not to take certain drugs while on the pill and warning of the increased risk of vascular disease, especially among smokers. On the other hand, the package insert for the low-dose pill (30 mcg of estrogen) emphasizes the method's benefits and downplays its possible side effects, but it still warns users against smoking while on the pill.

OTHER SOURCES

Condoms and spermicides are available without prescription in pharmacies, counseling bureaus, drugstores, and via mail order (Dersjant et al. 1986). Other widespread sources of condoms are vending machines, supermarkets, newspaper and tobacco shops, and hair salons.

CLIENT PREFERENCES

The vast majority of family planning patients obtain contraceptives (primarily the pill) from their own doctors, but a significant minority utilize contraceptive services they get at family planning clinics. Family planning clinic services appeal to some women for a number of reasons. Clinics are considered places where services can be obtained anonymously and where women clinicians provide the privacy and reassurance sought especially by teenagers and members of cultural minorities. Another important feature of family planning clinics is that, in addition to offering actual medical services, they serve as the principal national source of information and counseling about problems related to sexuality and birth control.

A one-week survey of family planning clinics and counseling bureaus conducted by the Central Bureau of Statistics (CBS) in 1983 found that 94 percent of family planning clinic patients were registered with a family doctor (Engberts 1985). About two-thirds of the family planning clinic patients had Sickness Fund insurance and could have had free contraceptive services from their own doctors but chose to use the clinics, where services are not covered unless the family doctor refers the patient.

The CBS survey found that about 60 percent of all visits made to the clinics were for birth control services (mostly for the pill), and 11 percent were for problem counseling. Half of telephone requests from women were for information about birth control methods and questions related to sex (Engberts 1985, calculated from table 5). Although most visits for both counseling and services are made by young women, the survey found that about one-quarter of the women who received services at the clinics were over twenty-five.

The pill is particularly popular among the young. In a survey of young people in the 1981 *Sex in the Netherlands*, almost 90 percent of sixteen to twenty year-olds said that the pill was acceptable and effective, the condom acceptable but less effective, and the IUD less acceptable but effective enough (Jones et al. 1986). Far fewer knew about the diaphragm and other less effective methods. Most viewed rhythm and withdrawal as ineffective.

Among immigrant women, the main method used is the pill, although some get it from the hospital after childbirth without much explanation. There is some interest in the IUD, but little is known about the diaphragm. Some immigrant women are not interested in these methods because they do not like to touch their genitals. They dislike the condom because they associate condoms with prostitutes. Sterilization is considered only after many children, and vasectomy never. They are often very relieved following sterilization, but positive word about it is slow to spread.

The patterns of use among women of all ages reflect the overwhelming preference of the Dutch for highly reliable methods of contraception. In the mid-1970s, just ten years after the introduction of the pill, oral contraceptive use in the Netherlands reached by far the highest level reported anywhere in the world (Kols et al. 1982, A–191, A–193, and figs. 1 and 2). By 1975, 42 percent of Dutch women aged 15–49 were either using the pill or were protected by male or female sterilization (36 percent and 6 percent, respectively) (Ketting 1983a). By 1981, 49 percent of women in this age group were relying on the pill or sterilization (29 percent and 20 percent, respectively). As can be seen, the seven-point increase in the use of these highly effective methods was due entirely to an increase in the use of sterilization; pill use actually declined by seven percentage points during this period, mainly because of widely publicized reports about its possible long-term health effects (Ketting 1983a). A study on contraceptive use among birth cohorts from 1969 to 1982 reported a shift to more reliable methods (the pill, the IUD, and sterilization) as women approached the end of the childbearing ages (Cliquet and Moors 1986; van de Kaa 1987).

In an attempt to determine why women change methods, the 1982 Netherlands fertility survey, conducted by the CBS, asked each current contraceptor what her last method was before the present one and, if different, what was the most important reason for the change. Each current user, as well as each nonuser who was not sterile but had previously used another method, was also asked about future plans for contraceptive use and the most important reason for any changes contemplated. Responses were grouped into major categories of reasons related to reliability, convenience, medical reasons (including inconvenient side effects), and psychological reasons. Other reasons were grouped in a fifth miscellaneous category. Differences in the women's circumstances and reproductive intentions between giving up one method and adopting another probably affect the data. Planned changes may or may not materialize depending on the women's circumstances, the availability of new methods, and new information about existing methods. The reasons for changes in specific methods were analyzed for two age groups, those under thirty and those thirty or older (table 7.1). Basically, the findings indicate the levels of concern, satisfaction, or dissatisfaction with available contraceptive methods.

Findings from the 1982 Netherlands fertility survey indicate that method reliability is the principal reason women switch from less effective methods to sterilization or the pill (the two most commonly used methods among current contraceptors). Forty-four percent of women who had turned from use of the pill to sterilization, and 53 percent of women who had switched from use of the IUD or condom, had done so for this reason. Women who had turned to sterilization tended to be in their thirties or older, an age group in which most women are likely to have completed childbearing. Psychological reasons were given by fewer than one-quarter of the women and medical reasons by fewer than one-fifth. Women over thirty were somewhat more likely to have made the change for psychological reasons than younger women.

Among women who switched from the condom to the pill, 70 percent of those under thirty and 63 percent of those over thirty indicated that reliability was their main reason. The next most frequently cited reason for switching from condoms to the pill was convenience. Only small proportions of both age groups cited psychological or medical causes. In contrast, women switched from the pill to the IUD, the condom, or other less-effective methods principally for medical or psychological reasons.

Almost all the women who were using the pill or the IUD at the time of the survey (94 and 95 percent, respectively) intended to continue using the same method, with little disagreement between younger and older women (not shown). Women who were using other reversible methods (the minority of total users) were more likely to want to change their method. About three in ten of the young women using the condom or other less effective methods planned on switching, but only one in ten older women expected to do so. Only 8 percent of all users intended to switch methods. Most women who contemplated changing their method expected to adopt sterilization or the pill, mainly because of reliability.

Table 7.1 *Percentage distribution of women practicing contraception, by reasons for changing from previous method*

Current method, age, and previous method	Reason for changing					Total weighted N
	Reliability	Convenience	Medical reasons	Psychological reasons	Other	
1. Women using sterilization						
All ages						
Pill	44	4	14	22	16	651
IUD and condom	53	5	16	9	17	146
Pill, IUD, and condom	45	4	15	20	16	797
< 30						
Pill	48	5	12	15	20	98
IUD and condom[a]	60	5	15	10	10	18
Pill, IUD, and condom	50	5	13	14	18	116
≥ 30						
Pill	43	3	15	23	16	554
IUD and condom	51	6	16	9	18	128
Pill, IUD, and condom	45	4	15	21	16	682
2. Women using the pill						
All ages						
IUD, condom, other	65	18	9	3	5	443
< 30						
IUD, condom, other	69	16	6	3	6	283
≥ 30						
IUD, condom, other	60	21	12	4	3	159
Condom						
All ages	68	21	4	2	6	311
< 30	70	19	2	2	7	207
≥ 30	63	24	7	2	4	104
3. Women using the IUD						
All ages						
Pill	2	5	26	63	4	413
Condom, other[a]	49	29	8	6	8	34
Pill, condom, other	6	7	24	58	5	446
< 30						
Pill	3	5	25	61	6	212
Condom, other[a]	53	29	0	0	18	16
Pill, condom, other	7	7	23	56	7	229
≥ 30						
Pill	2	5	26	65	2	200
Condom, other[a]	42	26	16	11	5	18
Pill, condom, other	5	7	25	60	3	218
4. Women using condoms and other methods						
Pill						
All ages	1	4	24	59	13	284
< 30	2	4	19	59	16	157
≥ 30	1	3	28	59	9	128
5. Women using the IUD, condoms, or other methods						
Pill						
All ages	2	5	25	61	8	697
< 30	2	5	23	60	10	369
≥ 30	2	4	27	62	5	328

Source: Special tabulations from the Central Bureau of Statistics 1982 fertility survey. Percentages may not add to 100 because of rounding.

[a]Reasons for switching are probably based on small sample sizes.

One issue that causes some concern among medical and health professionals in the Netherlands is that wider acceptance of contraceptive sterilization may result in increased instances of sterilization regret. The most common cause for regret is "broken relationships," and the number of couples facing separation and divorce has been increasing (Ketting 1983b). Concern over the adverse long-term health effects of the pill is the principal reason for the rapid increase in the number of sterilizations, although resort to sterilization because of the drawbacks of reversible methods appears to increase the risk of regret. The desire for sterilization reversals may increase as the possibility becomes better known (Ketting 1983b).

To lower the risk of sterilization regret, Ketting points to the importance of providing preoperative information to help those contemplating sterilization to make well-considered decisions, including information on possible postoperative complications and the chances of reversibility. However, he says counseling should not in any way infringe on the patient's right to make his or her decision. In case of regret, sterilization reversal should be made as available as possible, and payment should be covered by insurance (Ketting 1983b). (Currently the Sickness Fund covers the costs of sterilization and sterilization reversals; data on how far private insurance companies cover these procedures are not available.)

INFORMATION AND EDUCATION

Organized Communication Efforts
Over the past twenty years, knowledge about reliable methods of contraception has improved greatly. Government-sponsored information programs and the media in particular have played a major role in disseminating birth control information to the public. The development of sex-education material and of information by professionals and private organizations is subsidized by government funds and financial support from the business sector.

Sex education. Although it has not been formally integrated into the curriculum, sex education is available in secondary schools to a limited extent. Some teachers provide information about contraception, and some conduct informal group discussions about sexuality.

The government gives financial support to work professionals and private organizations do to develop sex-education programs and material for schools. The University of Leiden teaches a sex-education course for high school biology teachers with funds from the Ministry of Education. The goals of the course are to enable teachers to feel comfortable about sex-related topics and to be able to discuss their own experiences in the classroom and relate to the youth's thoughts and feelings; to become more aware of their own values and accept others; to allow students to realize their own sex values and behavior, that is, that they are not necessarily the same as adults; and to transmit these to their own teaching situation.

The University of Leiden has also been involved in developing a high school biology textbook that includes information on contraception. The first version (1982), considered too explicit by many school authorities and parents, has since been revised; only 20 percent of schools currently use it. The university also continues to develop such materials as film and video programs and booklets in cooperation with both public and private sectors, for example, the Rutgers Stichting and pharmaceutical companies and distributors.

In August 1985, a law passed that opened the way for health education in primary schools, which may also offer information on sexuality and birth control. There has been little negative reaction from the public but, as of 1986, sex education had not yet been integrated into the school system.

General information. Eighty counseling bureaus across the country serve as information centers, providing guidance and referrals to anyone in need of assistance with problems related to sexuality and birth control. These bureaus are all operated by private and charitable organizations, principal among which are the Rutgers Stichting, the Protestantse Stichting voor Verantwoorde Gezinsvorming, and the Nederlandse Vereniging voor Hervorming. They provide medical, psychological, and social assistance as well as public information and referral services. Each week at least 6,000 people, three-quarters of them women, call or visit the centers for information or guidance (Engberts 1985, table 5 [CBS survey of counseling bureaus]). Nearly 53 percent of all requests are about sexual problems and birth control; 35 percent are to make appointments for checkups at family planning clinics or other facilities; 5 percent are for emergency referrals to doctors or family planning clinics, and the remaining 7 percent are for purchase of condoms and spermicides (5 percent) or to obtain general information (2 percent).

The government funds information and interpreter centers established specifically to assist young people and immigrants in gaining access to health services. The Children's Telephone Assistance Service has set up a hot line that operates daily from 4 P.M. to 8 P.M. for young people with problems; volunteers funded by the Ministry of Welfare, Health and Cultural Affairs provide the services. The hot line receives about 80,000 calls annually from young people aged six to eighteen.

About 25 to 30 percent of the calls are related to sexual matters and birth control, and another 15 to 20 percent are about relationships. Information requests are answered over the phone. Previously, calls for actual services were answered with information concerning existing sources of assistance, but this approach apparently worked poorly. Now young people with problems are advised to seek the help of a confidant of their choice. Translator's services are available to the public from interpreter centers, usually by telephone. Great effort is being made to provide translated information on all health topics. Doctors can get immediate translation by phone in all languages.

In 1976, the Ministry of Health, Welfare and Cultural Affairs established the Buro Voorlichting Gezondheidszorg Buitenlanders (Agency for information on health care for immigrants) to help assimilate into the health-care system immigrant workers who, because of language problems or lack of knowledge about the system, have difficulty in using the health-care system. The agency is fully subsidized by the government, works closely with a parallel organization for education and social welfare for immigrants, and is supervised by four or five national health organizations whose main activity during the past ten years has been to provide immigrants with translated, easily readable educational materials on all aspects of health care, including family planning. In addition, the agency sponsors a program that trains immigrant women to teach health education to their compatriots. A series of family planning educational materials, including information about the pill, injectables, the IUD, diaphragm, condom, sterilization, natural family planning, and abortion, are written in simple Dutch with simple translation and illustrations. For the illiterate the agency has prepared audiovisuals on family planning in drama or discussion form, which health workers use as a guide in communicating with migrants. The importance of communicating well is stressed. The counselor is urged to participate in the process, even when not bilingual, with the help of wordlists developed for this purpose. The goal of the agency for the next ten years is to shift these activities and transfer the responsibility for integrating immigrants into the health system to the national health agencies.

The decline in use of the pill attributed to increased publicity during the late 1970s about its health risks was followed by an increase in fertility and abortion rates (see chapter 4, figs. 1, 2, and 5). To counterbalance the bad publicity given the pill, pharmaceutical companies have become more involved in improving communication with the public. Journalists are invited to conferences where scientists discuss the risks and benefits of the pill. Booklets describing all methods are distributed through doctors, pharmacists, and women's magazines, without any advertisement.

Advertising of Methods and Services
Brand-name advertising of prescription contraceptives (pill, IUD, diaphragm) is forbidden by law, except in medical journals. The law requires, however, that package inserts contain information on the long-term risks of the method and important facts about symptoms related to method use that users can detect. Failure rates are not usually found in the package inserts; it is assumed that doctors know and discuss them with their patient. Pharmaceutical companies submit the text of patient leaflets to authorities for approval. Once the authorities have approved the text of an insert, consumers may not bring product liability suits, as U.S. consumers have done in the case of the IUD, for example. Lawyers are not compensated on the basis of awards to their clients as in the United States.

Direct advertisement of birth control services is not prohibited, but the Royal Dutch Union of Physicians abides by guidelines that consider advertising by doctors and clinics unethical. Brochures distributed by clinics in public education campaigns disseminate general information about the various methods or about sex-related problems.

No policy prohibits advertisement of condoms or other nonprescription contraceptives, but there is little product advertising about them. The market for the condom is stable, and sources and general information so widespread that companies have little motivation to incur the heavy costs of advertising. The scientific press on other nonprescription methods is very negative; little information about them is available to the general public, and ads are rarely considered.

Media Treatment of Contraception
Many people believe that the widespread use of reliable methods in the Netherlands has resulted mainly from open presentation and discussion in the media about matters related to sex and birth control. Media presentations and discussions range from the biological facts of reproduction to sexual problems. Radio, television, and magazine coverage of sexual issues and contraception is geared toward educating the public, not toward sensationalizing sexual topics.

A popular television program, produced by an interchurch radio program organization called IKON (Inter Kerkelijke Omroep Nederland), runs for two hours every week and covers topics ignored by others in the media. The topics are presented in the form of drama, documentaries, and talk shows, a number of which have won public acclaim and prizes. One-fourth of the programs produced for the format are aimed at young people. Apparently, a favorite among young people is a half-hour talk show in which the moderator, who is not a television personality, talks with five or six boys or girls from the studio audience about a different topic each week. The show often covers topics related to sexuality, relationships, and contraception. Emphasis is on personal choice, development, and acceptance of reality. The producers' aim is to break down stereotypes like "punk." They also believe there is a need for more programs aimed at young people and have planned on including a drama series on sexuality in future productions, with a script reviewed by school students.

There is no discussion of contraception on the adult part of the IKON format because the need for new contraceptives or methods for older women is not an issue in the Netherlands. Some discussion of sex in relation to divorce has been aired. AIDS is not covered in any of the programs in the format because other media give it a lot of attention. Abortion remains a difficult topic for the producers.

Libelle, the most widely read women's weekly magazine in the Netherlands, is a major source of birth control information. The magazine has a weekly circulation of 750,000 and reaches 52 percent of all women over fifteen. Its target group is women aged 20–40. The median educational level of its readers is three or four years of high school. The magazine presents sexuality and contraception in four ways:

Reporting. Libelle reports periodic interviews with women, for example, those married five years. These appear every one or two months.

Special item. A magazine insert, in the form of a booklet, provides information on the various methods of contraception, mainly the pill. It shows how a method works, the good and bad things about the pill (age, smoking), and other methods. Doctors contribute to the information and discussions found in the booklet. It does not provide failure rates for condoms and gives no information about foam. This booklet, produced in cooperation with a pharmaceutical company, appears once or twice a year.

Special monthly. Libelle subscribers have a choice of three supplementary monthly magazines. *Man and Woman* treats sexuality philosophically, often reporting interviews with experts. The *Medical* magazine may include reports on the various methods, but in greater detail, and it also notes the latest developments in contraception. The third monthly special is devoted to fashions.

Weekly rubriek. The *rubriek*, a question-and-answer section that appears in every issue of *Libelle*, has the biggest impact on the readers. Questions and answers go through a panel of specialists. Between 5 and 10 percent of the questions are on contraception. All questions are answered, but only some are selected for publication. A letter and a corresponding answer by an expert is published only if there is little information on the subject. A by-product of the *rubriek* is the *Libelle Samen-reeks* edition, a paperback series featuring the hundred most often asked questions about a subject, such as pets, buying a house, burial, or cremation. *Libelle* publishes a separate edition about the pill and another about other methods of contraception (Braam and Leemhuis 1983, 1978). These cover general information, such as what the various methods are and how to use them, their effectiveness (including failure rates), safety and convenience, health risks and possible side effects, where to get advice, whether advice is confidential, the cost of contraception and who pays for it, and new developments in contraceptives.

Libelle takes its educational responsibility very seriously, and women depend on it for reliable information. The editors strive consciously to avoid any writing that might contribute to a rise in unintended conceptions. They regret that an article in *Libelle* some ten years ago was part of a wave of negative publicity about the pill that was followed by a rise in pregnancy and abortion.

Libelle is a family magazine and has a certain sense of propriety about sex. It aims to provide reliable information about different aspects of life, including sex, in a practical and careful way, and it avoids sensationalism and uses discreet illustrations. AIDS is thought to be regarded by the average woman as related to "dirty" sex and is not written about. Abortion is considered a hot topic, not the subject for a major article but possibly woven into a story in the fiction section. Questions about AIDS and abortion are dealt with in the *rubriek*. Religious stands, such as recent statements by the pope against abortion and artificial family planning are considered the province of newspapers rather than the magazine.

Climate of Opinion Concerning Sex

Openness about sex increases continually. In the past few years, the press has covered AIDS extensively, and radio and television have brought the need for safe sex practices to public attention. In cooperation with the Ministry of Health, Welfare and Cultural Affairs, private organizations are conducting an information campaign about the disease. Widely distributed brochures describe the disease, its symptoms, how it is transmitted (and also that it cannot be transmitted by "normal" daily contacts), who is at risk, when testing is needed, and use of the condom for safe sex. The brochures include information on special telephone numbers to call and places to go for assistance, including municipal health centers for infectious diseases in every town, village, or city.

Recent research on sexual relationships by the Nederlands In-stituut voor Sociaal Sexuologisch Onderzoek indicates that, in addition to the openness with which society regards matters related to sex, men's respect for women in personal relations has contributed to the success of contraception in the Netherlands. Dutch boys turn early from a purely self-centered approach to sexual relationships to one based on a negotiation process seeking to enhance mutual enjoyment. This en-courages communication and cooperation about contraception.

ASSESSMENT

Proportion of Overall Need That Is Met
Of the five case-study areas, the Netherlands has the lowest fertility rate, the lowest abortion rate, and appears to have the lowest ratio of unplanned to planned pregnancies (see table 4.2). In the Netherlands, fertility rates declined dramatically during the 1970s and have been stable since, while abortion rates have remained at low levels (see figures 4.1 and 4.3). Use of effective methods of contraception is quite high: 56 percent of Dutch women aged 15–44 are protected by steril-ization, the pill, or the IUD (see figure 4.8). One reason for this impressive record is improved access to reliable methods through the national insurance system and government funding.

The provision of modern contraceptive methods has been included among health services covered by the government-sponsored national health insurance fund in the Netherlands since the early 1970s. Family physicians are the principal source of contraceptive services, and the fund covers most contraceptive services obtained from doctors. The government also subsidizes family planning clinics that serve women who are not reached by family doctors, namely adolescents and immi-grants. Both public and private sectors have supported widespread communication and information efforts. Books giving information about various methods of contraception are widely distributed. Infor-mation, guidance, and referrals for services are available to anyone needing assistance on sexual problems and birth control. Telephone services for young people with problems and translator services for immigrants are also widely available. In 1986, more than 1.2 million women obtained modern reliable methods of contraception, mainly the pill, from family doctors and family planning clinics financed or subsidized from public funds. Family physicians write about 90 percent of pill prescriptions, doctors in family planning clinics 5 percent, and obstetrician-gynecologists the other 5 percent. Pills are the most popu-lar method among young people, and unintended pregnancy is low among them compared to other industrialized countries. Contraceptive use among immigrant women has increased remarkably in the relatively short time they have lived in the Netherlands. Levels of use of effective methods among immigrant women are comparable to those of Dutch women.

Barriers to Service

People in the Netherlands have shown concern that the level of abortion among adolescents is not low enough. The relatively high proportion of abortions adolescents undergo is because many do not use reliable methods of contraception, particularly at first intercourse. A need is felt for greater access to sex education in schools, contraceptive information, and services for adolescents. The Dutch government has recognized the crucial role of the schools in reaching young people with information about sex, pregnancy and contraception before they have intercourse. It has established an interdepartmental committee to study ways of improving contraceptive behavior among groups with special needs, including adolescents, and subsidized the development of school material and training of schoolteachers to be sex educators. A law passed in 1985 paved the way for the introduction of health education, including sex education, in primary schools, but school authorities have been slow in integrating sex education in primary as well as high schools. Sex education in schools still largely dwells on the biological aspects of reproduction and informal group discussions about sexuality and contraception.

Adolescents do not need parental consent or notification to obtain contraceptive services from a doctor or clinic, but fear of adverse parental reaction and lack of awareness that doctors are required to respect their right to confidentiality combine to dissuade some adolescents from approaching their family doctor for contraceptives. In addition, lack of information about clinic locations, and the cost of clinic services, however small, may still present barriers to effective contraception among young people. It is not known how many teenagers who do not avail themselves of contraceptive services from their doctor attend a family planning clinic or go without.

Almost all immigrant women who were not currently using a method had never used one, yet a substantial proportion of nonusers and their husbands approve of contraception. Besides communication problems, cultural barriers, such as the fear of using condoms, may inhibit them from using the only methods they know about. Little information is available about nonprescription contraceptives other than the condom.

Data are not available that show how well people are counseled about the benefits and risks associated with the pill, but a significant proportion of telephone requests for guidance and information from counseling bureaus are about it. This suggests a need for more and better counseling from providers. Little follow-up activity seems to occur where the pill is concerned.

Relation of Services to Method Use
In the Netherlands, contraception is encouraged by the government, the medical profession, and the media, and it is widely accepted by the public. Changes in social attitudes toward sexuality and birth control, concern over the efficacy of traditional contraceptive methods and improved access to services, have stimulated the extensive use of reliable modern methods. Method reliability is extremely important both to clients and to their providers. Though the pill is the most prevalent method of contraception, increasingly women are relying on male or female sterilization. The fact that primary health care centers around family physicians who are likely to promote the pill may partially account for its rapid acceptance and continuing widespread use. Nevertheless, a very high proportion of couples eventually turn to surgical sterilization, perhaps in part because of concerns about the health risks involved in prolonging pill use into the later years of reproductive life.

The inclusion of contraception in the package of services covered by public health insurance has contributed to widespread use of effective methods of contraception. Contraceptive services and supplies provided by family physicians are free for most patients and those offered at some family planning clinics are partially subsidized by the government and are consequently inexpensive. It is not surprising to find high levels of pill use, particularly among young women for whom health risks associated with the pill are minor and for whom costs and alternative sources of family planning services are important issues (see table 4.7). Young women with more education, perhaps because they are better able to take advantage of the system than less educated women, are more likely to use medical methods, particularly the pill.

The availability of medical methods of contraception, made easier by their inclusion among services covered by the national health insurance fund, appears to account in part for the narrow gap in use of effective contraceptive methods (sterilization, pill, and IUD) between older lower- and upper-income women (see table 4.7). At older ages, combined use of effective methods is about the same among low-income as among high-income women. Low-income women, however, are much more likely to use the pill, the most effective method directly available from the family doctor without charge. Sterilization, a surgical method, requires referral to a specialist, which could present obstacles, but sterilization has become the method of choice among older women regardless of income or education. Improved access to sterilization services, as well as government and private efforts to extend information and guidance to those less able to take advantage of the health-care system, may explain in part why women with less education are just as likely to have contraceptive sterilization as women with more.

8

Great Britain

GENERAL DESCRIPTION

Great Britain has a nationalized health care system that covers people of all income groups. Like all health-care programs operated by the state, it competes with other national concerns for its share of the budget and places restrictions on access to some types of medical providers. In the mid-1970s, family planning services were included in the national scheme, although the organization and delivery of these services and the funding and payment arrangements with medical professionals had no precedent in the national health-care system.

People interviewed: Isobel Allen, Policy Studies Institute; John Ashton (M.D.), Department of Community and Environmental Health, Liverpool University; Toni Belfield, Family Planning Association; Margaret Bone, Office of Population Censuses and Surveys; Nick Boyd, Department of Health and Social Security; Anne-Marie Carlen, Family Planning Association, North West England; Joanna Chambers, Birth Control Trust; Elphis Christopher (M.D.), Senior Medical Officer, Family Planning; Deborah Colclough, Family Planning Association, South West England; Dilys Cossey, British Parliamentary Group on Population and Development; Paul Coveslant, London Weekend TV; Stan Drummond, Department of Health and Social Security; Karen Dunnell, Office of Population Censuses and Surveys; Yvonne Ford, Brook Advisory Centre; Alwon Frater, Brook Advisory Centre; Romie Goodchild, Press Officer, Family Planning Association; Helene Graham, Pregnancy Advisory Service; John Guillebaud (M.D.), Margaret Pyke Centre; Kathleen Kiernan, The City University; Audrey Leathard, Polytechnic of the South Bank; Helen Martins, Family Planning Association; Angela Mills (M.D.), Bloomsbury Health Authority; John Modle (M.D.), Department of Health and Social Security; Vivienne Nathanson (M.D.), British Medical Association; Zandria Pauncefort, Family Planning Association; Bruce Penhale, The City University; Fran Reader (M.D.), Tower Hamlets Health Authority; Bruce Rhodes, Pharmaceutical Society of Great Britain; Deirdre Sanders, The Sun; Pram Senanayake (M.D.), International Planned Parenthood

181

The following discussion attempts to describe the structure and pattern of health delivery, especially family planning services, in Great Britain. Although the health-care system is based on national policy, resources and services differ considerably both within and between England, Wales, and Scotland. Many policies and statistical data may apply to Great Britain as a whole. Much of the assessment of family planning service delivery, however, will focus on England, the only part of Great Britain where site visits were made.

Overall Health System

Comprehensive health care has been largely free to all residents of Great Britain since the establishment of the National Health Service (NHS) in 1948, when nearly all hospitals and clinics were nationalized. The NHS guarantees easy access to basic medical care through an extensive network of general practitioners, who control access to specialist physicians and hospitals. Services are free to the patient, although a nominal dispensing fee (about $3.00) is payable at the pharmacy for having prescriptions filled.[1] The old, young, chronically ill, and those with low incomes are exempt from these charges, leaving about one in five persons who must pay (*British Medical Journal* 1986a).

The NHS covers about 93 percent of Britain's medical bill, with revenues primarily derived from general taxation. Although the public and medical professionals continue to support the NHS overwhelmingly, it has increasingly come under attack from both groups for deteriorating conditions, outdated medical technology, long waiting periods, and substantial variation in services across geographic regions (*British Medical Journal* 1986b). Some have criticized the system for being too costly, even though health expenditures account for only about 6 percent of the gross national product and have grown more slowly than in many other industrialized countries. Others have accused the government of being too budget-conscious, at the expense of quality patient care (at hospitals, in particular) ("British Health Service" 1988). Many critics feel that the present government has a hidden agenda of actually encouraging growth in the private health-care industry.

The Department of Health and Social Security (DHSS) sets policy for the NHS but does not run the service. The Secretary of State for Social Services is responsible for its supervision. Actual planning and man-

---

Federation; Alastair Service, Family Planning Association; Howard Seymour, Liverpool Regional Health Promotion; Gordon Snow, FP Sales; Robert Snowden, University of Exeter; Deborah Thom, Family Planning Association; Martin Vessey (M.D.), Oxford University; Kaye Wellings, Family Planning Association; Denise Wynn, Cosmopolitan.

1. British pounds have been converted to U.S. dollar amounts using the 1986 average exchange rate of $1.467 to £1.

agement as well as the reduction of services are, however, decentralized operations.

There are fourteen Regional Health Authorities in England and one in Wales, and within each of these are smaller District Health Authorities (DHAs). The regional authorities allocate money among the DHAs, review their plans, manage construction, and provide some services. The approximately 190 DHAs in England and Wales are the basic policy and management units for planning and administering services. Decisions are made at this level on services that a particular district will offer.

Community Health Councils exist in every district to protect and represent the interests of the public in their local health service. Councils have access to information about any changes in the service in their districts and act as a vehicle for consumer complaints about gaps or defects in current service delivery (except those relating to clinical judgment).

In the two-tier British health-care system, the general practitioner is the first point of contact for the patient and provides all primary medical care. Instead of making appointments directly with a specialist, an NHS patient must first consult with and obtain a referral from his or her general practitioner.

In 1984 there were approximately fifty-five general practitioners per 100,000 population in Great Britain (calculated from BMA 1987 and FPIS 1986a). In 1983, the average number of consultations per year for males and females was four and five, respectively (OPCS 1983, 151). Most general practitioners are thirty-five or older (64 percent) and are men (82 percent) (BMA 1987). Group practice is replacing solo practice as the typical working arrangement, especially among younger doctors and those in densely populated areas. Although some physicians have joined traditional group practices, others have become staff members at health centers, a more recent alternative setting. Health centers, established by District Health Authorities, are typically staffed with general practitioners, health visitors, and district health nurses.

The general practitioners (also the dentists, pharmacists, and opticians) in an area have contractual agreements with Family Practitioner Committees (FPCs) that are responsible for administering all general practitioner services (Wells 1982). FPCs have recently become health authorities in their own right, resulting in considerable independence of this group within the NHS. The FPC in an area maintains a list of general practitioners providing services as well as a list of the special services that some but not all general practitioners extend, such as obstetric or family planning services. FPCs are also instrumental in appointing general practitioners to employment vacancies, although the final decision is left to the Medical Practices Committee (a more central body that also controls the number of general practitioners allowed to practice in any one area).

In Great Britain, all individuals sixteen and older register with a general practitioner, who is responsible for the medical care of everyone on his or her "list." The general practitioner receives a capitation fee (a flat payment for each person seen), plus additional item-of-service payments for such other duties as treating patients over sixty-five, practicing in a group or in a rural area, making night visits, providing maternity services, or treating temporary nonresidents. The General Medical Services Committee (GMSC) of the BMA negotiates terms and conditions of service for general practitioners with the DHSS.

The NHS uses health visitors as liaison between the patient and the formal medical system and as an extension of the work of the general practitioner. The DHAs employ health visitors, who are concerned with "the promotion of health and the prevention of ill health in families by giving them education, advice, and support, and by referring them to general practitioners or to other services if they need special help" (Central Statistical Office 1985, 116). A midwife visits all mothers and newborn infants at home (for a minimum of ten days after delivery) and then places them in the care of a health visitor, who visits the home periodically to ensure that their health-care needs are being met.

Specialist physicians, who generally work in hospitals, have contractual agreements with the Regional Health Authorities. Unlike general practitioners, these physicians are salaried employees of the NHS. Negotiations for their terms and conditions of service are the responsibility of the Central Committee for Hospital Medical Services of the BMA. The average number of hospital inpatient visits in 1983 was 0.11 for males and 0.14 for females, while for outpatient attendances (excluding prenatal and postnatal visits) it was 1.17 and 1.15, respectively (OPCS 1983, 152).

Doctors in general practice and in hospitals are entitled to spend part of their time in private practice. While most general practitioners rely almost exclusively on the NHS for their incomes, many hospital doctors have opted for part-time involvement in private practice.

Patients also have the right to purchase private health insurance and receive their medical care through the private sector. Although the market for private insurance has been steadily increasing, it accounts for only a small proportion of the population. In 1983, 4 percent of people aged sixteen and over held a private medical insurance policy, and such policies covered 7 percent of the population (OPCS 1983, 152). The average fee in 1983 for private coverage was approximately $270 per subscriber (Central Statistical Office 1985, 118). Private insurance is available on an individual or a group basis. Group membership is usually linked to the place of employment, and the company may pay all or part of the employee's subscription. Members of some subgroups are more likely to be private policy holders than others, including individuals in the professional socioeconomic group and those living in the outer metropolitan area in southeast England. People in Wales and Scotland are much less likely to have private medical insurance, regardless of their socioeconomic status.

In 1983, only 5 percent of all inpatient hospital stays and 2 percent of all outpatient attendance by people sixteen and over were paid for privately (Central Statistical Office 1985, 118). Three-quarters of private inpatient stays were in private hospitals and the rest in NHS hospitals. The private sector may also be utilized by NHS patients who do not have private medical insurance but, for a variety of reasons, are unable to obtain specialized services like abortion or sterilization, or who are frustrated by excessive waiting periods for hospital beds.

Family Planning Services

Free family planning services were not always available within the NHS. Indeed, the NHS existed for almost twenty-five years before coverage of family planning services was included.

Britain has a long history of organized family planning services, going back to the first clinic, established by Marie Stopes in 1921. Opposition by religious groups and the medical profession pushed the National Birth Control Association (a forerunner of the current Family Planning Association) into developing its own network of family planning clinics for married women (Leathard 1980). By 1930, attitudes toward birth control services were somewhat more favorable (except within Roman Catholicism and among conservative parts of the medical profession) and local health authorities were empowered to provide birth control advice to married women for whom pregnancy was contraindicated. The opposition of the Catholic church and the lack of interest among physicians encouraged the Family Planning Association (FPA) to increase its clinics and services and pursue the long-term goal of comprehensive family planning services provided by the state. Toward this goal, it avoided controversial issues like sterilization and abortion and developed good working relationships with government officials.

An important event occurred in 1955, when a popular and respected minister of health made an official visit to an FPA clinic. This opened the media to FPA news and altered the attitudes of local authorities to its clinics. The 1960s were critical years in the campaign for free family planning services. One overwhelming factor was the introduction of oral contraceptives, which significantly changed patterns of contraceptive use and, as a prescription drug, captured the interest of the medical profession. Further developments came quickly.

In 1967, local health authorities were allowed (at their discretion) to provide birth control services to women of any marital status, on social or medical grounds, and following passage of the 1967 Abortion Act (Leathard 1980), free abortions were permitted within the NHS. Due to the controversial nature of these reforms, the public sector rarely offered these services, and the nonprofit organizations took the major responsibility. Brook Advisory Centres, providing free NHS services, were established in the 1960s to serve young, unmarried people in particular, and charitable organizations like the Pregnancy Advisory Service and the British Pregnancy Advisory Service tried to meet the growing demand for abortions.

Two issues, overpopulation and abortion, were crucial in the final push for the inclusion of free family planning services within the NHS. In the 1960s, the population lobby tied its campaign closely with the push for free contraceptive services. In addition, more widespread use of contraceptives was seen by political groups as a better alternative to the growing number of abortions. These issues offered the necessary leverage for the Birth Control Campaign (a lobbying offshoot of the FPA) to gain acceptance of free family planning services nationwide in 1973.

In 1974, the FPA began the process of handing over its established network of more than a thousand clinics to the NHS. Up to that time the FPA had been the largest organization outside the NHS to offer a nation-wide medical service. Since then it has been mainly responsible for education and information, although it retains about twenty-four clinics for small-scale research and development work. The FPA receives grant aid from the DHSS in support of its efforts and maintains an informal consultative role with the DHSS by keeping it informed about the current and future status of family planning services.

The two main providers of family planning services are general practitioners and family planning clinics staffed by doctors with special training in providing contraceptive methods. (In some instances, clinic doctors may be gynecologists, but that is not typical.) Patients who have serious gynecological problems or need surgery are referred to specialists (mainly gynecologists, urologists, and general surgeons) for treatment. Contraceptive advice and supplies may also be obtained at pharmacies and, depending on the area and availability, through home-visiting programs or from Brook Advisory Centres, whose clients are mainly young people. Maternity patients may receive contraceptive services while in the hospital or during postnatal visits by health visitors. Condoms are available at clinics, pharmacies, some supermarkets, through mail-order houses, in barbershops, and in vending machines, which are often located in pubs.

How the NHS provides family planning services differs in some ways from most other NHS care. As noted earlier, patients must consult their own general practitioner before they can be treated at a hospital or specialized clinic. In 1974, however, the DHSS acknowledged the "special nature" of family planning care by giving patients a choice of providers: the general practitioner and the family planning clinic (DHSS 1974). In addition, recognizing that some patients might be uneasy talking to their own general practitioner about contraception, the NHS agreed to permit patients to retain their regular general practitioner for routine medical care but visit a different one to obtain family planning services if the "new" general practitioner agreed to accept the patient.

Funding arrangements for family planning services are also anomalous. Two systems (general practitioners and clinics) are financed separately. General practitioners receive item-of-service payments (over and above the capitation fee) from the NHS central fund for every family planning consultation. Agreement on this special arrangement was crucial for enticing general practitioners, in 1975, to accept responsibility for providing family planning services within the NHS. Family planning clinics are funded locally through the DHAs, which receive a limited annual budget from the NHS for running all health services. This funding arrangement can work to the clinic's disadvantage, for although they rely entirely on the DHAs for funding, they constitute a very small part of the DHA's responsibilities and must compete with all its other services for funding.

Hospital-based specialist physicians also depend on allocations from DHAs. Because the service obligations spelled out in the specialist's contracts had not included family planning, the NHS was forced to offer item-of-service payments like those for general practitioners. Unlike the special payments made to general practitioners, however, the specialists' payments come from each DHA's budget rather than from the NHS central fund.

The aims of the family planning service, as stated by the DHSS in a 1974 health service circular, were to enable people to avoid unwanted pregnancy, to reduce the financial and emotional stress on families, and to improve the physical health of families through proper spacing and timing of births. Services must be made available to everyone who needs them—men and women, the married and the unmarried—and all people should be free to choose their source of advice from either a general practitioner or a family planning clinic. In order to remove all financial barriers, a precedent was set by eliminating all prescription dispensing fees for contraceptives. General practitioners, however, refused to provide condoms, reducing the range of methods they offered.

Present government guidelines make no stipulation regarding parental consent or notification requirements for teenagers seeking contraceptive services, although there have been fierce battles over this issue. For young people aged sixteen and under, physicians are encouraged to have the patients seek the involvement of their parents, but confidentiality remains the right of every patient.

Officially, general practitioners and clinics offer confidential advice; a choice of birth control methods, including postcoital contraception;[2] free contraceptive supplies;[3] male and female sterilization advice; pregnancy testing; advice on sexual problems; and advice and information regarding unplanned pregnancies. Basically all reversible methods of contraception are available in Great Britain, including injectables (banned in the United States). In 1984, the injectable Depo-Provera was licensed for long-term use, but only for women for whom other contraceptive methods were contraindicated or unsuitable (DHSS 1984). Oral contraceptives include monophasic, biphasic, triphasic, and progestrogen-only pills. The most widely used preparations are combined pills containing thirty or fewer micrograms of estrogen; no pills contain more than fifty micrograms (FPIS 1983).

The availability of such specialized services as subfertility counseling, sterilization, and abortion varies greatly in different regions. Since the 1967 Abortion Act, a woman can have a legal abortion if two registered medical practitioners agree that continuation of the pregnancy would threaten her life, involve risk to her physical or mental health or that of any existing children, or involve a substantial risk that she will give birth to a physically or mentally handicapped child. Although the Abortion Act does not specify an upper limit on the gestation period, the Infant Life Preservation Act has established twenty-eight weeks as the time of viability, and twenty-six weeks is now generally considered to be the latest time for a legal abortion, to be sure of being within the limit. The DHSS has asked private abortion clinics to restrict the upper limit to twenty-four weeks, based on a recommendation from the Royal College of Obstetricians and Gynecologists and other medical organizations. Specialists (usually gynecologists) per-

2. Postcoital methods consist either of two doses (two tablets each) of an oral contraceptive containing 50 mcg of ethinyl estradiol, taken seventy-two hours apart, or an IUD that is inserted within three to five days of unprotected intercourse. Postcoital contraception is available as an emergency method following unprotected intercourse, failure of a mechanical method, or rape.

3. A general practitioner gives a patient a prescription, but the woman must obtain her supplies (free of charge) at a pharmacy; a clinic generally provides supplies on site.

form all NHS abortions. There are few outpatient facilities for abortions within the NHS. According to 1985 statistics, 60 percent of NHS abortions performed on residents of England and Wales were inpatient procedures (OPCS 1986, table 5). Most women spend one or two days in the hospital.

A conscientious-objection clause in the Abortion Act allows general practitioners, gynecologists, or nurses to refuse to recommend or perform the procedure. If they believe that the woman's situation would meet one of the criteria for an NHS abortion, however, they are strongly advised to refer the patient to another colleague.

The attitudes of the referring doctor and the gynecologist are important factors in whether a woman will or will not receive an NHS abortion. The woman is often reluctant to seek help and advice from her own general practitioner. A study designed to explore how well abortion services satisfy the needs of the consumer found that many women viewed each visit to a general practitioner and gynecologist as a battle in their effort to be granted an abortion (Allen 1981). That study also identified other factors that delay women, such as inefficient pregnancy testing services provided by general practitioners and delays in referring to specialists. Furthermore, if an area has only a few gynecologists, and they do not perform abortions, the service is not available. General practitioners seem to know which gynecologists in an area are willing to perform abortions and generally refer women only to them.

Although only 3 percent of abortions in England and Wales take place at gestations of eighteen or more weeks, considerable attention has been paid to the link between the provision of abortion services by the NHS and delays in obtaining abortions. Inefficient pregnancy testing services, general practitioners' unsympathetic attitudes or reluctance to approve abortions, the narrow range of reasons for which consultant gynecologists will perform abortions, and inadequate district resources have all been identified as key factors in causing delay into the second trimester of pregnancy and in forcing women to obtain abortions from private-sector providers (Roe 1988).

Despite the legal availability of abortion, therefore, several barriers exist. A woman's ability to obtain an abortion within the NHS is limited not only by her physician's attitudes and by delays in the referral process, but also by the uneven availability of services across regions and the long waiting lists for the operation. As a result of these conditions, approximately half the abortions in Great Britain are performed outside the NHS by such private agencies as the Pregnancy Advisory Service, the British Pregnancy Advisory Service, and Marie Stopes House. The current fee for an abortion by the Pregnancy Advisory Service is approximately $215 for the operation and $40 for the counseling and consultation with two doctors.

Target Groups for Family Planning

In 1974, the DHSS Memorandum of Guidance on the Family Planning Service acknowledged two groups requiring special attention: (1) adolescents, and (2) women who "cannot bring themselves to seek help or who have difficulty in getting to a surgery or clinic." In an effort to increase effective use of contraceptives by adolescents, the DHSS recommended that either special clinic sessions or more informal clinics be established so that teenagers could have their special needs met in a congenial setting. As a result, some clinics offer special Youth Advisory Services and, where they are available, teenagers can also attend Brook Advisory Centres, which are especially sensitive to the needs of young people. In 1984, there were 118,200 pregnancies to women under twenty in England and Wales; and 33 percent of these ended in abortion (Brook Advisory Centres 1986a). The Bristol Bookings Study (Ineichen 1982) revealed that two-thirds of teenage pregnancies going to full term were unplanned.

Research has demonstrated a trend toward earlier sexual experience among teenagers over the last two decades (Farrell 1978). Their birth and abortion rates, however, do not reflect this trend. Since 1973 abortions have stabilized between 6.5 and 7.5 per thousand fifteen-year-old girls, while the birthrate has fallen from 3.90 per thousand in 1973 to 2.42 in 1982 (FPIS 1986b). These figures suggest that sexually active young teenagers have become better contraceptors. Concurrent with these trends, clinic attendance by clients under sixteen has steadily increased. From 1976 to 1984 the number of clients under sixteen more than doubled (FPIS 1986b).

The provision of contraceptive services to these young teenagers has been a topic of much controversy in recent years. In 1983 Mrs. Victoria Gillick took legal action against her local authority and the DHSS charging that it was unlawful for physicians to give contraceptive advice or treatment to girls under sixteen without parental consent. The House of Lords in 1985 upheld the DHSS guidelines, and the decision to prescribe contraception to a person under sixteen without parental consent rests ultimately with the doctor.

The second group of people for whom the DHSS has encouraged special arrangements are defined as those unwilling or unable to receive services from established sources. These people may have mental or physical handicaps, have language and other cultural barriers, or be locked in social and environmental conditions that militate against their use of formal contraceptive services. Domiciliary services, in which family planning personnel visit patients at home, were set up to meet the needs of such subpopulations. Although there is no formal definition of the targeted women, they have typically been from lower socioeconomic groups and more recently seem to include larger numbers of immigrant women from India and the West Indies.

An analysis of immigrant fertility patterns between 1971 and 1981 in England and Wales found greater convergence among certain immigrant groups with the fertility levels of those born in the United Kingdom (Yusuf and Werner 1987). Women from the Irish Republic, parts of Europe, North America, and the Old Commonwealth displayed the greatest convergence. The highest marital fertility rates were found among immigrants from the Commonwealth countries of South Asia and Pakistan. The FPA has taken the initiative to identify other groups whose needs the current delivery system does not adequately address, including men, certain ethnic groups, and the blind.

Contraceptive services for men are almost nonexistent within the NHS, even though 40 percent of couples who practice contraception depend on the condom or on vasectomy (Rowlands 1985). General practitioners do not offer the condom as a family planning method, and clinics make little or no effort to publicize their provision of condoms. Some clinics do not give out free condoms, and those that do generally require that the man receive some counseling or at least register his name and address. Many men are embarrassed to use clinics because they are primarily staffed and attended by women. A study conducted by the Birth Control Trust revealed that the provision of free condoms by clinics was limited for several reasons, ranging from ambivalence among clinic staff about encouraging condom use to concern about draining already limited and threatened clinic budgets (Birth Control Trust 1984). In 1984 the FPA launched the "men too" campaign to promote men's increased involvement in contraceptive decisionmaking, handing out special posters and leaflets for this purpose.

In the course of our interviews, teenagers and people living in rural areas were most typically identified as groups with unmet needs. Several of those with whom we spoke had difficulty grasping the question about target groups. This suggests that many assumed the policy of free contraceptive services for everyone to have eliminated issues of accessibility and availability.

GENERAL PRACTITIONERS AND FAMILY PLANNING SERVICES

General practitioners offering family planning services are more common than family planning clinics and continue to increase in numbers as clinic facilities decrease. In 1982, 97 percent of all general practitioners (22,130) were taking care of family planning services in

England, and they served 2.2 million patients, or 22 percent of all women aged 15–44 (approximately one general practitioner for every 446 women in this age group) (FPIS 1984). In 1983, 62 percent of the approximately 3.8 million people who utilized medical family planning services in England visited general practitioners. The situation is similar in Wales and Scotland (60 and 64 percent, respectively).

General practitioners receive no fees directly from family planning patients within the NHS, but because they are paid a set amount from the central NHS budget for each contraceptive patient on their list, plus additional amounts depending on the method of contraception provided, family planning funding for general practitioners is "demand led": the more they do, the more they earn. On average, general practitioners earn $1,540 per annum for contraceptive services, the second largest contribution to their income from item-of-service payments, after maternity services (Warburton 1986). Physicians receive a standard payment of about $14 per patient for providing contraceptive advice, prescriptions for the pill, and follow-up. The standard payment covers helping a woman to determine the contraceptive she wants, even if she actually obtains it elsewhere. General practitioners who provide methods other than the pill, such as the diaphragm, the cervical cap, or the IUD get paid more. For example, reimbursement for an IUD fitting is an additional $50.

Women who visit a general practitioner for family planning services tend to be older and are more likely to be married and have children than are those who go to clinics. They also are typically more interested in spacing their pregnancies than in postponing or ceasing childbearing (Snowden 1985). General practitioners are the most natural source of contraceptive advice for such women, since they usually provide postnatal services and subsequent care for the women's children.

Although nearly everyone has contact with a general practitioner at some point for routine medical care or for referral to a specialist, and thus presumably talks to the physician about a variety of health issues, this does not mean that the general practitioner initiates discussion of contraception; some general practitioners wait for the woman to bring it up. General practitioners with special certificates in contraceptive technology[4] are more likely than those without special training to

4. The Certificate of Contraceptive Technology is awarded to doctors and other professionals who have attended a course in family planning and who have been judged by the instructing physician to have reached an adequate standard of efficiency. Such courses may be organized by voluntary bodies (e.g., the FPA), by professional bodies (e.g., the Royal College of Midwives) or by clinics (e.g., the Margaret Pyke Centre of the Marie Stopes Memorial Centre). The Joint Committee on Contraception, which includes representatives from the Royal College of Obstetricians and Gynecologists, the Royal College of General Practitioners, the National Association of Family Planning Doctors, and the FPA approves the courses.

introduce the topic with any patient who they think is at risk of pregnancy (Kevern 1981a).

General practitioners make no effort at formal outreach to advertise their family planning services or to recruit new patients. While almost everyone knows that general practitioners provide free family planning services, it is less well known that women can go to a general practitioner other than their own for family planning advice and care, an especially important option for young people. Names of doctors offering family planning services are available at post offices, libraries, and from Family Practitioner Committees, which keep the lists of all physicians practicing in an area. These lists contain special codes that indicate whether a general practitioner provides family planning services and whether he or she will accept another physician's patient solely for contraceptive care. Patients register on the family planning list of a general practitioner for a period of one year.

General practitioners who provide family planning services are generally characterized as being widely available and easy to find, having convenient hours on a daily basis, and are most likely to be men (Snowden 1985). Patients are usually able to obtain an appointment within a day of the request.

Despite the additional payments that general practitioners receive for providing methods such as the IUD or diaphragm, they typically offer a very restricted range of contraceptive methods. A study found that a relatively high proportion of general practitioners said they would like to provide contraceptive services to more patients, but only 36 percent said they would like to provide a greater range of contraceptive methods (Kevern 1981a). They often recommend only the pill, and most women are likely to receive the pill from a general practitioner regardless of their age.[5] In 1983, about 90 percent of the family planning patients of general practitioners obtained the pill, 5 percent were fitted with an IUD, and the remaining 5 percent received other contraceptives like the diaphragm, the cervical cap and spermicides (FPIS 1986c). As part of their 1975 negotiations with the DHSS general practitioners officially refused to provide or prescribe condoms. They do prescribe spermicides and clinical thermometers and temperature charts for women choosing to use the rhythm method.

Why have general practitioners not provided more comprehensive family planning services, despite the apparent financial incentive? First, although the majority of general practitioners register to provide contraceptive services, only 43 percent of those under forty-five and 32 percent of those over have received professional training in contraception (Kevern 1981a). Even if general practitioners have had some

5. Recently, the upper age limit for pill use was raised from forty to forty-five for nonsmoking women with no medical problems.

training, they may not get enough practice in, say, fitting IUDs to keep their skills at an acceptable level. In addition, many general practitioners find it much easier, less time-consuming, and more financially rewarding to prescribe only the pill and refer to clinics those patients who request other methods.

Despite the actual limits on provision of contraceptive methods by general practitioners, one survey found that most women expect them to provide the IUD and diaphragm in addition to the pill (Snowden 1985). But when it comes to choosing a provider source, most women who want an alternative to the pill are more likely to go to a family planning clinic than a general practitioner.

In an attempt to rectify this situation, the organizational structure of general practitioner practices has been changing. Partnerships, group practices, and health centers have evolved as a way for general practitioners to provide a greater variety of services. For example, by having at least one partner who is trained to fit IUDs, the general practitioner gains the additional item-of-service payment for providing the method and then for all the necessary follow-up care. The patient also benefits from this arrangement, because the partner who can extend such a service is better able to maintain and enhance his or her skills, since it occupies a larger proportion of the work load. As another option, general practitioners can often arrange to have a district authority nurse, trained in family planning, join the practice. The nurse may be able to fit diaphragms, prescribe pills (after the initial prescription by a doctor), and do follow-up care.

In a survey of general practitioners, about half the respondents stated that they use health visitors, midwives, and practice nurses in family planning care (Kevern 1981a). Most use them to prepare equipment, record blood pressure, and do weight checks, fewer have them advise patients about contraception.

It is becoming more common these days for young medical trainees to obtain certification in contraceptive care if they are considering going into general practice. Research has shown that general practitioners who do become certified are more likely to offer alternative methods of contraception than those who do not. For example, 71 percent of general practitioners with training fit IUDs, compared with 25 percent of those with none. The training process may also increase cooperation between general practitioners and clinics. Kevern (1981a) found that general practitioners with certification were more likely to refer a patient to a clinic.

Most people expect general practitioners to refer patients desiring contraceptives that they cannot provide—as well as those who are having a problem with a contraceptive method requiring more expertise—to a clinic. Patients who have gynecological problems or require surgery are referred by general practitioners to a specialist at a hospital. In each instance, the general practitioner may provide the follow-up care.

The DHSS issues its *Handbook of Contraceptive Practice* to all general practitioners. This publication describes all the available methods, their medical contraindications, and the clinical examination women using the pill should have. It also gives advice on the distinctive nature of family planning counseling. For oral contraceptives, the handbook encourages the physician to use the lowest possible dose of estrogen and progestogen to minimize the long-term risks of adverse effects, to consider all relevant medical history, and to weigh the adverse effects of the contraceptive method against those of a pregnancy, especially an unwanted one. Virtually all pills used now in Great Britain have less than 35 micrograms of estrogen (most have 30 mcg or less), and the trend is toward increasing use of biphasics and triphasics. A patient beginning to take the pill is supposed to return to the physician first after three months and then every six months if there are no problems. It is strongly recommended that the general practitioner receive practical training at a recognized training center before attempting to insert IUDs.

The primary complaint about many general practitioners (especially from clinic physicians and other medical professionals) is that they have no uniform standards of care. While the recommended components of a clinical examination for women desiring or taking the pill include testing blood pressure, checking body weight, and doing breast, vaginal, and cervical cytological examinations, none are mandatory, and monitoring of blood pressure is the only one that is strongly encouraged.

The impression from the interviews conducted for this study was that general practitioner services vary widely in quality. Some of the persons interviewed expressed special concern about general practitioners who prescribe the pill based on what they considered incomplete medical information. Others suggested that general practitioners may be less likely than clinic physicians to present a balanced discussion of the risks and benefits of the pill. Most British general practitioners, however, believe that the actual dangers of the pill are few and therefore view it as the method of choice for most women.

Information about the risks and merits of the pill is not necessarily included with the pill package, as package inserts are not required in Great Britain. If they are included, however, they must provide all the facts about possible side effects. The Contraceptive Foundation (a consortium of manufacturers, the FPA, the Health Education Authority, and other organizations) is working to update and improve package inserts so that they are more "consumer-friendly" and give consistent information from all manufacturers.

FAMILY PLANNING CLINICS

In comparison to the relatively large number of general practitioners, there were only 1,739 family planning clinics in England in 1982 (FPIS 1984), approximately one clinic for every 5,700 women of reproductive age. Most clinics in Great Britain are located in nonhospital facilities and in urban centers. Approximately two in five patients using medical contraceptive services in Great Britain choose a family planning clinic as their source of care (Snowden 1985).

According to DHSS policy, every district has family planning clinic services, although the number and availability of sessions varies greatly. The distribution of specialized clinic services is particularly variable nationwide. Of 162 DHAs in England and Wales in 1982–83, 59 percent did not offer any subfertility counseling; 23 percent did not offer psychosexual advice; 56 percent had no young people's sessions; 44 percent had no domiciliary service; and in 1984, 15 percent did not offer postcoital contraception (Leathard 1984a).

DHAs allocate their budgets among the competing demands of all the programs and services for which they are responsible. Family planning services often seem to fare poorly in these decisions, especially if authorities think that contraceptive patients can obtain services even if clinic sessions are cut. In other words, clinic users can transfer to general practitioners, who are paid from unrestricted central NHS funds.

The two funding sources for clinics and general practitioners are not ultimately separate, because general taxes support both. Despite the trend toward substituting general practitioners for clinics, research has shown that clinic services are more cost-effective than those of general practitioners (Laing 1982). In 1982, the cost to the NHS for fully comprehensive clinic services (including information and education, prescriptions, and such services as cytologic screening) was $15 per patient, while the cost through the general practitioner was $20 for prescribing the pill and $40 for fitting an IUD (FPIS 1986d). The shift of patients toward general practitioners simply transfers the costs from the local to the central government budget, and from the patients' perspective, the two sources are not equivalent. Many clinic patients might not transfer to a general practitioner, and for those who did it is probable, given the current status of general practitioner services, that the range of methods available to them would be greatly restricted.

Clinic clients are more likely than patients of general practitioners to be young, single, childless women interested in postponing child-birth or older women who have completed their families and who often need an alternative to the pill (Snowden 1985). Because clinics are generally located in urban areas, they tend also to attract professional and middle-class women who are looking for specialized services.

Of the total female population aged 15–44, 14.3 percent were seen at family planning clinics in 1985. This included 3 percent of those under age sixteen, 12 percent of 16 and 17-year-olds, 17 percent of 18-year-olds, 19 percent of 19-year-olds, 18 percent of those aged 20 to 34, and 9 percent of women 35 years of age and over (DHSS 1986b, table 5B).

One of the most typical complaints about clinic services revealed in a national survey on family planning services, was the difficulty con-sumers have finding out where their local clinics are, and especially the days and hours of clinic sessions (Snowden 1985). Theoretically, clinic information can be obtained at libraries, hospitals, health centers, from midwives and health visitors, in the telephone directory or classified directory under "family planning," from the FPIS (run by the FPA), FPA regional centers, and the Health Education Authority. The FPA seems to keep the most current information about hours, as well as travel directions to all the clinics in a region. Apart from the FPA, some health authorities (for example, the Bloomsbury Health Authority in Lon-don) have taken the initiative of preparing brochures detailing the choice of clinics, hours, telephone numbers, maps, and any special services available at a particular clinic. Individual clinics usually do little formal outreach, in part because NHS clinics are not permitted to put ads in newspapers (although private clinics can).

Contraceptive Services
The provision of family planning services at clinics has a long history in Great Britain. Their experience with contraceptive provision coupled with the availability of a wide range of contraceptive methods has earned clinic providers the reputation of being "family planning spe-cialists." Due to this expertise, clinics are almost entirely responsible for training doctors and nurses for Certificates in Contraceptive Technol-ogy.

Physicians who have undergone special training in contraceptive technology, in addition to that received in their prequalification courses, staff family planning clinics, and female doctors are more common at family planning clinics than in general practitioners' offices (Cardy 1984). Clerical staff deal with administrative tasks so that spe-cially trained nurses are free to play a more important role in patient care by taking medical histories, counseling patients about contracep-tive methods, and doing routine medical checks. Other district health personnel such as health visitors, midwives, and district nurses may also be part-time staff members of a clinic (if they have family planning training), in addition to their work in the community. Some clinics have interpreters available so that they can serve immigrant populations better.

Clinic sessions during which clients may receive counseling and obtain contraceptives are held in every district, although the clinic site may range from a discrete facility (such as a freestanding or hospital-based clinic) to a temporary, neighborhood location (a school or church basement). Clinic schedules vary considerably from one facility to another. Some have daily and evening sessions; others have only one session each week or even each month. Visits are generally by appointment, but walk-in patients are not necessarily turned away, and a few clinics operate entirely on a walk-in basis. To increase accessibility for patients who need immediate help, some health authorities have instituted centralized appointment systems so that any clinic user who urgently needs an appointment can call in and be referred to the clinic in her area that has the earliest family planning session.

At a woman's first clinic visit, the staff take complete individual and family medical histories, as well as the name of the patient's general practitioner. A nurse explains the various methods of contraception and helps her choose an appropriate one. After the patient's blood pressure and weight are recorded, she sees the physician. At this time a breast examination is done, and a pelvic examination may be done, or it may be postponed to a later visit if it causes the patient too much anxiety. The doctor prescribes a contraceptive, and the patient returns to the nurse to receive instructions regarding proper use of it. The first visit normally takes an hour or less (not including waiting time). There is no guarantee that a patient will see the same doctor at each visit, and there is no formal follow-up of patients who do not keep their appointments.

For pill users, a Pap smear is normally taken at the first clinic visit and then every two or three years following a negative report. The official DHSS recommendation is every five years. All pill users normally receive a medical consultation and have their blood pressure and weight checked after six and twelve months.

Before a patient has an IUD inserted, family planning doctors are instructed to check for any pelvic pathology or abnormality. The IUD is generally viewed as an unsuitable method for young, nulliparous women because evidence shows that this population group is at increased risk of pelvic inflammatory disease.

Most family planning clinics offer all available contraceptive methods: oral contraceptives, injectables (Depo-Provera and Noristerat), IUD, diaphragm, cervical cap, condom, spermicides, natural family planning, and postcoital contraception. Some perform sterilizations. The sponge is rarely available in NHS family planning clinics. In 1983, 58 percent of new clinic patients obtained pill prescriptions; 16 percent, the IUD; 8 percent, the diaphragm or cap; 10 percent, the condom; 6 percent, nothing; and 2 percent obtained spermicides or were sterilized (FPIS 1986c). Most clinics dispense supplies free. Free condoms are technically available at all clinics. This fact is not publicized for fear of being inundated by increased demand and high costs.

Relatively little communication and sharing of information takes place between clinic doctors and general practitioners. With the patient's permission, clinic doctors may inform the patient's general practitioner (in writing) of the contraceptive method prescribed for the patient. This provides the general practitioner with the opportunity to inform the clinic doctor of any medical contraindications. Other professional boundaries between clinic doctors and general practitioners must be observed in the treatment of patients. For example, in the course of a family planning visit, a clinic doctor may be asked by her patient to consult about a minor gynecological problem such as vaginitis. Although clinic doctors may carry out the clinical examination, they are not authorized to treat the problem. The results of the tests usually go to the individual's general practitioner, who will treat the condition. According to a survey of general practitioners, 42 percent thought that clinic doctors should not be authorized to provide treatment for minor gynecological disorders (Kevern 1981a).

Whereas general practitioners appear to favor prescribing the pill for most women, clinic physicians encourage a more wide-ranging sequence of method use across women's sexual careers: condoms during initial sexual experiences, the pill while postponing childbearing and when involved in a steady relationship, other reversible methods while spacing births, and the IUD or sterilization when the woman has completed her childbearing.

SPECIALIZED SERVICES:
FEMALE AND MALE STERILIZATION

According to the 1983 General Household Survey, sterilization has replaced the pill as the most popular method of contraception among married or cohabiting women aged 18–44 (Wellings 1986a; also see chapter 4, table 4.6 and figure 4.9, above). Sterilization for women increased during the late 1960s with the introduction of simpler laparoscopic techniques and between 1977–79 and during 1983 with reports of adverse health consequences from pill use. The number of men undergoing vasectomy has been on the increase since 1972, when local authorities were empowered to provide vasectomies under the

NHS, and more recently in response to concerns about the pill and IUD. It has been estimated that in 1983 approximately 90,000 female sterilizations and an equal number of male sterilizations were performed in Britain. Typical candidates for male or female sterilization are married couples in their thirties who have completed their families (Wellings 1986a).

Women usually go to a hospital for sterilization and stay overnight or for a few days. Outpatient sterilizations, though increasing, are not the norm. In most cases a general practitioner refers a woman to a hospital specialist. In some areas, it is a common practice for a family planning clinic doctor to counsel a woman about the procedure but then send her back to her general practitioner for referral. Vasectomies are performed in NHS clinics and hospitals, in private clinics, by private surgeons, and by specially trained general practitioners. The operation can be an outpatient procedure, since it is typically carried out under local anesthesia and takes about ten minutes.

One clinic we visited would not sterilize women under twenty-five or those under thirty without children. In addition, they required a woman to have a referral from a general practitioner who had also counseled her about her family situation. Although a partner's consent is not legally necessary, it is standard practice to seek the partner's agreement before performing a sterilization. Counseling is considered an integral part of the delivery of both male and female sterilization services, although there is a good deal of variation in both quality and quantity. The position generally espoused is that counseling for sterilization should include: discussion of alternative methods of contraception, the irreversibility of the procedure, and commonly believed myths surrounding the consequences of sterilization. The decision to perform the surgery includes an assessment of the patient's age, parity, marital stability, and the potential for regret. A study of sterilization counseling services found that women have to go through more red tape than men in order to be sterilized (Allen 1985). Most of the women in the study felt they had had enough or too much counseling, since they had made up their minds before ever approaching their general practitioner. The patients would have appreciated more description of the actual surgery and its effects earlier on in the process. During counseling with the gynecologist, some women are apparently reluctant to ask too many questions or to seem unsure for fear of being denied the operation.

Female and male sterilization come free of charge under the NHS, but the services cannot be had in all areas. In 1984, 65 percent of the DHAs in England and Wales made no provision for vasectomy in family planning clinics, and 88 percent indicated no provision for female sterilization (Leathard 1985a). (A small proportion of these authorities remarked that services were available in local hospitals.) Waiting lists are often long. One study found the average waiting time six months or longer for female sterilization and about three months or less for vasectomies (Birth Control Trust 1981). Although annual data on the provision of sterilization are not systematically recorded, some have estimated that, because of the uneven distribution of services and the long waiting lists (up to three years in some areas), one-third of all married couples are likely to obtain sterilizations through private providers (FPIS 1986e). The average fee for a vasectomy is approximately $100–$130, the fee for female sterilization, $205–$235, depending on the technique and the length of stay (FPIS 1986f).

Funding arrangements are an important reason for the inability of the NHS to meet the demand for sterilization. Before the NHS routinely covered family planning services, it paid for sterilizations only if they were done for "medically necessary" reasons; specialists deemed procedures done for "social reasons" as being outside their contractual agreement. To ensure the wider availability of sterilization, the NHS instituted item-of-service fees in 1976 for specialists performing it. In 1986, a specialist received about $65 for each vasectomy and $90 for each female sterilization (DHSS 1986a). Funding, however, is at the discretion of the DHAs, and some allocate no money at all, while others earmark only a small amount. When the money runs out, many specialists postpone vasectomies and female sterilizations until the next fiscal year begins.

If a health authority cannot meet the demands for sterilization in an area, it may be able to make arrangements with a nonprofit agency to provide the service for the NHS. This can result in cheaper services in the long run, since specialist agencies (such as the Marie Stopes House) are more likely to use methods requiring only a local anesthetic or a maximum of a one-day stay.

PRIVATE AND NONPROFIT AGENCIES

Private clinics and nonprofit facilities thrive on the inability of the NHS to meet the demand for specialized services and are generally perceived as providing specialized, high-quality care. The Pregnancy Advisory Service, the British Pregnancy Advisory Service, and the Marie Stopes House are all important providers of abortion and sterilization. Some also offer pregnancy testing and postcoital birth control.

The FPA has retained about two dozen of its family planning clinics. Some of these do vasectomies only; others provide general contraceptive services; some offer menopausal and well-women services, psychosexual counseling, well-men services and small-scale research and development facilities. In general, these are fee-paying services, although the consumer can get some services free, at the expense of the relevant NHS authority.

DOMICILIARY SERVICES

Domiciliary family planning services, by which family planning personnel visit hard-to-reach women at home, have been available in Britain since the late 1950s. The women targeted were those defined as unwilling or unable to obtain services from established sources. The implicit goal of the domiciliary service is to enable patients eventually to receive family planning services from either clinics or general practitioners. In 1984, 19 percent of the previous year's patients had transferred to the established services (FPIS 1986g).

Domiciliary services are under the control of the DHAs and are subject to the same budgetary constraints as family planning clinics. They are even more vulnerable to extinction since they serve a relatively small number of people who often need more intense, personalized interaction and a combination of family planning and social services. Despite these demands, it has been suggested that the often-cited higher per patient cost for domiciliary services compares favorably with those for general practitioners and clinics, which exclude overhead costs (Christopher, Kellaher, and von Koch 1980).

About 140 domiciliary services were in existence when the NHS assumed responsibility for family planning services, but by 1980 their number had dwindled to about fifty. In 1984 domiciliary programs in England reached approximately 15,000 patients, including 52,210 visits by family planning staff (FPIS 1986g). Of the patients seen, 13 percent were under twenty, 73 percent 20–34 years of age, and 14 percent thirty-five and over. In Wales (1983) 245 patients, totaling 1,987 visits, were seen through a domiciliary service, in Scotland (1984) family planning staff served 3,078 women and made 21,147 visits.

Referrals to the domiciliary service can come from general practitioners, health visitors, social workers, midwives, hospital family planning nurses, and the patients themselves (Christopher, Kellaher, and von Koch 1980). The primary source of referral is the health visitor, who is required to visit every new mother at her home. The strength of the referral network depends on how well the domiciliary service has made itself known and has clearly outlined suitable cases for referral, as well as on the attitudes of other members in the medical and paramedical community regarding the need for the service. The domiciliary services have been criticized for being too expensive, encouraging dependency ("spoonfeeding the feckless"), failing to reach the targeted group, and for inadequate or nonexistent evaluations of services (Allen 1976).

The investigating team visited one model domiciliary program near London that does not seem to be vulnerable to these criticisms. The demographics of the population served by this particular program has changed through the years—from Cypriots, Greeks, Turkish, Irish, and West Indians to a more recent inclusion of Bangladeshi women. The program appeared to be meeting the needs of women who would be unlikely to approach another provider and who would not maintain effective use of a contraceptive method without personal attention and understanding of their life situation and culture.

All methods of birth control are available through the domiciliary service. Patients are counseled and referred to specialists for sterilization and abortions. In 1984 (in England), at the time of the patient's first visit, the pill was recommended, chosen, or already in use by 36 percent of patients; the IUD, 18 percent; condom, 16 percent; the cervical cap, spermicides, male and female sterilization, 1 percent each; withdrawal and other less effective methods, 16 percent. Nine percent used no method at all (DHSS 1986c, table 2B).

BROOK ADVISORY CENTRES

The Brook Advisory Centres, which are funded primarily by NHS grants DHAs health authorities and private donations, serve nearly 60,000 clients annually. Their intent is to be especially sensitive to the contraceptive needs of young people in order to reduce teenage abortions and unwanted births. In 1985, 77 percent of their clients were twenty-five or younger. Women under twenty accounted for 32 percent of all Brook Advisory Centre clients, in comparison to 17 percent of all clients seen in family planning clinics in England and Wales and 15 percent of all clinic patients in Scotland (Brook Advisory Centres 1986b).

The centers charge no fee and are typically staffed by doctors, nurses, and counselors who are particularly interested in working with young people. In an effort to create a less "medical" atmosphere, the staff in some facilities do not wear uniforms, and the interiors look more cheerful and casual than at the typical family planning clinic. Counseling is an important component of service delivery for the role it can play in building up self-esteem in teenagers, increasing their effective use of contraceptives, and helping those who wish to "say no" to sex.

Brook facilities are discreetly located in places that are easily accessible by bus or the tube, and most are open during the evening and on Saturday mornings so teenagers can attend easily. Each session leaves some time free to accommodate clients who show up without an appointment. Pregnancy testing is available along with counseling and referral for abortion, if requested. Young men are welcome to come with their partners, to come alone for counseling, or to obtain free condoms, but few men come to Brook facilities for services. Most patients find out about the clinics by word of mouth. Leaflets are also distributed through the FPIS, through youth clubs, and to a limited extent in the schools. Schools sometimes invite clinic counselors to address school nurses and teachers.

The pill is the most popular contraceptive method among Brook Advisory Centre clients. In 1985, 80 percent of clients used the pill; 8 percent, condoms; 6 percent, the cap; 4 percent, the IUD; and 2 percent used other methods (Brook Advisory Centres 1986b). Brook facilities first prescribe the pill for two months, then extend it to a maximum of six months. Pelvic examinations are not done during the initial visit but are postponed to a later date. Follow-up procedures vary from one center to the next, but staff generally make some attempt to contact patients who miss appointments. Although there are currently eleven Brook Advisory Centres in the London area, nationwide there are only about seventeen. Like other NHS family planning clinics, Brook Advisory Centres have had their funding cut by local health authorities.

PHARMACIES

Pharmacies are the primary source for both prescription and non-prescription contraceptives in Great Britain, although most clinics and some general practitioners dispense them. Pharmacies do not charge for either medical or nonmedical methods if they are obtained with a prescription from a general practitioner or a clinic doctor. Since most clinics do not advertise their free condoms, however, and since most men do not frequent clinics, condoms are generally purchased at the pharmacy or from other sources. (Condoms cannot be obtained from general practitioners.) In addition to providing contraceptive supplies and advice, a number of pharmacies (31 percent of the sample in the FPA/Pharmaceutical Society study) also offer pregnancy testing services (Meredith 1982), so that the pharmacist may be the first professional contact for a woman confronted with an unintended pregnancy.

In recent years, the FPA has taken an interest in extending and formalizing the role of the community pharmacy as a resource center for educational materials and advice on family planning. Motivating factors for this include an overtaxed national health service that was not reaching all the women and men potentially needing information about birth control or family planning services, the underutilization of pharmacists' training and skills in dispensing medicines, and the un-tapped potential of over 12,000 pharmacies in the United Kingdom to disseminate health information to millions of people (Meredith 1982). Pharmacists were already the primary suppliers of the pill, and it was not difficult to imagine expanding their role to include advice and information about side effects or about other available methods and family planning services. The FPA looked on pharmacies as an excellent venue for a third family planning resource. They have the added benefit of being a nonmedical, nonthreatening, and easily accessible source of information for both men and women.

In 1986 the FPA, the Health Education Authority, and the Pharmaceutical Society of Great Britain initiated the first national health-education campaign in community pharmacies. All pharmacies received display racks and pamphlets, and contraceptive handbooks were given to all pharmacists to aid them in their role as advisors. Local health education officers are kept abreast of the materials, and press releases, picked up by newspapers and radio stations, tell the public about the availability and nature of the materials they can obtain at their community pharmacy. A preliminary assessment of the project reveals a high degree of participation of the pharmacies and a high degree of public interest, as measured by the number of pamphlets taken and the response to tear-off slips on the leaflets. Less participation occurs in inner-city areas, most likely due to language barriers (Morley et al. 1986).

Since the deluge of media attention to AIDS, condoms have moved from under the counter to more prominent positions on the prescription counter at most pharmacies.

CLIENT PREFERENCES

According to a 1985 national survey, 55 percent of women stated a preference for consulting a general practitioner for family planning advice, compared to 33 percent who preferred a clinic and 12 percent who had no preference (Snowden 1985). These results parallel the proportions of women using each type of provider, suggesting that women are generally going to the type of provider they prefer. In another study on family planning services, Allen had found that women have adopted a functional approach to family planning providers: they view both family planning clinics and general practitioners as suitable sources of advice and supply at different periods of their lives (Allen 1981).

Women who prefer general practitioners do so mainly because they provide care in a familiar setting, are more likely than a clinic to have daily office hours, and provide greater continuity of care; moreover, the purpose of the woman's visit is less obvious to friends and neighbors. Clinics tend to attract women who want a wider range of methods, greater expertise, and more thorough care. In addition, some women find it less embarrassing to discuss sexual matters with a clinic staff member than with their family doctor and like having the choice of consulting a female physician. Clinics' disadvantages include their inconvenient hours, long waiting times, less personal knowledge of the patient's medical history, less continuity of care (patients generally see a different doctor on each visit). They are also difficult to find.

The movement between provider types highlights the contributions of both clinics and general practitioners. Patients tend to transfer from a general practitioner to a clinic if they experience side effects from their present method or are interested in changing to another. Sixty-eight percent of the women who switched from a general practitioner to a clinic did so either on their own initiative or on the recommendation of a friend or other clinic patient (Kevern 1981b).

Clinic patients tend to switch to a general practitioner if they have an acute problem with their method and need to be seen on short notice (Kevern 1981b). (As mentioned, general practitioners are in most cases accessible on a daily basis, whereas some clinic doctors may hold only weekly or monthly sessions.)

The International Health Foundation (IHF) conducted a survey in Great Britain in 1984 and 1985 that focused in part, on opinions and attitudes about contraceptive methods (Riphagen, Van der Vurst, and Lehert 1986a). The survey asked women to rate each contraceptive method according to four attributes: reliability, moral and religious acceptability, disturbance of one's sex life, and health effects. Sterilization was considered the only fully reliable method, followed most closely by the pill. There was more doubt about the reliability of the IUD and barrier methods, and both rhythm and withdrawal were considered unreliable. All the methods were considered acceptable from a moral and religious perspective except for some doubt regarding the pill. Only the pill and the IUD were perceived as completely unobtrusive to one's sex life. The pill, followed by the IUD, caused the greatest concern about effects on health. More in-depth analysis of perceptions of the pill revealed that although women are aware of its advantages, they also tend to believe that it has serious long-term risks.

An exploratory study of women's attitudes about the pill suggested that even long-term pill users are never fully committed to the method (Coulter 1985). Rather, women recognize potential dangers but weigh the risks against the consequences of pregnancy in their current life situation. Most women believe that the pill is the best method for teenagers or young single women. They looked on use of less effective methods as a rational alternative for women who could risk becoming pregnant, were spacing their children, and, more important, wanted to avoid the risks associated with the pill.

Most clinic physicians with whom we spoke said that women do fear the pill, but most use it because it is easy and effective. One provider summarized the decision about which contraceptive method to use as a "choice among negatives."

INFORMATION AND EDUCATION

It should be noted that this discussion antedates the very intensive national attention that has recently been given to controlling the spread of AIDS. Even during our two-week visit to England in March 1987, we were witness to quantum changes in information, advertising, and programming efforts aimed at encouraging "safer sex." In the course of our interviews we learned that much of what we were seeing and hearing would have been unheard of only a short time before. If this trend continues, the barriers being torn down for the sake of AIDS may also have a significant liberalizing effect on the attention given to sex-education programs, contraception, and contraceptive services.

Organized Communication Efforts
Formal dissemination of information about family planning methods and services became the key responsibility of the FPA after they relinquished most of their clinics to the NHS in the mid-1970s. The national headquarters in London houses a bookstore that stocks a wide range of titles dealing with sexuality, birth control, family planning, and other related topics. The FPA Medical Department, through its Medical Advisory Panels, evaluates current research and data on fertility, contraception, and related issues. Some of the remaining FPA clinics are used for research and development purposes. All of these activities contribute to the knowledge base of the Information Resource Center of the FPA.

The Family Planning Information Service (FPIS) was organized in 1977 by the FPA and the Health Education Council (now Health Education Authority), with the aid of government funding. Its function is to provide information on family planning services, contraceptives, sexuality, and so on to both the public and health-care professionals. In 1985, the FPIS distributed over six million leaflets and received 155,000 inquiries (by phone, letter, or personal visit) from consumers and professionals. It compiles "Fact Sheets," which are brief statistical, historical, or analytical compilations of data on fertility, contraception, and population issues. The FPIS responds to inquiries about clinic services as well as questions about method effectiveness, side effects, and drug interactions. In the current NHS environment, where the continued viability of clinic family planning services is threatened, and where general practitioners have limited training and skills with regard to family planning, the FPA is an invaluable source of information and expertise. It is not only important as a repository of accurate and current information for both the public, medical professionals, and the DHSS, but also for keeping a watchful eye on the fate of family planning resources.

The FPA press office is very active in providing information, reacting to articles in the paper about methods or services, and releasing policy statements. The press office also initiates media interest by producing press releases for FPA projects, leaflets, reports, statistics, and other initiatives.

In recognition of the language barriers that exist for immigrant groups, the FPA has set up an Ethnic Communities Working Group to research the needs of ethnic communities and develop appropriate family planning materials. Some FPIS literature has already been translated into braille for the blind.

Sex education. The overwhelming majority of parents and their teenage children believe that schools should provide sex education (Allen 1987). This research revealed that the main reason for the small amount of parental dissatisfaction with the sex-education program at the secondary school level was that the school had given too little sex education or had taught it in insufficient detail. But sex education remains a delicate and potentially controversial issue for the government, local education authorities, the media, and some conservative citizen groups. In the 1960s and 1970s, sex-education programs focused almost exclusively on reproduction and contraception. In the 1980s, the Department of Education and Science defined sex education in the broader context of personal and social development. It aimed to include such topics as values clarification, decisionmaking, communication, and sensitivity, as well as the development of nonexploitative relationships and the promotion of responsible sexual behavior. The ideal sex-education program is viewed as one that integrates topics into the students' regular curriculum. Unfortunately, the coordination required to avoid duplication and omission of topics is generally lacking, and many teachers are not comfortable teaching the subject and have had little or no training. The FPA and to a lesser extent the National Marriage Guidance Council are the only national organizations training teachers and youth workers in this field, and education authorities are short of funds for sending their teachers to these courses.

In 1986, an amendment to the British government's Education Bill stated that whether and how sex education is provided in the schools should be the decision of local school officials. As a result, schools vary widely in the priority given to sex education and in the content of what is taught.

A recent study on sex education, limited to three cities in England, found that 94 percent of sixteen-year-olds, 85 percent of fifteen-year-olds, and 65 percent of fourteen-year-olds said that they had covered contraception in a course at their secondary school, and it was one of the topics teenagers remembered best (Allen 1987). Some indications suggested that boys received less education about sex and personal relationships than did girls, from school and particularly from home. The study concludes, "If education in sex and personal relationships were left to parents alone many adolescents would receive no education in these matters from any authoritative source" (Allen 1987, 187). The two topics most frequently discussed at home were pregnancy and childbirth and changes in the female body at puberty.

About two-thirds of the teenagers cited school as the primary source of their information about sex and contraception. Although the teenagers reported that they would turn first to their parents and friends for consultation on questions about sex, contraception, and personal relationships, they also revealed a "healthy skepticism" about the accuracy of the information coming from these sources—particularly from their peers.

Advertising of Methods and Services
Advertising contraceptive products by brand name is banned on television and radio but is permissible in print, although only after all statements and visual depictions have been approved by a committee of the Advertising Standards Authority (ASA). One researcher has described the advertisements usually approved as "non-persuasive, ambiguous and usually euphemistic" and "couched exclusively in terms of couples needing family planning" (Hayman 1977).

The Independent Broadcasting Authority (IBA), which authorizes commercial television and radio, and the ASA are the two self-regulatory organizations that protect the public from "offensive" advertising. The Birth Control Trust has argued that these organizations engage in "selective prudery" by allowing sexually explicit tobacco and alcohol advertisements and yet refuse contraceptive advertising for fear of offending and embarrassing the public.

The IBA allows advertising of family planning services. Public service announcements about family planning services and motivational messages about the use of contraceptives in general have appeared on television, but they are often scheduled at times when the target audience is unlikely to be watching. Recently, increasing competition between radio stations has led to decreasing public service programming in lieu of more entertainment.

Services offered by such agencies as the Pregnancy Advisory Service are not permitted to advertise on television. They are also severely restricted in the posters they may display. Although it displays many suggestive advertising posters in the underground, the Pregnancy Advisory Service cannot mention the word *abortion* unless it is accompanied by the words *help* or *advice*.

Media Treatment of Contraception

Media treatment of contraception in Great Britain resembles that in the United States. Popular television programming makes little if any mention of contraception or contraceptive methods, and the print media give far more attention to reports about the dangers of methods than to their health benefits.

An analysis of the media coverage of the 1983 "pill scare" found a proliferation of articles in the national and local press (34 and 161, respectively) in response to two papers in a medical journal linking the pill to breast and cervical cancer (Wellings 1985). This was in stark contrast to one mention in the national press following a report, at about the same time, that suggested a protective effect of the pill on breast cancer (Kalache et al. 1983). One study found the content of the articles factually accurate but deficient in omitting "any concept of relative risk" (Wellings 1985). Efforts on the part of the press to rectify this omission (by declaring "don't panic") came days later and may only have served to confuse the public with conflicting messages.

A credible source of information to all people, but to teenagers in particular, are the "agony auntie" columns (advice columns) that appear in magazines and newspapers. Questions regarding sexuality appear frequently (about 50 percent of all letters) and those concerning contraception represent about 10 percent of all personal topics that are addressed. Not only are all letters answered with carefully researched responses, but relevant literature and pamphlets (often provided or prepared by the FPIS) are also enclosed.

Women's magazines, for example, *Cosmopolitan*, devote one page every month to health issues, which often include some discussion of contraceptives such as instructions for use or new developments in the field. Most women's magazines have one major article on contraception every year.

Another source of information, especially for young people, is the phone-in shows on radio. Sexual and relationship problems are a common focus for many of the programs (Birth Control Trust 1984). The topic of contraceptives is even more commonplace when a representative from an organization like the FPA is asked to appear as the "expert" host.

Climate of Opinion Concerning Sex

The climate of opinion concerning sex in Great Britain is filled with contradictions, just as in the United States. If one uses the amount of nudity that appears in newspapers, magazines, and on television as an indicator of the society's norms, then Great Britain would be described as sexually more open than is the United States. The extent of premarital sex and early initiation of sex is on a par with other developed countries.

If the climate of opinion concerning sex in a society is truly open, however, one might expect contraception to be treated as a normal and natural part of present-day sexual behavior. The fact that contraceptives are still grouped with hemorrhoid and scalp treatments as unacceptable products for advertising suggests this is not the case (Hayman 1977). Thus the contradiction in Great Britain. On the one hand, the government recognizes the importance of family planning and makes it universally free, while on the other, the mention of contraception is greatly restricted and in some cases conspicuously absent from general programming and advertisements which typically include sexually explicit content.

The relationship between public policies and private attitudes is not clear. Thus far, it appears that those in power in Britain have misjudged or exaggerated the public's sensitivities to issues involving sex. Surveys of attitudes about such topics as premarital sex and sex education have found the majority of people to be quite liberal in their views. An organization called the Responsible Society (recently changed to Family and Youth Concern), a conservative group in Great Britain with aims similar to those of the Moral Majority in the United States, does stir up controversy on subjects like sex education and abortion, but it does not have so large a following or the same political power as equivalent groups in the United States.

Most recently, in response to the AIDS crisis, concern over public sensitivities has been replaced by the government's perceived need to communicate explicit and accurate information about the spread of the disease and how to avoid it. During one week in March 1987 the public was bombarded by visually explicit prime-time television programs on AIDS that had special emphasis (and instructions) on the use of condoms. What effect these dramatic changes will have on future messages about contraception remains to be seen.

ASSESSMENT

Proportion of Overall Need That Is Met

Since 1974, when free family planning services were first provided within the NHS, use of contraceptive methods and services has increased significantly (Allen 1981; Wellings, 1986b). Despite the shortcomings of the family planning delivery system, women in Great Britain are more likely to practice contraception, particularly with the more effective methods, than are women in the United States.

According to the 1983 General Household Survey, it is conservatively estimated that some method of contraception was being used by approximately 85 percent of all women surveyed (aged 18–44) who were at risk of an unintended pregnancy. Married women and those aged 25–39 were more likely to be using a method (97 and 90 percent, respectively) than single women (58 percent) and those aged 18–19 (57 percent). About three-quarters of contraceptors were using the most effective methods (sterilization, pill, and IUD), followed by about 17 percent using the condom (OPCS 1983, calculated from tables 5.1 and 5.2, p. 51). As mentioned in chapter 4 ("Background for Country Reports"), one of the reasons overall use looks high for married or cohabiting women is the relatively large proportion using the condom, especially among women aged 35–44.

Fertility and abortion rates for adolescents in Great Britain, although significantly lower than those in the United States, are of considerable concern to those involved in family planning delivery, as is the relatively large proportion of late abortions that occur within the NHS. Similarly, the fertility patterns for immigrant women, especially those from the New Commonwealth and Pakistan, are much higher than those of U.K.–born women. Without data on the intention status of these births, however, it is not possible to know if the high fertility rates reflect desired family size or difficulty in obtaining contraceptive advice and services.

Many of the people with whom we spoke seemed to feel that, since services are free, there is no unmet need. Based upon the evaluation studies of family planning services and discussions with people on the "front lines," this complacency appears not to be justified. Poor women, immigrant women, men, and people in rural areas are examples of some of the groups that still have problems getting contraceptive services from the NHS. Access can be hampered by limited availability of services because of budget cuts or by a multitude of social, cultural, and linguistic factors that militate against utilization of available services.

Barriers to Service

Based on our interviews and on studies that have systematically evaluated the family planning delivery system (Leathard 1984a, 1984b, 1985a, 1985b), a number of barriers to service can be identified. One critical barrier is the lack of widely disseminated, visible information about family planning services. In particular, there is a paucity of information, especially at the local level, about family planning clinic hours and locations as well as such policy issues as the freedom to consult with a general practitioner other than one's own for contraceptive services. Although each of the eleven regional FPA offices maintains information on the location and schedule of all NHS clinics in their region, barriers still exist for people who are not aware of this service or who are unable to take the initiative to get the information.

The major barrier to comprehensive service provision seems to be the very funding arrangement that was instituted to ensure widespread availability of these services from a choice of providers. The existence of separate funding mechanisms for general practitioners and clinics has led to a competitive rather than a cooperative relationship. General practitioners may feel that their patients are being poached and that efforts are being duplicated, clinic doctors may feel that their specialty is threatened and that patients who see general practitioners receive inferior service. The DHAs are primarily interested in providing as many services as possible within a limited budget, so if family planning services can be removed from their budget and transferred to the central budget from which general practitioners are paid, then it is in their interest to force the movement of patients from clinics to general practitioners. Clinics, however, have no financial motivation to seek out new clients or expand their services even in areas not well covered by general practitioners.

As a result of budgetary problems, the number of clinics offering Youth Advisory Services and the number of Brook Advisory Centres for teenagers are very limited, and domiciliary services have dwindled. Access to specialized services—vasectomy, female sterilization, abortion—is scattered across the districts, and waiting lists are sometimes unacceptably long. Substantial numbers of people are forced to pay for these services in the private sector.

The special item-of-service payments for general practitioners succeeded in gaining their participation as a major component in the contraceptive delivery system. But only a minority of them are adequately trained to provide a range of methods, and most general practitioners who offer family planning services prescribe the pill for most women most of the time. Women who do not fit the common pattern may have a difficult time obtaining services, especially if they do not have access to a clinic.

Relation of Services to Method Use
The fundamental factor contributing to greater utilization of family planning services in Great Britain and the use of highly effective methods is that contraceptive services are free to people of all ages. Another critical factor is that general practitioners offer family planning services. Given their wide distribution and key role as coordinators of all medical services in Great Britain, general practitioners have a significant effect on the contraceptive-use patterns of the population, since most women at one time or another will come into contact with

one, either for themselves or for their children. Specifically, general practitioners' services account in large part for the widespread use of the pill, for several reasons. First, most general practitioners seem favorably disposed toward the pill as a generally safe, effective, and simple method for most women to use. Second, there is probably some degree of self-selection of women who have decided that they want the pill and who associate the general practitioner with it. Finally, general practitioners have a financial incentive to provide the pill, since they need no additional training and can prescribe the pill for a large volume of patients without deflecting much time from the treatment of their general medical patients.

Although the pill is the most popular method prescribed to young women by both general practitioners and family planning clinics, the contraceptive service offered by general practitioners has been criticized because of its apparent bias toward prescribing the pill without offering alternatives. Clinics are more likely to give at least equal time to alternative methods (IUDs, diaphragms, cervical caps) depending upon the age of the woman, the nature of her sexual relationship, and her childbearing intentions. Evidence suggests that women choose either a general practitioner or a clinic based on their particular needs (Allen 1981). As long as there are significant differences in the services offered by clinics and general practitioners, the existence of a choice of providers will probably remain a key element in the successful use of contraception in Great Britain.

A relatively large proportion of the population in Britain relies on condoms. Although they are available without charge at clinics, most people buy them at pharmacies or other nonmedical outlets. Before the advent of the pill in the 1960s, the condom was the most popular birth control method among married couples (Wellings 1986b). Although it has never regained its former status, use of the condom still tends to rise with negative publicity about the pill.

The high proportion of sterilizations among older women seems to reflect the determination of these women to obtain an effective method even if it entails overcoming substantial obstacles. Long waiting times and limited availability of services again force many to use the private sector.

Chapter 4 presented some interesting findings about the relationship between income and method use among younger and older married women in Great Britain. Regardless of age, married women in the lowest income category are more likely to use effective methods like sterilization and the IUD than those in the higher income group, and they are less likely to use less effective methods like the condom (see table 4.7). It may be that young women in low-income groups reach their desired family size at an earlier age than older, affluent women and are, therefore, more interested in and more likely to be counseled about obtaining the most effective methods that require the least effort on their part, such as sterilization and the IUD. Young married women who are better off financially may be of lower parity and find the condom an acceptable alternative for the purpose of spacing their births.

Women aged 35–44 who are in the low-income category are much more likely to be sterilized than women in the high-income group, and sterilization is used more by less educated than by more educated women. Again, this could reflect greater motivation among these women to end their childbearing. Perhaps service providers also view low-income women as less likely to be successful with reversible methods and thus tend to recommend sterilization to them. Older women who are better off financially may have fewer children, feel uncomfortable with the permanence of sterilization, be unwilling to continue using the pill or have an IUD inserted (because of negative publicity), and may therefore resort to the condom as their method of choice. According to Wellings, the condom has a popular following among older married couples (Wellings 1986b).

The relationship between the distribution of methods and the service delivery system is perhaps best understood by imagining other potential arrangements. In particular, one can see that the general practitioner's focus on the pill is really a two-edged sword. If clinic services were expanded to the point where they attracted a much larger share of all users, the net effect could potentially be that a larger proportion of women would be using less effective methods. But if clinics were virtually edged out by general practitioners because of budgetary constraints (thereby removing both choice of provider type and, to some extent, choice of method options to patients), the net effect could be an even greater level of pill use or perhaps even more women opting for sterilization. Although this is a simplistic model and does not take into account women's preferences for type of provider and their willingness to adopt the pill in lieu of other nonmedical methods or no method at all, it does highlight the fact that the current dependence on general practitioners, despite its shortcomings, contributes to having a large proportion of women use a very effective method.

If current trends continue, it is most likely that the family planning delivery system in Great Britain will undergo some changes in the near future. A steadily increasing number of young general practitioners are receiving the necessary training to allow them to provide a more comprehensive contraceptive service. In time, this could mean that more women will perceive general practitioners as a reliable and convenient source for most reversible methods, although the pill may still be the physician's method of choice for most patients.

Clinics, on the other hand, have developed an excellent reputation in the field of family planning in Great Britain and will probably play an even greater role as "experts" in dealing with method problems, sterilizations, and special services (such as subfertility and psychosexual problems), and as key providers for special groups like adolescents.

9

Conclusions

This study reveals much that is of interest and importance concerning the relationships between contraceptive services, method use, and level of unintended pregnancy. Many of the findings of the overview examination of twenty countries are inconclusive because of the very small number of units of observation, incomplete coverage of data, inappropriate temporal relationships between sets of observations, and serious underlying problems of intercountry comparability. At the same time, much of the evidence produced in the case studies is qualitative and to some extent subjective. Yet the results of the two investigations support and complement each other to point clearly toward a number of generalizations.

Of the twenty Western countries in the study, the United States has a total fertility rate that falls somewhat above the middle. Its total abortion and pregnancy rates, however, are higher than those of most other Western countries. Because unplanned births as well as abortions are common in the United States, the unplanned pregnancy rate is also relatively high. Fully half of all conceptions are unintended.

Detailed comparisons of the United States with Ontario, Quebec, the Netherlands, and Great Britain show that the birthrate in the United States is significantly higher only among women under twenty-five. Although the U.S. abortion rate is higher at most ages, the contrast between the United States and the other countries is again much greater among younger than among older women. Consequently, it is at ages under twenty-five the U.S. pregnancy rate stands out most. The proportion of births that is unplanned varies markedly among the five study areas but is greatest in the United States, and unplanned pregnancies are also most common here. Unplanned conceptions tend to be concentrated early in reproductive life; unplanned pregnancies and the frequency of early pregnancies in the United States represent different aspects of one phenomenon.

The proportion of all women of reproductive age who use one of the three modern, highly effective methods of contraception is lower in the United States than in many other Western countries. The level of pill use in the United States is moderate. Both young, unmarried women and older women are less likely to use the pill than their peers in the other study areas. In addition, few U.S. women chose the IUD even before the major IUD manufacturers took their products off the U.S. market. Although sterilization is relatively common in the United States, especially among younger women, its prevalence does not raise the combined level of use of these three highly effective methods above the middle of the range for all twenty countries. In the United States, less reliance on the most effective methods is associated with a high proportion of women using no method at all. Somewhat fewer U.S. women may be exposed to the risk of conception, but this is almost certainly not the main explanation of low overall use. In some other countries where use of the most effective methods is low (for example, Greece and Italy), many women report use of less effective methods—mainly the condom and withdrawal—and the proportion not using any method is smaller than in the United States.

The principal effect of using a highly effective method of contraception is to reduce the incidence of abortion. The proportion of women relying on one of these three methods is strongly negatively associated with the abortion rate. Evidently the determination to limit childbearing is deeply entrenched in modern, developed societies, and women often resort to abortion if an unintended pregnancy occurs.

Use of the most effective methods of contraception also results in fewer unplanned births, especially those that are wanted eventually but occur sooner than desired. This is of particular relevance to early childbearing in the United States. Because these effective methods provide a high measure of security concerning postponement and spacing of pregnancies, they enable young people, especially young women, to prepare for parenthood and integrate family building into other aspects of their lives.

Because the use of each of these three methods requires medical intervention, reliance on them is dependent on access to services. Access has a number of dimensions, the most important of which are probably cost, proximity, and familiarity. Most of the countries covered in this study are similar with respect to the cost: a complete range of medical contraceptive care is offered to everyone free of charge or at a very low price. Typically, such care is also integrated into the primary health services of the country, making it available locally at places that people frequent for a variety of purposes. Thus proximity and familiarity are maximized as well. The United States differs from the usual pattern in that contraceptive care is not offered to everyone at little or no expense and, like most other health care, is delivered primarily through medical specialists.

This study shows that use of the most effective methods of contraception is likely to be high where general or family practitioners are the usual source of primary health care, including contraceptive services. In such countries, family practitioners meet all three accessibility criteria very well. But use of effective methods is likely to be relatively low where the usual source of contraceptive service is specialist physicians, mainly obstetricians and gynecologists, as in the United States. Specialists may charge high fees for their services, they are often not located nearby, and women may not be familiar with them.

Because of the pervasiveness of specialist services in the United States and the accompanying absence of a unified system of primary health care provision, people depend less on family practitioners, and their function is not the same as in many other countries. Although this situation may be, in many respects, beyond the scope of policy manipulation, general and family practitioners could be encouraged to provide contraceptive services and to increase awareness of such services among their patients. Access to physicians providing contraceptive services could be improved by further reducing financial barriers. Some forms of organization in the United States that link physician services, such as group practices and health maintenance organizations, hold promise for improving access within the existing system.

A notable finding of the case studies is that reliance on family doctors for basic contraceptive care appears to be associated with widespread use of and confidence in the pill. Family doctors often do not have the necessary training and skill to insert IUDs or to fit diaphragms. They rarely perform sterilization operations. The pill is simple to prescribe, and most women have no contraindications to its use. The risk of long-term side effects is low, especially for the low-dose formulations that are used almost exclusively everywhere except in the United States. Such short-term side effects as breakthrough bleeding pose minimal problems when the patient can contact the doctor easily. Favorable experience with the method seems to foster positive attitudes on the part of both doctors and their patients. In addition, although no evidence was found to suggest that economic advantage was ever a major consideration, in many systems continuing supervision of patients on the pill provides an easy source of income for the doctor. Utilization of family physicians as service providers may not make the greatest choice of methods available, but the resulting emphasis on the pill does tend to promote effective fertility control.

The pill is not viewed either by the medical profession or by the public at large as a method to be used indefinitely, however. The need for a highly effective alternative to the pill apparently provides much of the impetus for sterilization in the four countries where it is commonly relied on (Canada, the Netherlands, the United Kingdom, and the United States). Couples everywhere are concerned about the permanence of sterilization, but choice of methods is very limited, and couples and providers alike evidently give higher priority to effectiveness than to reversibility. High levels of sterilization, even at young ages, seem to be due more to favorable assessment of the advantages and disadvantages of this method compared to others than to inability to use reversible methods successfully. Sterilization is likely to be less prevalent where the IUD is widely accepted (for example, Finland, Norway, and Sweden). Cultural or religious opposition to sterilization may be an overriding consideration, leading in some cases to continued use of the pill throughout a woman's reproductive life or to use of less effective methods backed up by abortion (Belgium is an example of the first; both occur in France and Italy).

Family doctors are the principal source of contraceptive services in all countries where sterilization is common except the United States, and they apparently cooperate in making this option available to their patients even though they seldom provide it themselves. Although referral of a patient for sterilization may result in a decrease in remuneration for a family doctor, the specialist performing the operation often stands to gain financially, whether the case comes by referral or from his own practice. In Britain, sterilization constitutes a partial exception to the accessibility of free contraceptive services, because the waiting time for elective surgery under the National Health Service is often so long that many people turn to private services.

The existence of a choice of sources is another critical factor contributing to extensive use of the three most effective methods. Some potential clients are unwilling or unable to take advantage of the primary service provider, and for some this type of service is unsuitable. In particular, neither general practitioners nor specialists typically spend more than minimal time with their patients, and they give very little counseling. Family practitioners often do not offer a full range of methods. Many couples who want or need a method other than the pill, and those who require more extensive counseling must look for another source of service. If no other source of medical advice is available, they may use a nonmedical method or go without. Clinics are often successful as a secondary source of contraceptive services because they can more easily combine great expertise with a wide choice of methods and such features as female personnel.

In this connection, first-time users of contraception, most of whom are young people, are an obvious focus of concern, and many countries have made special provision for them. That effort has been less successful in the United States than elsewhere, as extensively documented in the AGI study of adolescents (Jones et al. 1986). Young people everywhere tend to seek an anonymous source of service where confidentiality can be maintained, frequently a place other than the one used by adult women in their communities. Counseling is often very important at this stage—about the responsibility involved in sexual activity as well as about the comparative risks and benefits of various contraceptives and about proper method use. Even if most new users end up with the pill, it takes time to explain the regimen carefully and to make sure the instructions have been understood. Especially in Canada, most women seem, at some point early in their reproductive lives, to attend family planning clinics where they are exposed to extensive group and individual counseling that helps to prepare them for responsible decisionmaking concerning sex and contraception. Medical professionals in Canada, the Netherlands, and England believe that detailed discussion of possible adverse long-term effects of the pill, now required in the United States, promotes a degree of anxiety about the method that is unwarranted in view of the actual risk involved. In other countries, for new, young pill patients, the pelvic exam is often postponed to an early follow-up visit.

The most essential feature of the choice of sources is that all potential clients have open access to all options and view them as equally acceptable places to go. In England, everyone can decide for her or himself whether to go to a general practitioner or a family planning clinic. In the Netherlands and Canada, all those who are uncomfortable with the services of their family doctor, want a wider choice of methods, or need additional information can go to a family planning clinic. In any of these three countries, a family doctor who wants to refer a patient for special help or counseling about contraception in most cases recommends a clinic instead of a specialist. The assumption, stressed more in Canada and the Netherlands than in England, is that such clients will return to the mainstream source of service when their special need is no longer pressing.

In contrast, the family planning clinic system in the United States exists primarily to serve the low-income population. Many women who would prefer to go to a private doctor do not have the money to do so. At the same time, some of those who might be attracted by a clinic arrangement, especially young people, find these facilities unattractive because they are seen as services for the poor and are thought to provide a lower standard of medical care. U.S. clinics are more apt to refer clients to doctors for special help than the reverse. Young, more affluent people who elect to go to clinics because of the greater confidentiality they provide often switch to private doctors when this consideration ceases to be so important. Poor clinic clients, however, do not have this option. In the United States, selection of the type of source is determined chiefly by financial resources, not by the nature and extent of service needed.

Outside the United States, no need for special services for low-income women is generally perceived. Poverty is recognized as an important social problem in Britain, but there, as in the other case-study areas, officials, and much of the general public as well, are convinced that because public medical services are open to everyone at little or no cost, people with low incomes are not at a disadvantage when it comes to health care. Whether this is true is another question. In Britain especially, observation suggests that the existence of a national health service could become an excuse for overlooking people who cannot take advantage of what is offered because they remain caught in a web of physical and psychological problems stemming largely from their poverty. Groups with special problems like language difficulties do receive special attention in many countries, including the United States. The universal well-baby programs in Britain and the Netherlands offer an advantageous opportunity to reach women who are likely to respond positively to family planning assistance but might not otherwise be aware of it.

Socioeconomic differentials in the proportion of births that are unplanned and unwanted as well as in the proportion of women practicing contraception exist in all the case-study areas. They appear to be less marked in the Netherlands than elsewhere. The relative frequency of unplanned and unwanted births is consistently higher among lower-status than among higher-status women. Of the most effective methods of contraception, sterilization is often more prevalent and may occur at an earlier age among less advantaged couples. Use of less effective methods is frequently positively related to both income and education, at least among married women.

In general, effectiveness is stressed much more as a criterion for contraceptive method choice, both by providers and by users, in the other case-study areas than in the United States. The range of effective contraceptive alternatives is also narrower in the United States. This is unfortunate, because each method tends to be particularly appropriate for some persons and in some situations. Provision of services through specialists and clinics ought to facilitate access to a wide variety of methods in the United States, but other pressures, including the cost of liability insurance and litigation, have slowed the development and marketing of new methods. The withdrawal from the American market of nonmedicated IUDs since the U.S. data on contraceptives used in this study were collected seriously narrowed the choice of effective methods open to couples in this country (although a copper IUD has now become available). Certain methods that are not available in the United States play a small but possibly very important role in increasing the success of contraceptive practice in all the other case-study areas. The morning-after pill is widely available in the Netherlands and Great Britain and to a lesser extent in Canada. The injectable Depo-Provera is used under certain circumstances in the Netherlands and Great Britain. More access to the cervical cap exists in Canada and Great Britain than in the United States. In contrast, methods like the *Today* sponge, which has not been found to be highly effective, are either not approved for distribution in the three other countries, or their use is actively discouraged.

The level of training and the gender of personnel involved in the delivery of family planning services is usually a function of the type of provider. Male professionals predominate, but there may be a demand for female personnel on the part of teenagers and immigrants from countries where women traditionally lead very sheltered lives. Much of the routine work involved in contraceptive care, including prescription of the pill and supervision of its use, does not require a high level of training, and reservation of these tasks for physicians, as in the United States, may be both inappropriate and unnecessarily expensive.

Use of the most effective methods is greater where there is broad dissemination of information about contraceptive methods and how they can be obtained. Potential new users are especially in need of such information. Sex-education courses in school provide an obvious vehicle, although other avenues can be found—the media, for example, in the Netherlands. The British initiative, enlisting pharmacists as distributors of literature on specific health topics like contraception, is a promising example of a way to capitalize on existing resources in the private sector. A distinction should be drawn between information and counseling. Counseling can include presentation of information, but counseling services do not suffice to distribute the facts about methods and sources, nor does provision of information obviate the need for any discussion on an individual basis.

Information about contraception is both distributed and assimilated much more easily where open, tolerant attitudes about sex prevail. Although there seems to be little association between advertising of contraceptives and contraceptive practice, this is probably due to such factors as the nonexistence of television advertising in many countries. In the United States, media executives' refusal to allow advertising of condoms and other nonprescription contraceptive products on network television and in most print media cuts off a principal routine means of disseminating product information. The present study was not successful in identifying how messages concerning contraception received by the general public in the United States differ from the other case-study areas, except to reinforce the impression that contraception is treated in the United States as something special and a little taboo, reflecting an apparent underlying ambivalence about any topic closely related to sexuality. Elsewhere, especially in Quebec and the Netherlands, sex and contraception tend to be accepted simply as a part of the content of everyday communication.

In sum, how family planning services are provided seems to have a substantial impact on the pattern of contraceptive practice. The service-delivery system in the United States is different from other Western countries' in ways that make it less conducive, on the whole, to use of the modern, highly effective methods of contraception. In addition, readily available information about contraceptive methods and services is lacking in the United States, especially simple, objective materials in the mass media. The high U.S. incidence of abortion and unplanned births can be attributed at least partially to these circumstances.

APPENDIX A

Data Sources

Abbreviations used in this appendix:

AGI   The Alan Guttmacher Institute
COE   Council of Europe, *Recent Demographic Developments in the Member States of the Council of Europe*
INED   Institut National d'Etudes Démographiques
IPPF   International Planned Parenthood Federation
UN   United Nations

FEMALE POPULATIONS

General source: G. Calot, INED, unpublished data.
Additional specific sources
  1. Austria 1983, 1985:
       COE, 1984 and 1986 editions, table 1.
  2. Belgium 1980–82:
       Institut National de Statistique, *Annuaire statistique de la Belgique* Vol. 104, 1984, table 9.
  3. Canada 1983:
       AGI, S. Henshaw, unpublished data.
  4. Ontario 1977–82:
       Statistics Canada.
  5. Denmark 1983:
       UN, *Demographic Yearbook, 1984*, table 7;
       1984–85: COE, 1984 and 1985 editions, table 1.
  6. Finland 1983:
       AGI, S. Henshaw, unpublished data.
  7. France 1985:
       COE, 1986 edition, table 1.

8. Federal Republic of Germany, 1984:
   COE, 1986 edition, table 1.
9. Greece 1982, 1985:
   COE, 1984 and 1986 editions, table 1.
10. Ireland 1983:
    UN, *Demographic Yearbook, 1984*, table 7;
    1984–85: COE, 1984 and 1985 editions, table 1.
11. Italy 1983:
    AGI, S. Henshaw, unpublished data.
12. Netherlands 1983:
    AGI, S. Henshaw, unpublished data;
    1984: UN, *Demographic Yearbook, 1984*, table 7.
13. New Zealand 1983:
    AGI, S. Henshaw, unpublished data.
14. Norway 1984:
    COE, 1986 edition, table 1.
15. Portugal 1980–84:
    Instituto Nacional de Estatistica, *Estatisticas demograficas, 1984*,
    table 4.
16. Spain 1980:
    Instituto Nacional de Estadistica, *Movimiento natural de la población
    española ano 1980* Vol. 1, Madrid, 1986, table 1;
    1981: UN, *Demographic Yearbook, 1984*, table 7;
    1984–86: COE, 1984, 1985, and 1986 editions, table 1.
17. Sweden 1984:
    COE, 1984 and 1985 editions, table 1;
    1985: COE, 1985 and 1986 editions, table 1.
18. Switzerland 1984–85:
    COE, 1985 and 1986 editions, table 1.
19. United Kingdom 1984–85:
    COE, 1985 and 1986 editions, table 1.
20. England and Wales 1984:
    Office of Population Censuses and Surveys, OPCS *Monitor: Popula-
    tion Estimates for England and Wales*, PP1 85/1, table 1.
21. Scotland 1983:
    AGI, S. Henshaw, unpublished data.
22. United States 1974–81
    U.S. Census Bureau, *Preliminary Estimates of the Population of the
    United States by Age, Sex and Race: 1970–1981*, table 2;
    1982–84: U.S. Census Bureau, *Current Population Reports*, series
    P-25, no. 965, table 2.

BIRTHS

General source: G. Calot, INED, unpublished data
Additional specific sources
1. Belgium 1975–78:
   UN, *Demographic Yearbook, 1981*, table 23;
   1979–82: Institut National de Statistique, *Annuaire statistique de la
   Belgique* Vol. 104, 1984, table 26.

2. Canada 1981–84:
   AGI, S. Henshaw, unpublished data;
   1985: Statistics Canada, *Births and Deaths*, 1985, table 1.
3. Ontario and Quebec 1975–76:
   Statistics Canada, *Vital Statistics, Births, 1975–1976*;
   1977: Statistics Canada, *Births, 1977*;
   1978–85: Statistics Canada, *Births and Deaths*, 1978–85 editions, table 4.
4. Denmark 1983:
   UN, *Demographic Yearbook, 1984*, table 10.
5. Finland 1983:
   AGI, S. Henshaw, unpublished data.
6. Greece 1982:
   UN, *Demographic Yearbook, 1984*, table 10.
7. Italy 1980:
   COE, 1985 edition, tables 1 and 3.
8. Ireland 1983:
   UN, *Demographic Yearbook, 1984*, table 10.
9. Portugal 1980–82:
   Instituto National de Estatistica, *Estatisticas Demograficas, 1980–82*, Tables 15.1–3;
   1983: 1983 edition, table 15;
   1984: 1984 edition, table 27.
10. Spain 1980:
   Instituto Nacional Estadistica, *Movimiento natural de la población española ano 1980*, vol. 1, Madrid, 1986, table 1.1.
11. Sweden
   1975–80: UN, *Demographic Yearbook, 1981*, table 23;
   1981: UN, *Demographic Yearbook, 1983*, table 10.
12. England and Wales 1984:
   AGI, S. Henshaw, unpublished data.
13. Scotland 1983:
   AGI, S. Henshaw, unpublished data.
14. United States 1981–84:
   National Center for Health Statistics, *Monthly Vital Statistics Report: Advance Report of Final Natality Statistics*, 1981–84 numbers, 32(9) supplement, 33(6), 34(6), and 35(4) supplement, table 2.

AGE-SPECIFIC FERTILITY RATES

Countries and years for which population and/or birth data were not available—Austria, 1984; Denmark, 1984–85; F.R.G., 1984; Greece, 1983–84; Ireland, 1982, 1984–85; Italy, 1981; Netherlands, 1984; Norway, 1984; Sweden, 1984–85; Switerland, 1984; United Kingdom, 1984–85: COE, 1986 edition, table 3.

TOTAL FERTILITY RATES

Countries and years for which population and/or birth data were not available—Belgium, 1983; Finland, 1984; France, 1984–85; F.R.G.,

1985; Greece, 1982; Italy, 1982–84; Spain, 1981–83; England and Wales, 1984–85: INED, "Quinzième rapport sur la situation démographique de la France," *Population* 41(4–5), 1986, table 5.

ABORTIONS, IN FIVE-YEAR AGE GROUPS UNLESS OTHERWISE NOTED

General source: AGI, S. Henshaw, unpublished data.
Additional specific sources
  1. Australia 1980 (total):
     S. Siedlecky, personal communication, December 22, 1983.
  2. Belgium 1979:
     Marcel Vekemans and Brigitte Dohmen, "Induced Abortion in Belgium: Clinical Experience and Psychosocial Observations," *Studies in Family Planning* 13(12): 355–64, December 1982.
  3. Ontario 1981–85:
     Statistics Canada, *Therapeutic Abortions*, 1981 edition, table 5; 1982 edition, table 12; 1983–84 edition, table 16; 1985 edition, table 16.
  4. Quebec 1980–85:
     M. Rochon, Ministry of Health and Social Services, Quebec, unpublished data.
  5. Federal Republic of Germany 1978–82 (totals):
     Joachim von Baross, "Schwangerschaftsabbruche an Frauen aus der Bundesrepublik," *Pro Familia Magazin* 27–30 (1986) table 4.
  6. France 1979–82:
     Chantal Blayo, "L'avortement légal en France," *Population et société*, no. 187, January 1985.
  7. Greece 1981 (total):
     Jeremy Hamand, "Abortion—A Way of Life in Greece," *People* (3) 1985, p. 20.
  8. Ireland 1981:
     Raymond Illsley and Matthew Melliar-Smith, *Family Planning: Structural and Cultural Barriers to Change*, World Health Organization Europe, Copenhagen, 1985, table 2.5.6.
  9. Italy 1983:
     Simonetta Landucci Tosi et al., "Legal Abortion in Italy: 1980–81," *Family Planning Perspectives* 17(1): 19–23, 1985.
 10. Netherlands 1975–77, 1984 (totals), 1978–83:
     Evert Ketting and Paul Leseman, *Abortus en anticonceptie 1983/4*, Stimezo-Onderzoek, 1986, tables 2.1 and 2.3.
 11. Switzerland, 1975, 1980, 1982 (totals):
     P. A. Gloor et al., "Der Swangerschaftsabbruch in der Schweiz: Entwicklung nach 1979 bis 1981," Schweiz. Rundschau Med. (PRAXIS) 74, no. 17, 1985: 434–38, fig. 1.
 12. United States
     1980, 1981: Henshaw et al., "A Portrait of American Women Who Obtain Abortions," *Family Planning Perspectives* 17(2), 1985, table 1.

1982, 1983: S. Henshaw, "Characteristics of U.S. Women Having Abortions, 1982–83," *Family Planning Perspectives* 19(1), 1987, table 1.

CONTRACEPTIVE USE

General sources:

Evert Ketting and Willem A. A. van Os, "IUD Use in Western Europe," in Zatuchni, G. J., A. Goldsmith, and J. J. Sciavra, eds., *IntraUterine Contaception: Advances and Future Prospects*, Philadelphia: Harper and Row, pp. 37–45, 1985, table 7–1.

Evert Ketting and Philip van Praag, *Schwangerschaftsabbruch: Gesetz und Praxis im internationalen Vergleich*, Tübinger Reihe 5, Tübingen, 1985, table 7.6.

Adrienne Kols, Ward Rinehart, and Phyllis T. Piotrow, "Oral Contraceptives in the 1980s," *Population Reports* series A, no. 6, May–June 1982, table 1.

Henri Leridon, "Fertility and Contraception in 12 Developed Countries," *Family Planning Perspectives* 13(2), March/April 1981, pp. 93–102, table 7.

Laurie Liskin, "IUDs: An Appropriate Aontraceptive for Many Women," *Population Reports* series B, no. 4, July 1982, table 4.

John A. Ross, Sawon Hong, and Douglas H. Huber, *Voluntary Sterilization: An International Factbook*, Association for Voluntary Sterilization, 1985, table B.

National sources

Australia

David Lucas, "Australian Family Planning Surveys: Some Problems of Comparability," *Journal of Biosocial Science* 15(3): 357–66, 1983, table 1.

Austria

Rainer Munz, ed., *Leben mit Kindern: Wunsch und Wirklichkeit*, Schriften des Instituts für Demographie der Österreichischen Akademie der Wissenschaften, Franz Deuticke, Wien, 1985, table 6.2.

Belgium

Economic Commission for Europe, survey data master file (1976 survey). Population and Family Study Center, Brussels, unpublished tabulations from 1982 survey.

Canada

T. R. Balakrishnan, University of Western Ontario, special tabulations from 1984 survey.

Denmark

Economic Commission for Europe, survey data master file (1975 survey); Gert Schmidt, "Use of Contraceptives in 1975 among Danish Women 18–49 years," *Scandinavian Population Studies*, no. 5: 245–57, 1979, table 3.

Finland

Economic Commission for Europe, survey data master file (1977 survey).

France

Economic Commission for Europe, survey data master file (1978 survey); Institut National d'Etudes Démographiques, *Fertility Survey in France, 1978: A Summary of Findings*, World Fertility Survey, no. 2, October 1981, tables 1 and 8.

Federal Republic of Germany

F. E. Riphagen, J. Van der Vurst, and P. Lehert, *Contraception in the Federal Republic of Germany*, International Health Foundation, 1986, table 1.

Greece

Centre of Social Research, Athens, unpublished tabulations from 1983 survey.

Ireland

Raymond Illsley and Matthew Melliar-Smith, *Family Planning: Structural and Cultural Barriers to Change*, World Health Organization, Copenhagen, 1985, table 2.2.4 and p. 57ff.

Italy

Economic Commission for Europe, survey data master file (1979 survey).

Netherlands

Central Bureau of Statistics, Voorburg, abridged data tape of 1982 survey; Central Bureau of Statistics, Voorburg, *Onderzoek gezinsvorming 1982: Verontwoording en uitkomsten*, The Hague, Staatsuitgeverij/ cbs-Publicaties, 1984, table 2.1; Evert Ketting and Paul Leseman, *Abortus en anticonceptie 1983/4*, Stimezo-Onderzoek, 1986, tables 3.5– 8.

New Zealand

Janet Sceats and Ian Pool, "Fertility Regulation in New Zealand," chapter 2 in: escap, Population Division, eds., *The Population of New Zealand*, Country Monograph Series, no. 12, New York: United Nations (in press).

Norway

Central Bureau of Statistics of Norway, *Fertility Survey 1977*, Norges Offisielle Statistikk, Oslo, 1981, tables 1 and 57; Economic Commission for Europe, survey data master file (1977 Survey).

Portugal

Instituto Nacional de Estatistica, Centro de Estudos Demograficos, *Inquerito portugues a fecundidade, relatorio principal, volume 2: Quadros estatisticos*, Lisbon, 1983, tables 1.6.1 and 4.4.1.

Spain

Economic Commission for Europe, survey data master file (1977 survey); Instituto Nacional de Estadistica, *Encuesta de fecundidad 1985: Avance de resultados*, I.N.E. Artes Graficas, Madrid, 1986, tables 2.19.3 and 2.9.4.

Sweden

Central Bureau of Statistics, Stockholm, abridged data tape of 1982 survey.

Switerland

Franz Kühne, *Kontrazeption in der Schweiz*, Hedingen, 1984, tables 5 and 23.

United Kingdom

Karen Dunnell, *Family Formation 1976*, Her Majesty's Stationery Office, 1979, tables 2.1, 2.2, 8.1, 8.2, 9.2; Office of Population Censuses and Surveys, Social Survey Division, *General Household Survey 1983*, London: Her Majesty's Stationery Office, 1985, table 5.1; Office of Population Censuses and Surveys, unpublished tabulations from 1983 General Household Survey.

United States

Christine A. Bachrach, "Contraceptive Practice among American Women, 1973–82," *Family Planning Perspectives* 16(6): 253–59, November/December 1984, tables 1 and 2; Data file of 1982 National Survey of Family Growth.

LAW AND POLICY VARIABLES

Overall family planning policy

General source: UN, *World Population Trends, Population and Development: Interrelations and Population Policies*. 1983 monitoring report, vol. 2, table 101.

Additional source:

Greece: IPPF, *Family Planning in Five Continents*, 1983.

Advertising of contraceptive methods

General source: IPPF Europe, *Planned Parenthood in Europe: A Human Rights Perspective, 1986*, Country profiles.

Abortion laws

General source: UN, *World Population, Trends and Policies*. 1981 monitoring report, vol. 2, table 43.

Additional sources:

1. Federal Republic of Germany: E. S. O. Smith, "Family Planning Programs in Britain, German Federal Republic, Denmark and Sweden with the Implications for Canada," *Canadian Journal of Public Health*, vol. 68, September/October 1977, pp. 369–70.

2. Netherlands, Spain: IPPF, *Family Planning in Five Continents*, pp. 97–99.

3. Portugal: IPPF Europe, *Planned Parenthood in Europe in the 1980s: A Human Rights Perspective*, 1985.

Recognition of target groups

General source: AGI, International Contraceptive Practice and Services country survey.

Teaching of contraceptive methods in school

General source: AGI, International Adolescent Pregnancy Project Country Survey.

Sterilization laws

General source: UN, *World Population Trends and Policies*. 1981 monitoring report, vol. 2, table 44.

Additional source:
Austria, Denmark, Federal Republic of Germany, Greece, Portugal,
Spain: Association for Voluntary Sterilization, *International Factbook*,
1985, table 31.

SERVICE DELIVERY VARIABLES

Main source of contraceptive services
Combination of major family planning sources
Method recommended for termination of childbearing
Special efforts to assist young people
Special efforts to assist low-income people
Special efforts to assist immigrants
Contraceptive access for unmarried minors
Payment for female sterilization in hospital
Payment to obtain pill prescription
Payment for pill supplies
Variation in access to sterilization
Reasons for variation in access to sterilization
Variation in access to the pill
Sterilization requirements
Pelvic exam before pill prescription
    General source: AGI, International Contraceptive Practice and Services
    Country Survey.
Contraceptive access for unmarried minors
    General source: AGI, International Adolescent Pregnancy Project Country Survey.

INFORMATION DELIVERY VARIABLES

Overall information effort
Special information efforts for target groups
Proportion of female students receiving instruction on contraceptive methods
Advertising of condoms
    General source: AGI, International Contraceptive Practice and Services
    Country Survey.
Proportion of female students receiving instruction in contraceptive methods
    General source: AGI, International Adolescent Pregnancy Project Country Survey.

Statistical Data

Age-specific fertility rates											
Year	Age	Aus-tralia	Aus-tria	Bel-gium	Can-ada	On-tario	Que-bec	Den-mark	Fin-land	France	F.R.G.	Greece
	15–19	39.9	48.1	28.0	36.0	—	19.7	26.9	27.5	34.0	27.3	45.0
	20–24	133.2	130.7	119.3	115.3	—	98.6	136.7	105.5	133.7	92.5	154.0
	25–29	148.8	100.2	118.4	134.6	—	136.6	136.0	113.9	122.8	96.2	139.0
1975	30–34	73.7	51.9	54.9	66.8	—	69.8	63.6	59.6	62.3	48.1	80.6
	35–39	25.9	28.5	20.7	21.9	—	23.2	18.2	24.7	26.6	19.8	35.5
	40–44	6.1	8.3	5.2	4.9	—	5.1	3.4	5.9	6.8	5.5	8.7
	45–49	0.3	0.5	0.4	0.4	—	0.5	0.1	0.4	0.5	0.3	1.1
	15–19	33.5	42.1	26.7	34.1	33.7	20.5	23.1	26.1	31.2	25.6	48.4
	20–24	128.0	121.6	118.0	111.5	105.6	100.1	121.2	103.8	128.4	92.8	160.1
	25–29	145.9	96.9	120.7	131.5	124.6	137.1	125.0	116.3	119.8	99.6	141.3
1976	30–34	72.4	47.5	55.0	66.5	64.6	70.0	59.1	65.6	59.1	48.6	77.8
	35–39	24.0	24.1	19.1	21.4	20.6	22.4	18.2	25.2	22.6	18.7	33.4
	40–44	5.5	7.0	4.6	4.4	4.3	4.4	3.2	5.7	5.5	5.0	8.2
	45–49	0.4	0.4	0.3	0.3	0.3	0.3	0.1	0.5	0.4	0.3	1.0
	15–19	32.1	37.6	24.9	32.3	31.2	19.6	21.9	24.2	30.2	23.0	48.6
	20–24	121.9	119.6	116.2	108.6	103.0	97.4	115.3	99.2	132.2	88.1	155.2
	25–29	145.5	94.5	122.7	130.9	123.5	137.5	119.9	115.2	124.7	98.2	137.8
1977	30–34	74.1	47.3	54.6	67.7	66.2	70.2	55.7	67.8	61.3	48.7	73.5
	35–39	23.8	21.9	18.6	20.8	19.8	22.1	16.7	25.6	21.4	16.9	31.5
	40–44	5.0	6.7	4.2	3.7	3.3	3.6	2.8	5.9	5.0	4.3	7.6
	45–49	0.3	0.5	0.3	0.3	0.2	0.3	0.1	0.4	0.4	0.3	1.0
	15–19	29.9	35.9	23.4	30.0	28.6	17.6	19.9	21.3	27.2	21.5	51.4
	20–24	118.1	124.1	121.7	114.8	104.5	104.5	111.4	90.4	125.9	87.0	168.2
	25–29	143.9	97.8	124.4	128.8	121.4	134.6	124.7	113.7	125.0	98.5	137.1
1978	30–34	73.4	47.5	54.1	67.6	66.1	69.3	56.0	67.4	61.8	50.2	72.1
	35–39	23.5	19.5	17.4	19.4	18.8	19.7	17.0	26.5	20.8	15.8	29.3
	40–44	4.5	5.9	3.6	3.6	3.3	3.5	2.4	5.7	4.6	3.6	7.2
	45–49	0.2	0.4	0.3	0.3	0.2	0.3	0.1	0.3	0.3	0.3	0.9
	15–19	28.4	34.8	21.8	28.2	26.0	17.1	17.6	19.2	25.0	20.2	53.9
	20–24	108.7	117.5	115.0	102.2	94.5	94.6	107.8	93.6	127.9	82.9	159.6
	25–29	141.9	98.1	126.7	131.3	122.4	139.4	120.7	113.1	130.7	99.6	138.9
1979	30–34	73.7	49.0	54.2	69.4	67.8	71.7	54.6	68.3	64.1	53.3	68.8
	35–39	23.5	19.1	17.5	19.7	19.4	20.1	16.7	27.5	21.5	15.8	27.7
	40–44	4.5	5.3	3.4	3.4	3.5	3.0	2.6	6.4	4.4	3.3	7.1
	45–49	0.3	0.4	0.3	0.2	0.2	0.2	0.1	0.3	0.3	0.3	1.0
	15–19	27.6	35.4	20.3	27.9	25.1	16.1	16.3	18.9	24.5	20.2	53.1
	20–24	106.8	122.0	114.5	101.0	93.4	92.4	101.7	91.5	130.9	86.5	155.4
	25–29	140.7	103.0	128.9	128.9	122.9	135.1	117.9	114.6	138.6	104.8	131.4
1980	30–34	75.0	51.4	54.0	68.7	68.6	69.6	53.7	68.0	68.6	57.7	66.3
	35–39	23.6	19.0	16.9	19.4	19.7	19.6	16.3	27.1	22.7	16.8	26.0
	40–44	4.4	5.4	3.4	3.1	3.0	3.0	2.5	6.4	4.4	3.3	6.8
	45–49	0.3	0.4	0.4	0.2	0.2	0.2	0.1	0.3	0.3	0.3	1.1
	15–19	28.2	34.2	19.0	26.7	23.3	15.1	13.7	16.9	22.6	18.5	48.9
	20–24	107.5	118.9	113.6	97.3	89.1	88.3	92.3	88.7	127.1	84.1	147.7
	25–29	145.2	104.2	128.9	127.7	121.9	131.8	111.0	118.3	140.3	104.6	124.8
1981	30–34	77.6	52.8	54.2	68.5	68.6	68.2	51.4	69.5	70.5	58.6	64.4
	35–39	24.5	19.2	16.0	19.5	20.4	18.2	15.4	29.8	24.2	17.1	25.5
	40–44	4.5	5.1	3.2	3.2	3.4	2.8	2.3	6.1	4.5	3.2	6.1
	45–49	0.3	0.4	0.3	0.2	0.1	0.2	0.1	0.4	0.3	0.3	0.8

Age-specific fertility rates Year	Age	Ireland	Italy	The Netherlands	New Zealand	Norway	Portugal	Spain	Sweden	Switzerland	United Kingdom	Great Britain	United States
	15–19	22.8	32.5	12.6	55.2	40.3	38.1	21.6	28.8	15.3	36.8	36.9	56.8
	20–24	138.6	128.3	97.9	158.5	134.6	145.6	134.9	115.0	94.0	116.9	116.1	113.0
	25–29	216.1	138.2	137.6	157.5	129.2	148.0	189.1	123.3	120.6	124.9	123.7	108.2
1975	30–34	162.2	83.6	60.5	69.9	63.9	97.8	122.5	64.1	64.0	59.9	58.6	52.3
	35–39	100.1	40.3	19.9	25.1	24.3	59.9	64.5	20.7	23.0	21.0	20.1	19.5
	40–44	36.8	12.6	4.7	6.9	5.3	25.2	23.0	3.7	5.6	5.1	4.9	4.6
	45–49	2.6	0.9	0.4	0.6	0.3	2.6	2.2	0.2	0.3	0.4	0.4	0.3
	15–19	21.9	31.1	11.3	51.1	35.7	47.9	24.8	25.0	12.6	32.8	32.8	53.9
	20–24	133.7	124.1	94.5	152.3	126.0	160.6	142.1	107.1	88.7	111.9	111.0	110.3
	25–29	211.7	130.7	138.0	152.6	120.6	141.8	187.7	118.8	118.0	121.6	120.3	106.2
1976	30–34	162.2	80.5	60.4	69.5	63.0	89.0	119.2	62.4	63.6	59.1	57.8	53.6
	35–39	94.9	37.0	18.2	23.2	23.5	52.4	60.8	20.5	21.4	19.6	18.8	19.0
	40–44	34.8	11.3	4.4	6.1	5.0	22.4	21.1	3.6	4.8	4.7	4.4	4.3
	45–49	3.1	0.9	0.3	0.5	0.3	2.3	1.9	0.2	0.4	0.4	0.3	0.2
	15–19	21.2	27.2	10.1	46.8	32.4	48.6	25.8	22.1	10.5	30.1	30.1	53.9
	20–24	130.3	118.0	87.9	144.3	116.0	156.1	136.4	103.6	84.4	105.9	105.1	112.9
	25–29	205.5	123.7	136.6	150.3	117.5	138.5	177.2	117.9	120.0	120.4	119.1	111.0
1977	30–34	166.7	76.5	61.7	69.4	60.6	85.2	112.8	61.5	65.5	60.1	59.0	56.4
	35–39	93.9	33.1	17.2	21.7	20.9	45.3	56.4	20.7	21.3	19.1	18.3	19.2
	40–44	33.2	9.6	3.9	6.1	4.4	19.7	19.4	3.6	4.3	4.4	4.1	4.2
	45–49	3.0	0.9	0.3	0.3	0.2	2.5	1.8	0.2	0.3	0.3	0.3	0.2
	15–19	21.8	25.2	9.4	44.6	29.0	44.8	26.6	19.2	10.0	30.2	30.2	52.5
	20–24	141.4	111.1	87.1	144.4	117.4	159.0	144.0	89.1	76.2	109.7	108.4	121.8
	25–29	201.8	119.0	139.9	146.4	121.8	128.6	168.3	116.0	120.1	125.2	123.9	108.5
1978	30–34	167.8	72.8	63.3	68.7	63.4	79.3	107.6	62.4	66.5	64.9	63.7	57.8
	35–39	96.6	30.5	16.6	21.7	22.1	39.0	54.2	21.6	20.6	20.4	19.6	19.0
	40–44	31.1	8.7	3.5	5.3	4.5	17.2	17.6	3.7	4.2	4.3	4.1	3.9
	45–49	2.8	0.7	0.3	0.4	0.2	2.2	1.6	0.1	0.3	0.4	0.4	0.2
	15–19	22.7	23.1	8.9	41.2	27.4	41.4	26.7	17.3	9.7	31.0	31.0	53.4
	20–24	125.9	105.2	81.7	131.9	113.6	138.2	118.0	95.5	79.6	113.0	112.2	112.8
	25–29	202.4	114.8	139.2	152.6	121.1	123.5	153.6	122.7	122.6	134.2	132.9	111.4
1979	30–34	168.5	68.3	63.3	70.0	62.4	78.1	97.0	67.1	67.3	70.9	69.7	60.3
	35–39	94.1	28.2	16.9	21.9	22.2	35.7	49.0	24.4	20.7	22.4	21.4	19.5
	40–44	29.9	7.2	3.2	4.8	4.0	15.2	15.1	4.3	3.6	4.5	4.3	3.9
	45–49	2.3	0.6	0.3	0.5	0.2	2.0	1.4	0.1	0.2	0.4	0.4	0.2
	15–19	23.0	20.6	9.2	38.8	25.3	42.1	22.1	15.8	9.9	31.0	31.1	54.2
	20–24	125.4	99.7	80.1	125.2	108.3	137.3	110.6	95.6	79.5	114.7	114.0	114.8
	25–29	202.3	112.2	142.6	144.8	122.4	123.6	144.3	124.2	124.8	136.6	135.3	112.0
1980	30–34	165.7	65.6	66.7	67.8	62.8	76.3	89.9	70.7	70.4	72.1	70.9	61.3
	35–39	97.4	26.7	17.5	21.1	21.9	34.8	44.3	24.9	21.0	23.3	22.4	19.7
	40–44	29.6	6.5	3.5	4.3	4.1	14.4	14.4	4.3	3.7	4.5	4.3	3.9
	45–49	2.3	0.5	0.4	0.4	0.2	1.9	1.4	0.1	0.3	0.4	0.4	0.2
	15–19	22.4	18.0	9.0	38.2	23.8	39.6	—	14.5	9.6	28.5	28.3	53.3
	20–24	117.5	93.4	74.6	120.8	107.0	130.8	—	90.3	79.1	110.1	106.3	112.4
	25–29	191.4	110.0	139.8	144.2	120.5	124.6	—	120.6	123.5	130.3	129.5	111.5
1981	30–34	161.8	64.5	66.9	68.7	63.0	74.4	—	71.7	70.5	69.8	68.4	61.4
	35–39	93.8	26.0	17.5	20.0	22.0	34.3	—	24.8	21.4	23.3	21.6	20.0
	40–44	26.2	6.0	3.5	4.3	3.9	13.2	—	4.4	3.3	4.5	4.4	3.8
	45–49	2.4	0.4	0.4	0.2	0.2	1.7	—	0.2	0.2	0.5	0.5	0.2

Age-specific fertility rates Year	Age	Aus-tralia	Aus-tria	Bel-gium	Can-ada	On-tario	Que-bec	Den-mark	Fin-land	France	F.R.G.	Greece
	15–19	27.4	33.7	17.4	26.7	23.7	15.3	12.1	16.9	21.4	16.7	—
	20–24	104.0	117.3	107.6	95.8	87.9	84.5	87.3	90.0	123.4	80.9	—
	25–29	145.0	104.4	126.7	125.2	122.6	122.5	112.9	124.4	139.3	104.4	—
1982	30–34	80.6	52.5	53.7	68.9	71.5	63.1	54.1	73.7	70.1	58.1	—
	35–39	25.6	19.4	15.8	20.2	21.7	17.8	15.7	30.9	24.5	17.5	—
	40–44	4.5	4.7	3.0	3.2	3.1	2.7	2.3	6.9	4.6	3.0	—
	45–49	0.3	0.3	0.3	0.2	0.1	0.1	0.1	0.4	0.3	0.2	—
	15–19	—	30.4	—	25.0	22.3	14.5	10.6	15.8	19.3	14.0	43.7
	20–24	—	108.6	—	92.6	84.3	80.5	79.5	87.3	114.1	74.3	139.8
	25–29	—	100.7	—	125.0	124.7	118.8	111.6	126.7	131.4	100.5	116.5
1983	30–34	—	50.7	—	70.6	74.6	61.5	55.4	78.0	66.0	56.5	59.4
	35–39	—	18.8	—	20.6	22.6	16.5	15.2	33.2	23.1	17.6	23.0
	40–44	—	4.0	—	3.0	2.9	2.5	2.3	6.6	4.4	2.8	5.0
	45–49	—	0.3	—	0.2	0.1	0.2	0.2	0.4	0.3	0.2	0.6
	15–19	—	26.9	—	24.4	21.8	14.4	10.1	—	—	9.0	41.2
	20–24	—	105.5	—	88.8	82.7	76.6	77.5	—	—	62.1	131.5
	25–29	—	99.5	—	126.0	127.6	118.9	113.3	—	—	102.1	108.8
1984	30–34	—	50.9	—	73.0	79.1	62.4	59.2	—	—	62.1	56.7
	35–39	—	19.1	—	21.5	23.9	17.0	17.4	—	—	21.7	21.3
	40–44	—	3.6	—	3.0	3.3	2.5	2.3	—	—	3.3	4.6
	45–49	—	0.3	—	0.1	0.1	0.1	0.1	—	—	0.2	0.5

Total fertility rates

Year	Aus-tralia	Aus-tria	Bel-gium	Can-ada	On-tario	Que-bec	Den-mark	Fin-land	France	F.R.G.	Greece
1975	2.14	1.84	1.73	1.90	—	1.77	1.92	1.69	1.93	1.45	2.32
1976	2.05	1.70	1.72	1.85	1.77	1.77	1.75	1.72	1.83	1.45	2.35
1977	2.01	1.64	1.71	1.82	1.74	1.75	1.66	1.69	1.88	1.40	2.28
1978	1.97	1.66	1.72	1.82	1.71	1.75	1.66	1.63	1.83	1.38	2.33
1979	1.91	1.62	1.70	1.77	1.67	1.73	1.60	1.64	1.87	1.38	2.29
1980	1.89	1.68	1.69	1.75	1.66	1.68	1.54	1.63	1.95	1.45	2.20
1981	1.94	1.67	1.68	1.72	1.63	1.62	1.43	1.65	1.95	1.43	2.09
1982	1.94	1.66	1.62	1.70	1.65	1.53	1.42	1.72	1.92	1.40	2.04
1983	—	1.57	1.56	1.69	1.66	1.47	1.37	1.74	1.79	1.33	1.94
1984	—	1.53	—	1.68	1.69	1.46	1.40	1.70	1.81	1.30	1.82

General abortion rates

Year	Aus-tralia	Aus-tria	Bel-gium	Can-ada	On-tario	Que-bec	Den-mark	Fin-land	France	F.R.G.	Greece
1975	—	—	—	—	—	—	27.0	20.4	—	—	—
1976	—	—	—	—	—	—	25.7	18.7	—	—	—
1977	—	—	—	—	—	—	24.1	16.6	—	—	—
1978	—	—	—	—	—	—	22.3	15.8	—	—	—
1979	—	—	9.8	—	—	—	21.6	14.7	22.7	—	—
1980	13.9	—	—	13.2	—	9.3	21.4	13.9	22.4	12.4	—
1981	—	—	—	12.9	14.7	9.2	20.7	12.9	22.1	11.8	77.7
1982	—	—	—	13.0	14.9	10.3	19.3	12.6	21.8	11.8	—
1983	—	—	—	—	13.4	9.6	—	—	—	10.9	—
1984	—	—	—	—	13.1	10.2	—	—	—	10.6	—

Age-specific fertility rates				The Nether-lands	New Zea-land	Nor-way	Por-tugal	Spain	Swe-den	Swit-zer-land	United King-dom	Great Bri-tain	United States
Year	Age	Ire-land	Italy										
	15–19	20.9	—	8.2	34.7	22.0	39.3	—	13.1	9.4	27.8	27.7	53.6
	20–24	110.3	—	69.4	112.0	104.7	130.5	—	85.6	77.5	105.4	101.8	112.0
	25–29	184.7	—	132.5	141.5	123.0	124.7	—	121.3	125.3	127.9	126.0	111.1
1982	30–34	156.9	—	67.1	69.8	65.8	73.2	—	73.2	72.6	66.3	68.7	63.9
	35–39	91.8	—	18.0	21.0	22.4	33.6	—	25.5	21.1	25.2	22.6	21.2
	40–44	25.0	—	3.5	4.2	3.8	11.5	—	4.4	3.4	4.4	4.2	3.8
	45–49	2.2	—	0.4	0.4	0.3	1.5	—	0.2	0.2	0.4	0.4	0.2
	15–19	18.6	—	7.7	32.7	19.8	37.5	—	11.6	8.0	—	27.1	52.8
	20–24	101.0	—	66.5	111.2	97.3	121.8	—	82.5	74.0	—	98.7	108.3
	25–29	168.1	—	129.4	143.4	120.3	117.6	—	121.8	123.2	—	125.9	108.7
1983	30–34	144.0	—	69.9	73.3	67.8	69.1	—	74.7	72.8	—	70.9	64.6
	35–39	83.0	—	17.8	20.9	22.4	31.1	—	26.0	20.4	—	22.9	22.1
	40–44	24.6	—	3.2	4.1	3.6	10.8	—	4.7	3.4	—	4.3	3.8
	45–49	1.6	—	0.3	0.3	0.2	1.3	—	0.2	0.1	—	0.5	0.2
	15–19	18.3	—	7.4	—	19.2	36.8	—	10.7	5.2	27.8	—	52.0
	20–24	95.3	—	64.3	—	93.9	118.2	—	80.3	63.5	96.3	—	107.4
	25–29	161.6	—	131.5	—	123.7	114.6	—	125.8	125.3	126.7	—	109.0
1984	30–34	137.9	—	73.8	—	68.3	67.2	—	79.9	82.6	74.0	—	66.6
	35–39	79.3	—	18.5	—	22.2	30.2	—	28.1	25.0	24.0	—	22.9
	40–44	21.8	—	3.2	—	4.1	9.6	—	5.4	4.2	4.6	—	3.8
	45–49	2.0	—	0.4	—	0.2	1.2	—	0.2	0.2	0.4	—	0.2

Total fertility rates

Year	Ire-land	Italy	The Nether-lands	New Zea-land	Nor-way	Por-tugal	Spain	Swe-den	Swit-zer-land	United King-dom	Great Bri-tain	United States
1975	3.40	2.18	1.67	2.37	1.99	2.59	2.79	1.78	1.61	1.82	1.80	1.77
1976	3.31	2.08	1.64	2.28	1.87	2.58	2.79	1.69	1.55	1.75	1.73	1.74
1977	3.27	1.94	1.59	2.20	1.76	2.48	2.65	1.65	1.53	1.70	1.68	1.79
1978	3.32	1.84	1.60	2.16	1.79	2.35	2.60	1.56	1.49	1.78	1.75	1.82
1979	3.23	1.74	1.57	2.11	1.75	2.17	2.30	1.66	1.52	1.88	1.86	1.81
1980	3.23	1.66	1.60	2.01	1.72	2.15	2.13	1.68	1.55	1.91	1.89	1.83
1981	3.08	1.59	1.56	1.98	1.70	2.09	2.00	1.63	1.54	1.83	1.79	1.81
1982	2.96	1.57	1.50	1.92	1.71	2.07	1.88	1.62	1.55	1.79	1.76	1.83
1983	2.70	1.53	1.47	1.93	1.66	1.95	1.71	1.61	1.51	—	1.75	1.80
1984	2.58	1.50	1.50	—	1.66	1.89	—	1.65	1.53	1.77	—	1.81

General abortion rates

Year	Ire-land	Italy	The Nether-lands	New Zea-land	Nor-way	Por-tugal	Spain	Swe-den	Swit-zer-land	United King-dom	Great Bri-tain	United States
1975	—	—	5.1	0.0	—	—	—	20.3	21.7	—	10.9	11.2
1976	—	—	5.0	7.1	18.9	—	—	20.0	—	—	10.3	10.6
1977	—	—	5.3	8.0	19.4	—	—	19.1	—	—	10.2	10.4
1978	—	—	5.2	3.1	18.4	—	—	19.4	—	—	11.1	11.4
1979	—	—	5.6	5.3	17.7	—	—	20.9	—	—	11.7	12.1
1980	—	—	6.7	8.4	16.3	—	—	20.7	20.0	—	12.3	12.6
1981	5.3	—	6.5	9.4	16.4	—	—	19.4	—	—	12.1	12.4
1982	—	—	6.2	9.5	15.8	—	—	19.0	17.4	—	11.9	12.3
1983	—	27.7	5.9	—	15.7	—	—	17.9	—	—	—	12.1
1984	—	—	—	—	—	—	—	—	—	—	—	—

Age-specific abortion rates		Aus-	Aus-	Bel-	Can-	On-	Que-	Den-	Fin-			
Year	Age	tralia	tria	gium	ada	tario	bec	mark	land	France	F.R.G.	Greece
	15–19	—	—	—	—	—	—	25.0	21.2	—	—	—
	20–24	—	—	—	—	—	—	32.5	26.0	—	—	—
	25–29	—	—	—	—	—	—	32.0	22.0	—	—	—
1975	30–34	—	—	—	—	—	—	30.8	17.7	—	—	—
	35–39	—	—	—	—	—	—	24.3	17.1	—	—	—
	40–44	—	—	—	—	—	—	11.5	12.7	—	—	—
	45–49	—	—	—	—	—	—	1.0	2.2	—	—	—
	15–19	—	—	—	—	—	—	26.0	20.4	—	—	—
	20–24	—	—	—	—	—	—	31.5	25.0	—	—	—
	25–29	—	—	—	—	—	—	30.0	17.4	—	—	—
1976	30–34	—	—	—	—	—	—	28.3	16.3	—	—	—
	35–39	—	—	—	—	—	—	22.3	16.3	—	—	—
	40–44	—	—	—	—	—	—	11.0	12.0	—	—	—
	45–49	—	—	—	—	—	—	1.0	2.0	—	—	—
	15–19	—	—	—	—	—	—	25.5	19.6	—	—	—
	20–24	—	—	—	—	—	—	30.4	22.0	—	—	—
	25–29	—	—	—	—	—	—	28.0	16.1	—	—	—
1977	30–34	—	—	—	—	—	—	26.5	14.5	—	—	—
	35–39	—	—	—	—	—	—	21.4	13.4	—	—	—
	40–44	—	—	—	—	—	—	9.8	10.3	—	—	—
	45–49	—	—	—	—	—	—	1.0	1.8	—	—	—
	15–19	—	—	—	—	—	—	24.3	19.8	—	—	—
	20–24	—	—	—	—	—	—	29.0	21.4	—	—	—
	25–29	—	—	—	—	—	—	25.1	15.4	—	—	—
1978	30–34	—	—	—	—	—	—	23.0	13.0	—	—	—
	35–39	—	—	—	—	—	—	19.0	11.7	—	—	—
	40–44	—	—	—	—	—	—	9.4	9.7	—	—	—
	45–49	—	—	—	—	—	—	1.0	1.7	—	—	—
	15–19	—	—	8.0	—	—	—	22.5	19.5	15.4	—	—
	20–24	—	—	14.0	—	—	—	29.3	20.2	32.3	—	—
	25–29	—	—	12.0	—	—	—	24.8	13.6	28.8	—	—
1979	30–34	—	—	10.8	—	—	—	21.9	12.1	25.5	—	—
	35–39	—	—	8.4	—	—	—	18.1	10.4	19.3	—	—
	40–44	—	—	3.8	—	—	—	9.1	9.1	9.3	—	—
	45–49	—	—	0.5	—	—	—	1.0	1.7	1.3	—	—
	15–19	—	—	—	19.5	—	10.4	22.1	19.4	15.4	—	—
	20–24	—	—	—	21.1	—	14.3	29.4	19.7	31.8	—	—
	25–29	—	—	—	13.9	—	11.9	24.9	12.2	28.5	—	—
1980	30–34	—	—	—	9.0	—	8.1	22.2	11.0	24.8	—	—
	35–39	—	—	—	5.2	—	4.8	17.6	10.3	19.0	—	—
	40–44	—	—	—	2.2	—	1.8	9.0	8.2	9.2	—	—
	45–49	—	—	—	0.3	—	0.3	1.0	1.7	1.3	—	—
	15–19	—	—	—	19.0	21.9	10.3	20.4	17.9	14.9	—	—
	20–24	—	—	—	21.0	24.1	14.4	30.1	18.3	31.5	—	—
	25–29	—	—	—	13.8	16.0	11.5	24.6	11.5	28.4	—	—
1981	30–34	—	—	—	9.0	10.5	8.2	21.1	10.2	24.4	—	—
	35–39	—	—	—	5.1	6.1	4.7	16.5	9.9	19.2	—	—
	40–44	—	—	—	2.1	2.4	1.8	8.8	7.9	8.6	—	—
	45–49	—	—	—	0.2	0.3	0.2	1.1	1.4	1.2	—	—

Year	Age	Ireland	Italy	The Netherlands	New Zealand	Norway	Portugal	Spain	Sweden	Switzerland	United Kingdom	Great Britain	United States
	15–19	—	—	—	—	—	—	—	29.7	—	—	15.7	32.5
	20–24	—	—	—	—	—	—	—	26.9	—	—	15.0	34.3
	25–29	—	—	—	—	—	—	—	21.3	—	—	11.0	21.8
1975	30–34	—	—	—	—	—	—	—	18.0	—	—	9.8	14.0
	35–39	—	—	—	—	—	—	—	14.7	—	—	7.8	8.9
	40–44	—	—	—	—	—	—	—	7.3	—	—	3.6	3.2
	45–49	—	—	—	—	—	—	—	0.8	—	—	0.3	0.3
	15–19	—	—	—	10.1	22.7	—	—	28.5	—	—	15.2	35.8
	20–24	—	—	—	10.2	24.2	—	—	26.6	—	—	14.2	39.6
	25–29	—	—	—	6.6	19.0	—	—	20.9	—	—	10.4	24.1
1976	30–34	—	—	—	5.6	17.5	—	—	18.4	—	—	9.2	15.0
	35–39	—	—	—	4.1	15.5	—	—	15.0	—	—	7.3	9.3
	40–44	—	—	—	1.9	8.9	—	—	7.4	—	—	3.3	3.4
	45–49	—	—	—	0.2	1.1	—	—	0.8	—	—	0.3	0.4
	15–19	—	—	—	11.9	25.5	—	—	26.2	—	—	15.2	39.0
	20–24	—	—	—	11.5	24.9	—	—	25.8	—	—	14.3	44.3
	25–29	—	—	—	7.7	19.1	—	—	21.4	—	—	10.4	26.9
1977	30–34	—	—	—	6.1	17.6	—	—	17.5	—	—	8.8	15.7
	35–39	—	—	—	4.6	15.9	—	—	14.1	—	—	7.2	9.8
	40–44	—	—	—	2.1	9.0	—	—	7.8	—	—	3.4	3.5
	45–49	—	—	—	0.2	1.1	—	—	0.9	—	—	0.4	0.4
	15–19	—	—	4.7	3.8	25.4	—	—	23.9	—	—	15.6	41.1
	20–24	—	—	6.1	3.7	23.3	—	—	25.5	—	—	15.6	47.2
	25–29	—	—	5.9	3.2	18.1	—	—	21.2	—	—	11.5	28.4
1978	30–34	—	—	5.6	2.8	16.0	—	—	19.0	—	—	9.7	16.4
	35–39	—	—	5.0	2.3	13.8	—	—	15.8	—	—	7.7	9.8
	40–44	—	—	2.7	1.6	8.4	—	—	8.1	—	—	3.5	3.2
	45–49	—	—	0.4	0.2	1.1	—	—	0.9	—	—	0.3	0.4
	15–19	—	—	4.8	6.6	24.4	—	—	22.7	—	—	16.6	43.9
	20–24	—	—	7.0	7.0	23.4	—	—	27.5	—	—	17.0	49.9
	25–29	—	—	6.9	5.8	18.1	—	—	23.0	—	—	12.1	29.6
1979	30–34	—	—	6.1	4.6	15.3	—	—	20.7	—	—	10.1	16.5
	35–39	—	—	5.3	3.6	12.3	—	—	18.3	—	—	8.1	9.4
	40–44	—	—	2.3	2.1	7.5	—	—	10.1	—	—	3.5	3.1
	45–49	—	—	0.4	0.4	1.0	—	—	1.3	—	—	0.4	0.3
	15–19	—	—	5.7	10.8	22.6	—	—	22.2	—	—	17.5	44.3
	20–24	—	—	9.2	12.8	22.3	—	—	28.5	—	—	18.2	51.5
	25–29	—	—	8.2	9.4	16.3	—	—	22.1	—	—	12.9	30.7
1980	30–34	—	—	7.2	6.6	13.8	—	—	20.6	—	—	10.3	17.1
	35–39	—	—	5.5	4.6	11.4	—	—	18.2	—	—	8.2	9.3
	40–44	—	—	2.5	2.4	6.9	—	—	10.2	—	—	3.7	3.2
	45–49	—	—	0.4	0.3	0.8	—	—	1.1	—	—	0.4	0.3
	15–19	3.6	—	5.8	10.9	23.3	—	—	20.9	—	—	17.0	44.5
	20–24	10.9	—	9.2	15.2	21.8	—	—	27.3	—	—	18.2	51.5
	25–29	6.6	—	8.1	10.7	17.2	—	—	21.6	—	—	12.8	31.3
1981	30–34	4.2	—	6.8	8.0	14.2	—	—	19.2	—	—	9.9	17.7
	35–39	3.0	—	5.2	5.2	11.3	—	—	16.7	—	—	7.9	9.5
	40–44	1.2	—	2.2	2.5	6.2	—	—	8.8	—	—	3.4	3.1
	45–49	0.1	—	0.3	0.3	0.9	—	—	1.3	—	—	0.4	0.3

Age-specific abortion rates		Aus-tralia	Aus-tria	Bel-gium	Can-ada	On-tario	Que-bec	Den-mark	Fin-land	France	F.R.G.	Greece
Year	Age											
1982	15–19	—	—	—	19.0	22.6	11.8	18.2	17.9	14.7	—	—
	20–24	—	—	—	21.6	24.8	15.9	28.8	18.7	30.2	—	—
	25–29	—	—	—	14.1	16.2	13.3	23.5	11.0	28.7	—	—
	30–34	—	—	—	9.2	10.7	8.9	20.1	9.8	24.5	—	—
	35–39	—	—	—	5.2	6.2	5.1	15.2	9.5	18.8	—	—
	40–44	—	—	—	2.0	2.2	2.1	8.2	6.9	8.4	—	—
	45–49	—	—	—	0.2	0.2	0.3	1.0	1.3	1.2	—	—
1983	15–19	—	—	—	—	20.2	10.8	—	—	—	—	—
	20–24	—	—	—	—	22.4	15.2	—	—	—	—	—
	25–29	—	—	—	—	14.6	12.4	—	—	—	—	—
	30–34	—	—	—	—	10.0	8.9	—	—	—	—	—
	35–39	—	—	—	—	5.8	5.2	—	—	—	—	—
	40–44	—	—	—	—	2.0	1.7	—	—	—	—	—
	45–49	—	—	—	—	0.2	0.2	—	—	—	—	—
1984	15–19	—	—	—	—	19.5	12.0	—	—	—	—	—
	20–24	—	—	—	—	22.4	16.4	—	—	—	—	—
	25–29	—	—	—	—	14.7	13.1	—	—	—	—	—
	30–34	—	—	—	—	9.7	9.1	—	—	—	—	—
	35–39	—	—	—	—	6.0	5.2	—	—	—	—	—
	40–44	—	—	—	—	1.8	1.6	—	—	—	—	—
	45–49	—	—	—	—	0.2	0.2	—	—	—	—	—

Total abortion rates	Aus-tralia	Aus-tria	Bel-gium	Can-ada	On-tario	Que-bec	Den-mark	Fin-land	France	F.R.G.	Greece
Year											
1975	—	—	—	—	—	—	0.786	0.593	—	—	—
1976	—	—	—	—	—	—	0.751	0.547	—	—	—
1977	—	—	—	—	—	—	0.713	0.488	—	—	—
1978	—	—	—	—	—	—	0.654	0.464	—	—	—
1979	—	—	0.287	—	—	—	0.634	0.433	0.659	—	—
1980	—	—	—	0.356	—	0.257	0.631	0.411	0.650	—	—
1981	—	—	—	0.351	0.406	0.255	0.613	0.386	0.641	—	—
1982	—	—	—	0.356	0.415	0.287	0.575	0.376	0.632	—	—
1983	—	—	—	—	0.376	0.271	—	—	—	—	—
1984	—	—	—	—	0.372	0.288	—	—	—	—	—

Percentage of births unplanned and unwanted[1]

	Aus-tralia	Aus-tria	Bel-gium	Can-ada	On-tario	Que-bec	Den-mark	Fin-land	France	F.R.G.	Greece
Survey year			1976	1984			1975	1977	1978		
Lifetime experience											
Unplanned											
All ages	—	—	31.5	—	—	—	24.5	36.6	37.1	—	—
< 25	—	—	46.0	—	—	—	32.6	35.9	36.1	—	—
25–34	—	—	29.7	—	—	—	24.7	31.1	34.9	—	—
35–44	—	—	30.8	—	—	—	23.5	41.6	39.3	—	—
Unwanted											
All ages	—	—	8.4	—	—	—	8.6	10.2	11.3	—	—
35–44	—	—	11.0	—	—	—	9.8	13.3	15.5	—	—

Age-specific abortion rates		Ireland	Italy	The Netherlands	New Zealand	Norway	Portugal	Spain	Sweden	Switzerland	United Kingdom	Great Britain	United States
Year	Age												
1982	15–19	—	—	5.5	13.2	21.1	—	—	19.6	—	—	16.9	44.4
	20–24	—	—	8.9	14.8	22.3	—	—	27.6	—	—	18.0	51.2
	25–29	—	—	7.7	10.2	15.7	—	—	21.5	—	—	12.8	31.5
	30–34	—	—	6.5	7.3	13.9	—	—	18.7	—	—	9.7	17.7
	35–39	—	—	4.9	4.6	11.7	—	—	16.0	—	—	7.5	9.3
	40–44	—	—	2.3	2.2	6.0	—	—	9.0	—	—	3.2	3.0
	45–49	—	—	0.3	0.3	0.8	—	—	1.3	—	—	0.4	0.3
1983	15–19	—	—	—	—	20.8	—	—	17.9	—	—	—	45.2
	20–24	—	—	—	—	23.1	—	—	26.2	—	—	—	51.2
	25–29	—	—	—	—	16.2	—	—	20.7	—	—	—	31.1
	30–34	—	—	—	—	13.8	—	—	18.2	—	—	—	17.8
	35–39	—	—	—	—	10.7	—	—	15.3	—	—	—	9.6
	40–44	—	—	—	—	5.9	—	—	8.3	—	—	—	2.9
	45–49	—	—	—	—	0.8	—	—	1.2	—	—	—	0.3
1984	15–19	—	—	—	—	—	—	—	—	—	—	—	—
	20–24	—	—	—	—	—	—	—	—	—	—	—	—
	25–29	—	—	—	—	—	—	—	—	—	—	—	—
	30–34	—	—	—	—	—	—	—	—	—	—	—	—
	35–39	—	—	—	—	—	—	—	—	—	—	—	—
	40–44	—	—	—	—	—	—	—	—	—	—	—	—
	45–49	—	—	—	—	—	—	—	—	—	—	—	—

Total abortion rates

Year	Ireland	Italy	The Netherlands	New Zealand	Norway	Portugal	Spain	Sweden	Switzerland	United Kingdom	Great Britain	United States
1975	—	—	—	—	—	—	—	0.593	—	—	0.316	0.575
1976	—	—	—	0.194	0.545	—	—	0.588	—	—	0.300	0.638
1977	—	—	—	0.221	0.565	—	—	0.568	—	—	0.298	0.698
1978	—	—	0.152	0.088	0.530	—	—	0.572	—	—	0.319	0.732
1979	—	—	0.164	0.150	0.510	—	—	0.618	—	—	0.339	0.764
1980	—	—	0.193	0.234	0.471	—	—	0.615	—	—	0.356	0.782
1981	0.149	—	0.188	0.264	0.474	—	—	0.579	—	—	0.348	0.789
1982	—	—	0.180	0.263	0.457	—	—	0.569	—	—	0.342	0.787
1983	—	—	—	—	0.457	—	—	0.540	—	—	—	0.790
1984	—	—	—	—	—	—	—	—	—	—	—	—
1985	—	—	—	—	—	—	—	—	—	—	—	—

Percentage of births unplanned and unwanted[2]

Survey year	Ireland	Italy	The Netherlands 1982	New Zealand	Norway	Portugal	Spain 1977	Sweden 1981	Switzerland	United Kingdom	Great Britain 1976	United States 1982
Lifetime experience												
Unplanned												
All ages	—	—	—	—	—	—	9.5	—	—	—	—	—
< 25	—	—	—	—	—	—	9.9	—	—	—	—	—
25–34	—	—	—	—	—	—	9.9	—	—	—	—	—
35–44	—	—	—	—	—	—	9.0	—	—	—	—	—
Unwanted												
All ages	—	—	—	—	—	—	2.3	—	—	—	—	—
35–44	—	—	—	—	—	—	3.0	—	—	—	—	—

Percentage of births unplanned and unwanted, *cont.*[1]

	Aus-tralia	Aus-tria	Bel-gium	Can-ada	On-tario	Que-bec	Den-mark	Fin-land	France	F.R.G.	Greece
Experience of last five years											
Unplanned											
All ages	—	—	—	25.9	25.7	21.1	—	—	—	—	—
< 25	—	—	—	33.2	32.7	27.5	—	—	—	—	—
25–34	—	—	—	23.6	23.9	19.1	—	—	—	—	—
35–44	—	—	—	28.7	26.7	26.2	—	—	—	—	—
Unwanted											
All ages	—	—	—	7.8	8.0	4.7	—	—	—	—	—
35–44	—	—	—	13.1	11.2	6.5	—	—	—	—	—
Percentage of women practicing contraception[1][3]											
Survey year	1981	1982	1984	1984	1984	1975	1977	1978			1983
All ages											
Age limits	—	—	20–44	18–44	18–44	18–44	18–44	18–44	20–44	—	15–44
Marital status[5]	—	—	T	T	T	T	CM1	CM1	T	—	CM
Sterilization	—	—	11.5	30.4	29.9	30.0	—	4.3	4.1	—	1.7
Pill	—	—	32.0	21.5	21.6	24.6	21.4	10.8	27.9	—	2.0
IUD	—	—	7.4	6.3	5.9	6.3	8.5	26.6	8.9	—	2.3
Condom	—	—	5.5	6.3	6.8	5.2	24.1	29.7	5.2	—	27.8
All methods	—	—	71.1	69.0	68.8	71.3	—	75.5	72.2	—	77.9
Ages 20–29[6]											
Marital status	—	CM1	T	CMC	CMC	CMC	CMC	CM1	CM1	—	CM
Sterilization	—	1.3	2.2	13.2	13.9	11.5	—	0.6	0.7	—	0.7
Pill	—	40.2	41.8	32.3	32.1	35.4	23.9	14.8	34.9	—	3.2
IUD	—	8.4	7.3	7.6	6.5	8.8	8.9	26.4	8.9	—	2.2
Condom	—	4.0	4.7	9.6	9.4	11.2	24.3	30.2	5.4	—	25.1
All methods	—	71.3	64.4	68.8	69.4	72.8	—	74.0	72.6	—	76.8
Ages 35–44											
Marital status	—	—	T	CMC	CMC	CMC	CMC	CM1	CM1	—	CM
Sterilization	—	—	21.7	62.4	59.1	65.2	—	8.3	6.8	—	2.4
Pill	—	—	19.0	2.9	3.2	4.5	17.3	6.5	15.5	—	1.0
IUD	—	—	6.1	4.5	4.8	4.2	6.7	23.1	8.9	—	1.8
Condom	—	—	6.2	5.5	6.3	4.8	23.4	29.4	6.1	—	27.2
All methods	—	—	75.5	79.7	77.2	82.9	—	74.2	79.5	—	75.4
Overall assessment of contraceptive use											
Pattern of con-traceptive use[7]	2	2	2	1	—	—	2	3	2	2	5

1. Data for Belgium represent the Flemish part of the country only.

2. Data for the Netherlands represent ages 35–37 only.

3. Data for Greece represent the greater Athens area only; data for Great Britain include reporting of multiple methods currently used.

4. Data for Norway include reporting of multiple methods used in the four weeks before the survey.

5. Marital status codes: T = total; EM = ever married; CM = currently married; CMC = currently married including cohabiting; CM1 = currently married and in first marriage.

Percentage of births unplanned and unwanted, *cont.*[2]

	Ire-land	Italy	The Nether-lands	New Zea-land	Nor-way	Por-tugal	Spain	Swe-den	Swit-zer-land	United King-dom	Great Bri-tain	United States
Experience of last five years												
Unplanned												
All ages	—	—	6.7	—	—	—	—	14.0	—	—	19.8	30.3
< 25	—	—	12.7	—	—	—	—	29.4	—	—	27.1	45.1
25–34	—	—	5.3	—	—	—	—	11.3	—	—	15.6	24.5
35–44	—	—	11.8	—	—	—	—		—	—	30.3	26.1
Unwanted												
All ages	—	—	—	—	—	—	—	3.1	—	—	—	7.4
35–44	—	—	—	—	—	—	—	4.9	—	—	—	16.6
Percentage of women practicing contraception												
Survey year	1979	1982			1977	1980	1985	1981	1980		1983	1982
All ages[4]												
Age limits	—	18–44	18–37	—	18–44	15–49	18–49	20–44	—	—	18–44	15–44
Marital status[5]	—	CM1	T	—	T	EM	T	T	—	—	T	T
Sterilization	—	0.1	13.2	—	—	1.0	3.3	2.3	—	—	21.6	17.8
Pill	—	13.6	38.1	—	13.5	19.4	12.4	19.7	—	—	28.4	15.6
IUD	—	2.4	7.8	—	23.0	3.3	4.3	17.3	—	—	6.4	4.0
Condom	—	12.5	6.3	—	14.9	2.0	9.6	18.5	—	—	13.0	6.6
All methods	—	74.4	68.7	—	—	62.3	45.4	61.9	—	—	76.6	54.5
Ages 20–29[6]												
Marital status[6]	—	CM1	CMC	—	CM1	CM	T	CMC	CM1	—	CMC	CMC
Sterilization	—	0.5	5.6	—	1.2	0.8	0.6	0.3	8.7	—	3.9	13.3
Pill	—	17.4	51.6	—	19.2	25.9	19.9	29.8	32.0	—	47.3	28.0
IUD	—	2.2	9.2	—	32.0	5.4	3.8	16.1	10.9	—	5.5	5.8
Condom	—	11.6	7.2	—	15.6	6.5	9.9	19.1	7.7	—	9.6	7.6
All methods	—	72.0	76.3	—	73.2	72.7	43.9	69.1	68.0	—	72.0	67.8
Ages 35–44												
Marital status[2]	—	CM1	CMC	—	CM1	CM	T	CMC	—	—	T	CMC
Sterilization	—	0.6	21.4	—	14.0	1.1	6.1	4.6	—	—	40.2	38.3
Pill	—	9.0	18.4	—	8.1	14.0	7.5	13.3	—	—	7.5	2.2
IUD	—	1.4	7.3	—	21.2	3.6	5.1	21.4	—	—	6.7	4.0
Condom	—	13.1	7.0	—	18.8	6.8	11.4	26.8	—	—	16.3	8.1
All methods	—	75.1	78.3	—	76.5	68.5	53.8	73.1	—	—	76.4	62.7
Overall assessment of contraceptive use												
Pattern of con-traceptive use[7]	4	4	2	2	3	4	4	2	1	—	2	1

6. Data for Austria represent approximately ages 23–33; data for Portugal represent ages 25–34; data for Switzerland represent ages 20–31; data for Great Britain represent ages 18–29.

7. Codes are as follows:

1 = > 30% effective methods, main method is sterilization
2 = > 30% effective methods, main method is pill
3 = > 30% effective methods, main method is IUD
4 =   10–30% effective methods
5 = < 10% effective methods

Categorical Data and Codebook

DATA

	Aus-tralia	Aus-tria	Bel-gium	Can-ada	On-tario	Que-bec	Den-mark	Fin-land	France	F.R.G.	Greece
Laws and policies											
Overall family planning policy	2	1	2	1	—	—	1	1	1	2	1
Advertising of contraceptive methods	9	3	9	9	—	—	3	3	1	2	9
Abortion laws	3	2	4	2	—	—	2	2	2	3	3
Recognition of target groups	3	2	1	3	—	—	4	2	2	3	1
Teaching of contraceptive methods in school	3	2	3	3	—	—	1	1	2	2	3
Sterilization laws	1	1	2	2	—	—	1	1	2	1	3
Service delivery											
Main source of contraceptive services	1	1	2	1	1	1	1	3	1	2	2
Combination of main service sources	3	1	9	3	3	3	3	5	1	1	6
Method recommended for termination of childbearing	2	1	3	2	2	2	1	1	1	3	1
Special efforts to assist:											
Young people	2	5	9	1	—	—	5	5	5	9	9
Low-income people	3	9	9	3	—	—	9	9	9	2	9
Immigrants	3	9	9	9	—	—	4	9	9	5	9
Contraceptive access for unmarried minors	2	2	1	1	—	—	1	3	3	3	1

245

246

	Aus-tralia	Aus-tria	Bel-gium	Can-ada	On-tario	Que-bec	Den-mark	Fin-land	France	F.R.G.	Greece
Payment for female sterilization in hospital	1	3	2	1	1	1	1	1	2	1	4
Payment to obtain pill prescription	2	3	2	1	1	2	1	1	2	1	3
Payment for pill supplies	3	3	3	3	3	3	3	3	2	3	3
Variation in access to sterilization	3	2	2	3	1	4	4	4	2	1	9
Reasons for variation in access to sterilization	2	2	2	1	1	4	4	4	2	1	9
Variation in access to the pill	4	4	4	3	1	4	4	4	1	4	1
Sterilization requirements	1	2	1	1	1	1	2	3	3	1	9
Pelvic examination before pill prescription	1	1	1	1	1	1	1	1	1	1	1
Information delivery											
Overall information effort	3	3	3	3	3	2	4	3	3	2	3
Special information efforts for target groups	3	2	9	1	—	—	2	2	2	3	9
Proportion of female students receiving instruction on contraceptive methods	2	0	1	2	—	—	4	4	3	3	1
Advertising of condoms	1	1	2	2	2	2	1	1	2	1	2

	Ire-land	Italy	The Nether-lands	New Zea-land	Nor-way	Por-tugal	Spain	Swe-den	Swit-zer-land	United King-dom	Great Bri-tain	United States
Laws and policies												
Overall family planning policy	3	2	2	2	1	1	2	1	2	2	—	1
Advertising of contraceptive methods	1	2	9	3	9	3	3	3	9	3	—	2
Abortion laws	4	2	1	3	2	3	3	1	1	2	—	1
Recognition of target groups	1	1	4	2	2	2	2	2	1	2	—	3
Teaching of contraceptive methods in school	3	4	3	4	2	3	2	1	3		—	3
Sterilization laws	2	2	2	1	1	2	1	1	2	1	—	1

	Ireland	Italy	The Netherlands	New Zealand	Norway	Portugal	Spain	Sweden	Switzerland	United Kingdom	Great Britain	United States
Service delivery												
Main source of contraceptive services	1	2	1	1	1	3	2	3	2	1	—	2
Combination of main service sources	3	4	2	3	3	4	4	5	6	3	—	6
Method recommended for termination of childbearing	3	1	2	4	1	3	1	3	4	3	—	4
Special efforts to assist:												
Young people	9	9	4	4	3	3	5	1	9	1	—	2
Low-income people	9	9	9	9	9	9	9	9	9	9	—	1
Immigrants	9	9	4	9	9	9	9	9	9	9	—	1
Contraceptive access for unmarried minors	2	2	3	3	3	1	1	3	2	0	—	2
Payment for female sterilization in hospital	3	4	1	1	1	1	1	1	3	1	—	2
Payment to obtain pill prescription	3	1	1	3	2	1	3	1	1	1	—	3
Payment for pill supplies	3	2	1	1	3	1	3	2	3	1	—	3
Variation in access to sterilization	1	9	4	1	4	2	1	4	2	2	—	3
Reasons for variation in access to sterilization	3	9	4	1	4	1	2	4	3	2	—	1
Variation in access to the pill	2	4	4	4	4	4	2	4	2	4	—	4
Sterilization requirements	2	9	1	1	2	2	3	2	2	2	—	1
Pelvic examination before pill prescription	2	1	1	2	1	1	2	2	1	2	—	1
Information delivery												
Overall information effort	2	2	4	3	3	3	2	3	3	4	—	2
Special information efforts for target groups	9	9	1	3	2	3	2	2	9	2	—	1
Proportion of female students receiving instruction on contraceptive methods	0	1	2	2	3	1	1	4	4	0	2	2
Advertising of condoms	2	1	1	1	1	1	1	1	1	1	—	2

CODEBOOK

Variable Label

Laws and Policies
Overall family planning policy
    1 = direct support
    2 = indirect support
    3 = no support
Advertising of contraceptive methods
    1 = not permitted
    2 = permitted for nonprescription methods
    3 = permitted for any method
    9 = insufficient information
Abortion laws
    1 = minimum restrictions
    2 = some restrictions
    3 = substantial restrictions
    4 = illegal
Recognition of target groups
    1 = none
    2 = young people only
    3 = low-income people with or without others
    4 = other combinations of groups
Teaching of contraceptive methods in school
    1 = always done
    2 = officially encouraged, but not always done
    3 = no uniform policy, up to the individual school or school district
    4 = officially discouraged, but not prohibited
Sterilization laws
    1 = legal
    2 = not illegal but not specifically legalized
    3 = illegal

Service Delivery
Main source of contraceptive services
    1 = family physician
    2 = specialist
    3 = clinic
Combination of main service sources
    1 = family physician and specialist
    2 = family physician
    3 = family physician and clinic
    4 = specialist and clinic
    5 = clinic only
    6 = specialist only
    9 = insufficient information

Method recommended for termination of childbearing
    1 = IUD
    2 = sterilization, of self or partner
    3 = pill
    4 = pill or sterilization
Special efforts to assist young people
    1 = added clinics and other efforts except cost
    2 = added clinics and reduced cost
    3 = added clinics only
    4 = special training or outreach only
    5 = no special service efforts
    9 = no recognition of young people
Special efforts to assist immigrants
    1 = special clinics and special counseling
    2 = special training and special counseling
    3 = reduced cost and special counseling
    4 = special counseling only
    5 = no special service efforts
    9 = no recognition of immigrants
Special efforts to assist low-income people
    1 = reduced cost and other efforts
    2 = reduced cost only
    3 = no special service efforts
    9 = no recognition of low-income people
Contraceptive access for unmarried minors
    0 = data missing
    1 = most restrictive
    2 = some restrictions
    3 = no restrictions
Payment for female sterilization in hospital
    1 = service is free or only nominal payment is required
    2 = woman pays but is reimbursed
    3 = woman bears most or all of the cost
    4 = procedure is illegal or unavailable
Payment to obtain pill prescription (at main family planning source)
    1 = service is free or only nominal payment is required
    2 = woman pays but is reimbursed
    3 = woman bears most or all of cost
Payment for pill supplies
    1 = service is free or nominal payment is required
    2 = woman pays but is reimbursed
    3 = woman bears most or all of the cost
Payment for male sterilization
    1 = service is free or only nominal payment is required
    2 = man pays but is reimbursed
    3 = man bears most or all of the cost
    4 = procedure is illegal or unavailable
    9 = insufficient information

Variation in access to sterilization
    1 = urban/rural variation
    2 = regional variation
    3 = both urban/rural and regional variation
    4 = not much variation
    9 = procedure illegal or unavailable
Reasons for variation in access to sterilization
    1 = sources not conveniently located
    2 = negative attitudes of service personnel and/or local officials
    3 = negative public opinion
    4 = little variation
    9 = procedure is illegal or unavailable
Variation in access to the pill
    1 = urban/rural variation
    2 = regional variation
    3 = both urban/rural and regional variation
    4 = not much variation
Sterilization requirements
    1 = no requirements
    2 = age requirements over 25 and under 30 and/or husband's consent
    3 = age requirements 30 or more and/or number of children requirement
    9 = procedure illegal or unavailable
Pelvic examinations before pill prescription
    1 = regularly performed
    2 = not regularly performed

Information Delivery
Overall information effort (government and nongovernment)
    1 = no effort
    2 = weak effort
    3 = moderate effort
    4 = strong effort
Special information efforts for target groups
    1 = special information effort for more than one group
    2 = special information effort for one group
    3 = no special information effort
    9 = no recognition of target groups
Proportion of female students receiving instruction in contraceptive methods
    0 = data missing
    1 = less than one-third
    2 = between one-third and two-thirds
    3 = between two-thirds and nine-tenths
    4 = greater than nine-tenths
Advertising (practice) of condoms
    1 = commonly advertised
    2 = not commonly advertised

Country Survey Questionnaire
The Alan Guttmacher Institute, 1986

QUESTIONNAIRE ON FAMILY PLANNING SERVICES

This questionnaire covers topics that are of central importance to the international study and on which little information is otherwise available. It is divided into three sections: (A) contraceptive services, (B) methods of contraception, and (C) special activities. Although the last section is very brief, the response will receive particular attention.

Almost all of the questions can be answered simply by circling the appropriate option. You are invited to add comments or qualifications if you wish (feel free to use your own language). Your cooperation in completing the questionnaire without delay will be very much appreciated. Please return it to us by *air mail* in the envelope provided.

A.   Contraceptive Services

This section contains questions on the main features of the family planning
services in your country, including sources of information and education. The
focus is on the provision of methods of contraception and contraceptive sterilization, not abortion.

In questions A.1 to A.6, a single main source of contraceptive services
should be described, if possible. Use the second column *only* if there is no one
obvious choice—for example, if a second type of source serves as many as one-
third of contraceptive users.

		Main source	*Alternative main source*
A.1	Where is the average person most likely to go to obtain contraceptive services? (Please circle one option.)		
	• Family physician	1	1
	• Specialist physician	2	2
	• Clinic	3	3
	• Hospital	4	4
	• Pharmacy	5	5
	• Other (specify): _____	6	6
	Questions A.2 to A.6 refer specifically to the type of place identified in question A.1.		
A.2	Is this the same facility to which a person would go for routine health care? (Circle one option.)		
	• Yes	1	1
	• No	2	2
A.3	Is this contraceptive service operated by the government? (Circle one option.)		
	• Yes, directly	1	1
	• No, but it is subsidized or funded by the government	2	2
	• No, the government is not involved	3	3
	• Other (explain): _____	4	4
A.4	What personnel typically provide contraceptive services there? (Circle more than one option if applicable.)		
	• Male physician	1	1
	• Female physician	2	2
	• Other male professional (pharmacist, etc.)	3	3

	Main source	*Alternative main source*
• Other female professional (midwife, nurse, pharmacist, etc.)	4	4
• Nonprofessional person	5	5

A.5 What method of contraception would normally be recommended to a woman aged 20 who wanted to postpone childbearing, assuming that she herself had no strong preference and no method was medically contraindicated? (Circle no more than one option, if possible.)

• Pill	1	1
• Injection	2	2
• IUD	3	3
• Diaphragm	4	4
• Foam, jelly, suppository	5	5
• Condom	6	6
• Withdrawal	7	7
• Rhythm (periodic abstinence)	8	8
• Other (specify): _____	9	9

A.6 What method of contraception would normally be recommended to a woman aged 32 who wanted no more children, assuming that she herself had no strong preference and no method was medically contraindicated? (Circle no more than one option, if possible.)

• Pill	1	1
• Injection	2	2
• IUD	3	3
• Diaphragm	4	4
• Foam, jelly, suppository	5	5
• Condom	6	6
• Withdrawal	7	7
• Rhythm (periodic abstinence)	8	8
• Sterilization operation for herself	9	9
• Sterilization operation for her partner	10	10
• Other (specify): _____	11	11

A.7 Considering the existing services as a whole, are the contraceptive needs of most of the population well taken care of?

• Yes, very well	1
• Yes, fairly well	2
• No, not very well at all	3

A.8   Is advertising of contraceptive services and methods commonly carried in the following media? (Please circle at least one option for each service or method.)

	Services		Methods	
	Clinic services	Physician's services	Pill	Condom
• Yes, on radio and television	1	1	1	1
• Yes, in popular magazines and newspapers	2	2	2	2
• Yes, on billboards	3	3	3	3
• No, this method or service is not advertised	4	4	4	4
• No, this method or service is not available	5	5	5	5

A.9   How much effort is made to provide public information and education concerning contraceptive services by the government and by nongovernmental organizations? (Please circle one option in each column.)

	Government	Nongovernmental organizations
• Strong effort	1	1
• Moderate effort	2	2
• Weak effort	3	3
• No effort	4	4

B.   Methods of Contraception

Three of the most important methods of contraception that must be obtained from some appropriate facility are covered in this section: the pill (oral contraceptive), condom and surgical sterilization (female and male).

	Family physician	Specialist physician	Clinic	Hospital	Pharmacy	Other (specify): _____ _____	Method not available
B.1 Where can a prescription for the pill be obtained? (Circle the numbers under all usual sources.)	1	2	3	4	xxxx	6	7
B.1a Does the woman typically pay to obtain a prescription for the pill— including the attendant medical examination, if any? (Please an-							

	Family physician	Specialist physician	Clinic	Hospital	Pharmacy	Other (specify): _____ _____	Method not available
swer separately for each source circled in question B.1.)							
• Service is free or only nominal payment is required	1	1	1	1	xxxx	1	
• Woman pays but is reimbursed entirely or largely by insurance	2	2	2	2	xxxx	2	
• Woman bears most or all of the cost	3	3	3	3	xxxx	3	
B.2 Where can pill supplies be obtained? (Circle the numbers under all usual sources.)	1	2	3	4	5	6	7
B.2a Does the woman typically pay for pill supplies? (Please answer separately for each source circled in question B.2.)							
• Supplies are free or only nominal payment is required	1	1	1	1	1	1	
• Woman pays but is reimbursed entirely or largely by insurance	2	2	2	2	2	2	
• Woman bears most or all of the cost	3	3	3	3	3	3	
B.3 Where can condoms be obtained? (Circle the numbers under all usual sources.)	1	2	3	4	5	6	7

	Family physician	Specialist physician	Clinic	Hospital	Pharmacy	Other (specify): _____ _____	Method not available
B.3a Does the customer typically pay for condoms? (Please answer separately for each source circled in question B.3.)							
• Condoms are free or only nominal payment is required	1	1	1	1	1	1	
• Customer pays but is reimbursed entirely or largely by insurance	2	2	2	2	2	2	
• Customer bears most or all of the cost	3	3	3	3	3	3	
B.4 Where can a woman go to arrange for an operation to prevent her from becoming pregnant? (Circle the numbers under all usual sources.)	1	2	3	4	xxxx	6	7
B.4a Does the woman typically pay to obtain a sterilization operation? (Please answer separately for each source circled in question B.4.)							
• Service is free or only nominal payment is required	1	1	1	1	xxxx	1	
• Woman pays but is reimbursed entirely or largely by insurance	2	2	2	2	xxxx	2	

	Family physician	Specialist physician	Clinic	Hospital	Pharmacy	Other (specify): ____ ____	Method not available
• Woman bears most or all of the cost	3	3	3	3	xxxx	3	
B.5 Where can a man obtain an operation to prevent him from making his partner pregnant? (Circle the numbers under all usual sources.)	1	2	3	4	xxxx	6	7
B.5a Does the man typically pay to obtain a sterilization operation? (Please answer separately for each source circled in question B.5.)							
• Service is free or only nominal payment is required	1	1	1	1	xxxx	1	
• Man pays but is reimbursed entirely or largely by insurance	2	2	2	2	xxxx	2	
• Man bears most or all of the cost	3	3	3	3	xxxx	3	

	Pill	Condom	Female sterilization	Male sterilization
B.6 Does the ease with which contraceptive methods can be obtained vary according to where the couple resides? (Please circle at least one option for each method.)				
• Yes, the method is less available in small towns and rural areas than in cities	1	1	1	1
• Yes, the method is less available in some regions of the country than in others	2	2	2	2
• No, the availability of the method does not vary very much	3	3	3	3

	Female	*Male*
Pill Condom sterilization sterilization		

B.6a If the answer to question B.6
indicates that a given method is
more difficult to obtain in certain
places, why is this so? (Please
answer separately for each method
for which options 1 or 2 were
selected in question B.6, circling as
many options as apply.)

	Pill	Condom	Female sterilization	Male sterilization
• Sources for the method are not located conveniently	1	1	1	1
• Services are inconvenient in terms of opening hours, time spent waiting for attention, etc.	2	2	2	2
• Negative attitudes of service personnel or administrators	3	3	3	3
• Negative attitudes of local officials	4	4	4	4
• Negative public opinion	5	5	5	5
• Lack of publicity	6	6	6	6
• Lack of demand for the method	7	7	7	7
• Other (specify): _____	8	8	8	8

B.7 Is it necessary, in practice if not by law, for a woman to have a pelvic
examination in order to obtain a prescription for the pill? (Circle one
option.)

- Yes, a pelvic examination is
  regularly done before the pill is
  prescribed   1
- No, but a pelvic exam is regularly
  done within a few months of
  initiation of pill use   2
- No, a pelvic examination is not
  necessary   3

B.8 Is it necessary, in practice if not by law, for a woman to meet certain
requirements before she can obtain a sterilization operation? (Circle one
option, filling in the blanks if applicable.)

- Yes, a woman must be at least
  ____ years old to obtain a
  sterilization operation   1
- Yes, a woman must have at least
  ____ children to obtain a
  sterilization operation   2
- Yes, a woman must have the
  consent of her husband to obtain
  a sterilization operation   3
- No, there are no special
  requirements   4

C. Special Activities

Even when the family planning needs of most couples are met reasonably well, there may be concern about certain segments of the population where problems remain. This last section addresses this issue.

	Immigrants	Low-income families	Rural residents	Young people	Other (specify): _____ _____	None
C.1 Has the government identified any of the population subgroups listed to the right as needing special assistance with contraceptive services? (Circle the numbers under all groups so recognized.)	1	2	3	4	5	6
C.2 What kinds of efforts are made to meet the special needs of these groups? These may be activities carried out directly by the government or through nongovernmental organizations. (Please answer separately for each subgroup identified in question C.1, circling as many options as apply.)						
• Additional clinics or special clinics are provided	1	1	1	1	1	
• Regular clinics are open during additional hours or special hours	2	2	2	2	2	
• Regular clinic personnel have been given special training	3	3	3	3	3	
• Special counseling is available	4	4	4	4	4	
• Outreach workers actively seek contact with subgroup members	5	5	5	5	5	
• Additional or special effort is made with respect to public information and education	6	6	6	6	6	
• Oral and/or written communication in other languages is available	7	7	7	7	7	

	Immigrants	Low-income families	Rural residents	Young people	Other (specify): _____ _____	None
• Cost of service is reduced	8	8	8	8	8	
• Family planning is one component in a broad program designed to meet the overall health and welfare needs of this subgroup	9	9	9	9	9	
• Other (describe): _____ _____	10	10	10	10	10	
• Other (describe): _____ _____	11	11	11	11	11	
• No special effort is being made currently	12	12	12	12	12	

Comments:

References

Aday, Lu Ann, and R. M. Anderson. 1984. "The National Profile of Access to Medical Care: Where Do We Stand?" *American Journal of Public Health* 74/12: 1331–39.

The Alan Guttmacher Institute (AGI). 1984a. *Organized Family Planning Services in the United States, 1981–1983*. New York: AGI.

———. 1984b. "Private Physician Family Planning Services in the U.S." Report to the U.S. Department of Health and Human Services, Grant FPR 0030–01–0.

———. 1984c. "Final Report on a Study of the Provision of Voluntary Sterilization Services to U.S. Men and Women by Physicians in Private Practice" New York: AGI.

———. 1987. *Blessed Events and the Bottom Line*. New York: AGI. New York.

Aletta Jacobshuis (Rutgers Stichting). 1986. *Antikonseptiespreekuren voor turkse en marokkaanse vrouwen*. Amsterdam.

Allen, I. 1976. *Family Planning Services in the Home*, 18–27. London: PEP.

———. 1981. *Family Planning, Sterilisation and Abortion Services*. London: Policy Studies Institute.

———. 1985. *Counselling Services For Sterilisation, Vasectomy and Termination of Pregnancy*. London: Policy Studies Institute.

———. 1987. *Education in Sex and Personal Relationships*. Longmead: Blackmore Press.

The American College of Obstetricians and Gynecologists (ACOG). 1976. "Oral Contraception." ACOG Technical Bulletin, no. 41.

———. 1987a. "Premium Ranges of Professional Liability Insurance for Obstetrician-Gynecologists in the United States." Memorandum. July.

———. 1987b. "Oral Contraception." ACOG Technical Bulletin, no. 106.

American Health Consultants. 1987. "Results and Analysis: 1987 Oral Contraceptive Survey." *Contraceptive Technology Update*, 8/9:109–24.

American Hospital Association (AHA). 1986. *Hospital Statistics*. Chicago: AHA.

Arnett, R. H., III, C. S. Cowell, L. M. Davidoff, and M. S. Freeland. 1985. "Health Spending Trends in the 1980s: Adjusting to Financial Incentive," *Health Care Financing Review*. 6/3.

Association of State and Territorial Health Officers (ASTHO) Foundation. 1985. *Public Health Agencies 1983*. Vol. 2. *Services and Activities*.

Atsma, W. 1987. Personal communication.

"Average of 63% Approve of Legal Abortions; No Change over 15 Years," 1987. *Family Planning Perspectives Digest* 19/5:221.

Bachrach, Christine A. 1984. "Contraceptive Practice among American Women, 1973–1982." *Family Planning Perspectives* 16/6:253–59.

———. 1987. "Cohabitation and Reproductive Behavior in the United States." *Demography* 24:623.

Berent, Jerzy. 1982. *Family Planning in Europe and USA in the 1970s*. World Fertility Survey. Comparative Studies, no. 20. ECE analyses of WFS surveys in Europe and the U.S.A.

Berent, Jerzy, E. F. Jones, and M. K. Siddiqui. 1982. *Basic Characteristics, Sample Designs and Questionnaires*. World Fertility Survey. Comparative Studies, no. 18. ECE analyses of WFS surveys in Europe and the U.S.A.

Biesta, H. 1982. *Structure and Functioning of the Health Care System in the Netherlands*, Leidschendam: Ministry of Welfare, Health and Cultural Affairs.

Birth Control Trust. 1981. *Sterilisation and the National Health Service*. London: Family Planning Association.

———. 1984. *Men, Sex and Contraception*. London: Family Planning Association.

Boldt, Edward D., L. W. Roberts, and A. H. Latif. 1982. "The Provision of Birth Control Services to Unwed Minors: A National Survey of Physician Attitudes and Practices." *Canadian Journal of Public Health* 73 (November–December):392–95.

Bone, Margaret. 1978. *The Family Planning Services: Changes and Effects*. Office of Population Censuses and Surveys. Social Survey Division. London: HMSO.

Boulard, Richard, and D. DuFour. 1983. "La politique de repartition géographique des effectifs médicaux au Québec," *Cahiers québecois de demographie* 12, no. 83.

Braam, W., and A. Leemhuis. 1978. "100 vragen over andere voorbehoed middelen dan de pil." *Libelle/Spectrum Samen-reeks* no. 9.

———. 1983. "100 vragen over de pil," *Libelle Samen-reeks*, no. 1.

"British Health Service: 40 Years Later." 1988. *American Medical News* (September 2):25.

British Medical Association (BMA). 1987. Personal communication.

British Medical Journal. 1986a. "Inequitable and Anomalous Prescription Charges Should Be Reviewed." Vol. 292 (March):709.

———. 1986b. "Public Expenditure on the NHS—Recent Trends and Future Problems." Vol. 293 (September):638.

Brodie, Nicki. 1987. Personal communication from the Gallup Poll of Canada.

Brook Advisory Centres. 1986a. "Teenage Pregnancy, 1969–1984." C8.3/86.

———. 1986b. *Annual Report, 1985/86*.

Bureau of Community Health Services (BCHS). 1981 adopted. *Program Guidelines for Project Grants for Family Planning Services.* U.S. Department of Health and Human Services. Public Health Service.

Cardy, G. 1984. "Why We Still Need Family Planning Clinics." *British Journal of Family Planning* 10/1:22–23.

Central Bureau of Statistics (CBS). 1984. *Vademecum gezondheidsstatistiek nederland* (Compendium of health statistics of the Netherlands). Ministry of Welfare, Health and Cultural Affairs. Voorburg/Hearlen.

Central Statistical Office. 1985. *Social Trends,* no. 15. London: HMSO.

Chamie, Mary, S. Eisman, J. D. Forrest, M. T. Orr, and A. Torres. 1982. "Factors Affecting Adolescents' Use of Family Planning Clinics," *Family Planning Perspectives* 14/3:126–39.

Christopher, E., L. A. Kellaher, and A. von Koch. 1980. *A Survey of the Haringey Domiciliary Family Planning Service, 1968–1975.* Research Project No. 3. London: Polytechnic of North London.

Cliquet, R. L., R. Debusschere, F. Deven (M.M.V.), G. Delmotte, C. van Maele, and S. Wijewickrema. 1983. *Gezinsvorming in Vlaanderen: Resultaten van de nationale enquete gezinsontwikkeling 1975–1976 (NEGO-III).* C.B.G.S. Rapport 58/1983. Ministerie van de Vlaamse Gemeenschap, Centrum voor Bevolkings- en Gezinsstudien.

Cliquet, R. L. and H. G. Moors. 1984. "De anticonceptionele revolutie in Vlaanderen en Nederland." In D. J. van de Kaa and R. Lesthaeghe, eds., *Bevolking: Groei en krimp,* 59–69. Van Loghum Slaterus.

Cliquet, R. L., and E. Lodewijckx. 1986. "The Contraceptive Transition in Flanders." *European Journal of Population* 2/1 (May):71–84.

Conway, Brenda, and M. A. Ridley. 1984. *Teen Users of Family Planning Clinics.* Ontario Ministry of Health, Public Health Branch.

Coulter, A. 1985. "Decision-Making and the Pill: The Consumer's View." *British Journal of Family Planning* 11:98–103.

Dawson, Deborah Ann. 1986. "The Effects of Sex Education on Adolescent Behavior." *Family Planning Perspectives* 18/4:162–70.

de Haan, J. 1986. "De doktersassistente: Delegeren van taken in een huisartpraktijk" (The *doktersassistente* [doctor's assistant]: Delegation of tasks in a general practice). In *Meditekst,* 118–22. Lelystad.

Department of Health and Social Security (DHSS), 1974. "Family Planning Service Memorandum of Guidance Health Service Circular." May.

———. 1984. *Handbook of Contraceptive Practice.*

———. 1986a. Unpublished update of fees specified in 1976 publication "Health Circular: Pay and Conditions of Service, Family Planning in Hospitals."

———. 1986b. "Summary of Information from Form SBL708: 1985" (November). Statistics and Research.

———. 1986c. "Summary of Information from Form SBL709: 1985" (November). Statistics and Research.

Dersjant, M., J. Huls, I. Menalda, and M. van Walraven. 1986. *Polikliniek voor geboortenregeling anti-conceptie middelen en methoden.* Leiden: Academisch Ziekenhuis.

Engberts, L. 1985. "Statistieken eerste lijn maatschappelijke dienstverlening; Clienten van consultatiebureaus voor geboorteregeling en sexualiteits-vragen 1983." *Soc-cult kwartber.* 2:50–71. CBS Publications.

Family Planning Information Service (FPIS). 1983. *Contraceptive Handbook.*

———. 1984. *Fact Sheet K.3.*

———. 1986a. *Fact Sheet B.3.*

———. 1986b. *Fact Sheet F.2.*

———. 1986c. *Fact Sheet C.3.*

———. 1986d. *Fact Sheet C.5.*

———. 1986e. *Fact Sheet C.6.*

———. 1986f. *Fact Sheet K.2.*

———. 1986g. *Fact Sheet K.4.*

Farrell, C. 1978. *My Mother Said.* London: Routledge & Kegan Paul.

Forrest, Jacqueline D. 1986. "The End of IUD Marketing in the United States: What It Means for American Women." *Family Planning Perspectives* 18/2:52–57.

———. 1987a. Unpublished tabulations from the 1982 National Survey of Family Growth.

———. 1987b. "American Women—A Sexual Profile" *Contemporary Ob/Gyn,* 29/4:75–82.

Forrest, Jacqueline D., and S. K. Henshaw. 1983. "What U.S. Women Think and Do about Contraception." *Family Planning Perspectives* 15/4:157–66.

———. 1987. "Harassment of U.S. Abortion Providers." *Family Planning Perspectives* 19/1:9–13.

Forrest, Jacqueline D., and R. Fordyce. 1988. "U.S. Women's Contraceptive Attitudes and Practice: How Have They Changed in the 1980s?" *Family Planning Perspectives* 20/3:112–18.

42 CFR. 1978. Section 441.250, Subpart F. November 8.

The Gallup Poll. 1985. *Gallup Report No. 237.* Princeton, N.J.

Gold, Rachel B. 1987. Personal communication.

Gold, Rachel B., and A. M. Kenney. 1985. "Paying for Maternity Care." *Family Planning Perspectives* 17/3:103–11.

Gold, Rachel B., and J. Macias. 1986. "Public Funding of Contraceptives, Sterilization and Abortion Services, 1985." *Family Planning Perspectives* 18/6: 259–63.

Grady, William R., M. D. Hayward, and J. Yagi. 1986. "Contraceptive Failure in the United States: Estimates from the 1982 National Survey of Family Growth." *Family Planning Perspectives* 18/5:200–09.

Hatcher, Robert A., and J. Trussell. 1981. "Contraceptive Use among Family Planning Clinic Personnel." *Family Planning Perspectives* 13/1:22–23.

Hayman, S. 1977. *Advertising and Contraceptives.* London: Birth Control Trust.

Health Insurance Association of America (HIAA). 1986. *A Profile of Group Major Medical Expense Insurance in the United States.* Washington.

Henshaw, Stanley K. 1987. "Characteristics of U.S. Women Having Abortions, 1982–1983." *Family Planning Perspectives* 19/1:5–8.

Henshaw, Stanley K., and S. Singh. 1986. "Sterilization Regret among U.S. Couples." *Family Planning Perspectives* 18/5:238–40.

Henshaw, Stanley K., J. D. Forrest, and J. Van Vort. 1987. "Abortion Services in the United States, 1984 and 1985." *Family Planning Perspectives* 19/2:63–70.

Ineichen, B. 1982. "Bristol Bookings Study." University of Bristol, Department of Child Health.

International Planned Parenthood Federation (IPPF). 1983. *Family Planning in Five Continents*. London: IPPF.

Johnson, Jeannette H. 1985. "Individual vs. Group Education in Family Planning Clinics." *Family Planning Perspectives* 17/6:255–59.

Jones, Elise F., J. R. Beniger, and C. F. Westoff. 1980. "Pill and IUD Discontinuation in the United States, 1970–1975: The Influence of the Media." *Family Planning Perspectives* 12/6:293–300.

Jones, Elise F., J. D. Forrest, N. Goldman, S. K. Henshaw, R. Lincoln, J. I. Rosoff, C. F. Westoff, and D. Wulf. 1985. "Teenage Pregnancy in Developed Countries: Determinants and Policy Implications." *Family Planning Perspectives* 17/2:53–63.

———. 1986. *Teenage Pregnancy in Industrialized Countries*. New Haven: Yale University Press.

Kalache, A., K. McPherson, K. Barltrop, and M. P. Vessey. 1983. "Oral Contraceptives and Breast Cancer." *British Journal of Hospital Practice* 83:278.

Kennedy, Diana. 1987. Personal communication.

Kenney, Asta M., J. D. Forrest, and A. Torres. 1982. "Storm over Washington: The Parental Notification Proposal" *Family Planning Perspectives* 14/4:185–97.

Ketting, Evert. 1983a. "Contraception and Fertility in the Netherlands." *Family Planning Perspectives* 15/1:19–24.

———. 1983b. "Female Sterilization in the Netherlands: The Silent Revolution." In D. van Lith, L. Keith, and E. van Hall, eds., *New Trends in Female Sterilization*, Chicago: Year Book Medical Publishers. 15–26.

———. 1987. Personal communication.

Ketting, Evert, and P. Leseman. 1986. *Abortus en anticonceptie, 1983–84*. Stimezo-Onderzoek. The Hague: Vereniging Stimezo Nederland.

Ketting, Evert, and P. van Praag. 1985. *Schwangerschaftsabbruch: Gesetz und Praxis im internationalen Vergleich*. Tübingen: Tübinger Reihe 5.

Ketting, Evert, and W. A. A. van Os. 1985. "IUD Use in Western Europe." In Zatuchni, G. J., A. Goldsmith, and J. J. Sciavra, eds., *Intra-Uterine Contraception: Advances and Future Prospects*, 37–45. Philadelphia: Harper and Row.

Kevern, J. 1981a. "General Practitioner's Contraceptive Services." Exeter, England: Institute of Population Studies.

———. 1981b. "The Provision and Use of Contraceptive Services in Three Study Areas." Exeter, England: Institute of Population Studies.

Kirchner, Merian. 1986. "Are Fees Breaking All Restraints?" *Medical Economics* 60/20:122–55.

Kisker, Ellen E. 1984a. Unpublished tabulations from 1981 survey of factors affecting adolescents' use of family planning clinics.

———. 1984b. "The Effectiveness of Family Planning Clinics in Serving Adolescents" *Family Planning Perspectives* 16/5:212–18.

Kols, Adrienne, W. Rinehart, P. T. Piotrow, L. Doucette, and W. F. Quillin.

1982. "Oral Contraceptives in the 1980s." *Population Reports*. Series A, no. 6. May–June.

Laing, W. A. 1982. *Family Planning: The Benefits and Costs*. London: Policy Studies Institute.

Landelijk Informatie Systeem Ziekenfondsen. 1984. *Jaarboek Lisz*.

Leathard, A. 1980. *The Fight for Family Planning*. London: Macmillan.

———. 1984a. "Inequalities in Preventive Health Care: Birth Control Provision in Britain." Paper presented to the annual conference of the Social Administration Association, University of Kent.

———. 1984b. "The Politics of Birth Control." Paper presented at the British Sociological Association's Medical Sociology Conference, Sheffield University.

———. 1985a. *Family Planning Services in England and Wales*. London: Family Planning Association.

———. 1985b. "Family Planning: Facilities Surveyed." *British Journal of Family Planning* 11:62–63.

Leridon, Henri. 1981. "Les facteurs de la fécondité dans les pays développés." In D. Whitelegge and J. Casterline, eds., *Record of the Proceedings of the World Fertility Survey Conference* 1:411–51 Paper presented at the World Fertility Survey Conference, London, July 7–11.

———. 1987. "La seconde révolution contraceptive: La régulation des naissances en France de 1950 à 1985, présentation d'un cahier de l'INED." *Population* 42/2:359–67.

Lieblum, Sandra, and M. Burnhill. 1987. "Women's Evaluation of Their Gynecological Care." Submitted for publication.

Liskin, Laurie, and W. Rinehart. 1985. "Minilaparotomy and Laparoscopy: Safe, Effective and Widely Used," *Population Reports*. Series C, no. 9. May.

Lodewijckx, E. 1985a. "Het profiel van het I.U.D.–gebruik in Vlaanderen, 1982–1983." Centrum voor Bevolkings- en Gezinsstudien, Werkdocument no. 17. Brussels: Ministerie van de Vlaamse Gemeenschap.

———. 1985b. "Het profiel van het pilgebruik in Vlaanderen, 1982– 1983." Centrum voor Bevolkings- en Gezinsstudien, Werkdocument no. 19. Brussels: Ministerie van de Vlaamse Gemeenschap.

———. 1986. "Het profiel van het gebruik van condoom en diafragma in Vlaanderen." Centrum voor Bevolkings- en Gezinsstudien, Werkdocument no. 28. Brussels: Ministerie van de Vlaamse Gemeenschap.

Lodewijckx, E., and K. Impens. 1987. "The Impact of the Contraceptive Transition on the Recent and Future Development of Fertility in Flanders." Paper contributed at the European Population Conference, Jyväskylä, Finland.

Louis Harris and Associates. 1987a. "Sexual Material on American Television, 1986–87."

———. 1987b. "Television Station Managers' Attitudes to Contraceptive Advertising and Selected Issues."

Marcil-Gratton, Nicole, and E. Lapierre-Adamcyk. 1987. "La mesure du degré de satisfaction des femmes à la suite d'une stérilisation contraceptive." Unpublished report. University of Montreal.

Marcil-Gratton, Nicole, E. Lapierre-Adamcyk, and C. Duchesne. 1985. *Les facteurs associés au regret à la suite de la ligature des trompes: Une enquête auprès des obstetriciens et gynécologues du Québec*. Montreal: University of Montreal.

Marsiglio, William, and F. L. Mott. 1986. "The Impact of Sex Education on Sexual Activity, Contraceptive Use and Premarital Pregnancy among American Teenagers." *Family Planning Perspectives* 18/4:151–62.

Medical Economics Company (MEC). 1988. *Red Book Update* 6/3. Oradell, N.J.

Meredith, Philip. 1982. *Pharmacy, Contraception and the Health Care Role*. Project Report no. 3. London: Family Planning Association.

Meredith, Philip, and L. Thomas. 1986. *Planned Parenthood in Europe: A Human Rights Perspective*. Prepared on behalf of the IPPF, Europe Region. London: Croom Helm.

Miller, C. Arden, and M. Moos. 1981. *Local Health Departments: Fifteen Case Studies*. Chapel Hill, N.C.: American Public Health Association.

Morley, A., R. Panton, R. Taylor, and M. Jepson. 1986. "Health in the High Street: An Evaluation of the First National Health Education Campaign in Community Pharmacies." Unpublished report. University of Aston, Birmingham, England.

National Association of Boards of Pharmacies (NABP). 1987. *Survey of Pharmacy Law, 1986/1987*. Chicago.

National Center for Health Statistics (NCHS). 1986. *Health, United States, 1986*, DHHS Publication no. (PHS) 87–1232. Washington: U.S. Government Printing Office.

"Netherlands Liberalizes Abortion Law after 10 Years of Wide Availability, Low Abortion Rates." 1981. *Family Planning Perspectives Digest* 13/3:151–52.

Nolte, Judith. 1984. "Sex Education in Canadian Classrooms." *Tellus* 13 (Sept. 30). Ottawa: Planned Parenthood Federation of Canada.

Norland, J. A. 1983. *Common-Law Unions in Canada: Age Composition*. Interim Report no. 4, Statistics Canada.

Office of Population Censuses and Surveys (OPCS) 1983. *General Household Survey, 1983*. London: HMSO.

———. 1986. "OPCS Monitor." Reference AB 86/3. London: HMSO.

Office of the Ministry of Welfare, Health and Cultural Affairs. 1987. Personal communication.

Ontario Ministry of Health. 1986. *Family Planning Summary: Ontario Annual Report, 1985*.

Organization for Economic Cooperation and Development (OECD). 1985. *Measuring Health Care, 1960–1983*. Paris.

Orr, M. Terry. 1982. "Sex Education and Contraceptive Education in U.S. Public High Schools." *Family Planning Perspectives* 14/2:304–13.

Orr, M. Terry, and J. D. Forrest. 1985. "The Availability of Reproductive Health Services from U.S. Private Physicians." *Family Planning Perspectives* 17/2:63–69.

Orr, M. Terry, J. D. Forrest, J. H. Johnson, and D. L. Tolman. 1985. "The Provision of Sterilization Services by Private Physicians." *Family Planning Perspectives* 17/5:216–20.

Ortho Pharmaceutical (Canada). 1985. *Ortho Oral Contraceptive Tablets*.

Ory, Howard W., J. D. Forrest, and R. Lincoln. 1983. *Making Choices: Evaluating the Health Risks and Benefits of Birth Control Methods*. New York: AGI.

Parade. 1987. "Female Pharmacists" *Parade Magazine* (October 25).

Planned Parenthood Federation of America (PPFA). 1987. *Manual of Medical Standards and Guidelines*, part one—S & G, section 3. Powell, Marion. 1987. "Report on Therapeutic Abortion Services in

Ontario: A Study Commissioned by the Ministry of Health." Unpublished report. Toronto.

Public Health Foundation. 1986. *Public Health Agencies 1984*. Vol. 4. *An Inventory of Programs and Block Grant Expenditures*.

Ries, P. 1987. "Physician Contacts by Socioeconomic and Health Characteristics, United States." *Vital and Health Statistics*. Series 10, no. 161. Washington: National Center for Health Statistics.

Riphagen, F. E., J. Van der Vurst, and P. Lehert. 1984. *Contraception in Italy*. Geneva: International Health Foundation.

———. 1985. *Contraception in France*. Geneva: International Health Foundation.

———. 1986a. *Contraception in Great Britain*. Geneva: International Health Foundation.

———. 1986b. *Contraception in the Federal Republic of Germany*. Geneva: International Health Foundation.

———. 1986c. *Contraception in Spain*. Geneva: International Health Foundation.

Roback, Gene, L. Randolph, D. Mead, and T. Pasko. 1985. *Physician Characteristics and Distribution in the U.S., 1984 Edition*. Chicago: American Medical Association.

Roe, J., ed. 1988. *Reducing Late Abortions: Access to NHS Services in Early Pregnancy*. London: Birth Control Trust.

Ross, John A., S. Hong, and D. H. Huber, 1985. *Voluntary Sterilization: An International Factbook*. New York: Association for Voluntary Sterilization.

Rowlands, S. 1985. "Contraception for Men: Where Do General Practitioners Stand?" *British Journal of Family Planning* 11:109–10.

Rutgers Stichting. 1986a. *Bureaus voor geboorteregeling en seksualiteitsvragen: overzicht betreffende bezoeken aan de buroos van januari 1986–30 september 1986*.

———. 1986b. Summer campaign brochures.

———. 1987. Memorandum. February.

Sabia, Laura. 1986. Column in the *Toronto Sun* (October 1), p. 12.

Schoorl, J. J. 1985a. "Fertility and Contraception of Turkish and Moroccan Immigrant Women in the Netherlands: Some Exploratory Results of a Recent Survey." Paper presented at the International Union of the Scientific Study of Population (IUSSP) General Conference, Florence.

———. 1985b. "Geboortenregeling van Turkse en Marokkaanse vrouwen benadert Nederland niveau." *Demos*, (Netherlands Interuniversity Demographic Institute Bulletin) 1/6 (June).

———. 1987a. "Contraceptive Use among Turkish and Moroccan Immigrants in the Netherlands." Paper presented at the European Population Conference, Jyväskylä, Finland.

———. 1987b. Personal communication.

Shapiro, Robert Y., and J. T. Young. 1986. "The Polls: Medical Care in the United States." *Public Opinion Quarterly* 50:418–28.

Silverman, Jane, and A. Torres, 1987. *Barriers to Contraceptive Services*. New York: AGI.

Silverman, Jane, A. Torres, and J. D. Forrest. 1987. "Barriers to Contraceptive Services." *Family Planning Perspectives* 19/3:94–102.

Singh, Susheela. 1985. Unpublished tabulations from the 1984 Current Population Survey.

Sips, A. J. B. I. 1986. "Huisarts en anticonceptie." *Nieuw kompas voor de huisarts* 4/1 (December).

Snowden, R. 1985. *Consumer Choices in Family Planning*. London: Family Planning Association.

Sonenstein, Freya L., and K. J. Pittman. 1984. "The Availability of Sex Education in Large City School Districts." *Family Planning Perspectives* 16/1:19–25.

Springate, Russell, A. Danaher, and S. Morrison. 1987. "Family Planning Accessibility and Practices: A Local Survey of Family Physicians." *Canadian Journal of Public Health* 78:98–100. Statistics Canada. 1985. *Canada Year Book, 1985*. Ottawa.

———. 1986. *Therapeutic Abortions, 1985*, Ottawa.

Stichting Medisch Centrum voor Geboorteregeling (SMCG). 1986. "Fees." Mimeograph. The Hague.

Tanfer, Koray, and E. Rosenbaum. 1986. "Contraceptive Perceptions and Method Choice among Young Single Women in the United States." *Family Planning Perspectives* 17/6:169–277.

Tietze, Christopher, and S. K. Henshaw. 1986. *Induced Abortion: A World Review, 1986*. New York: AGI.

Torres, Aida. 1984. "The Effects of Federal Funding Cuts on Family Planning Services, 1980–1983." *Family Planning Perspectives* Vol. 16/3:134–38.

Torres, Aida, and J. D. Forrest. 1985. "Family Planning Clinic Services in the United States, 1983." *Family Planning Perspectives* 17/1:30–35.

———. 1987. "Family Planning Clinic Services in U.S. Counties, 1983." *Family Planning Perspectives* 17/2:54–59.

Torres, Aida, J. D. Forrest, and S. Eisman. 1980. "Telling Parents: Clinic Policies and Adolescents' Use of Family Planning and Abortion Services." *Family Planning Perspectives* 12/6:284–92.

Tyrer, Louise B. 1987. "Proposed Revisions to PPFA Medical Standards." Memorandum. Planned Parenthood Federation of America. July.

United Nations. 1982. *World Population Trends and Policies*. 1981 monitoring report. 2 vols. Department of International Economic and Social Affairs Population Studies, no. 79. New York: United Nations.

United Nations. 1984. *Recent Levels and Trends of Contraceptive Use as Assessed in 1983*. New York: United Nations.

United Nations. 1985. *World Population Trends, Population and Development Interrelations and Population Policies*. 1983 monitoring report. 2 vols. Department of International Economic and Social Affairs Population Studies, no. 93. New York: United Nations.

United States Bureau of the Census. 1986. *Statistical Abstract of the United States: 1987*. 107th ed. Washington.

van de Giessen, G. J. 1987. "Birth Control, 1982–1985." *Maandstatistiek van de Bevolking* 12/3:10–11.

van de Kaa, D. J. 1987. "Europe's Second Demographic Transition." Population Reference Bureau. *Population Bulletin* 42/1 (March).

Vaughan, Barbara, J. Trussell, J. Menken, E. F. Jones, and W. Grady. 1980. "Contraceptive Efficacy among Married Women Aged 15–44 Years." *Vital and Health Statistics*. Series 23, no. 5. U.S. Department of Health and Human Services. Waitzkin, Howard. 1985. "Information Giving in Medical Care." *Journal of Health and Social Behavior* 26:81–101.

Waldo, Daniel, K. Levit, and H. Lazenby. 1986. "National Health Expenditures, 1985." *Health Care Financing Review* 8/1:1–21.

Warburton, A. 1986. "Maximise Your Fees for Contraceptive Services." *Pulse* (October 25).

Washington Memo. 1988a. Washington: AGI. July 6, W–11.

————. 1988b. Washington: AGI. August 17, W–13.

————. 1988c. Washington: AGI. Forthcoming, W–17.

Wellings, Kaye. 1985. "Help or Hype: An Analysis of Media Coverage of the 1983 Pill Scare." *British Journal of Family Planning* 11:92–98.

————. 1986a. "Sterilisation Trends." *British Medical Journal* 292:1029–30.

————. 1986b. "Trends in Contraceptive Method Usage since 1970." *British Journal of Family Planning* 12:15–22.

Wells, F. O. 1982. "National Health Service Reorganisation and the General Practitioner." In Gee, J. L., and R. C. Gee, eds., *1982 GP Guide to Emergency and Medical Services*. Petersfield, England: Asgard Publishing Company.

Winter, Laraine, and A. S. Goldy. 1987. "Staffing Patterns in Family Planning Clinics: Which Model Is Best?" *Family Planning Perspectives* 19/3:102–06.

Yusuf, F., and B. Werner. 1987. "Immigrant Fertility Patterns and Differentials in England and Wales, 1977–1981." Paper presented at the European Population Conference, Jyväskylä, Finland.

Zelnik, Melvin, M. A. Koenig, and Y. J. Kim. 1984. "Source of Prescription Contraceptives and Subsequent Pregnancy among Young Women." *Family Planning Perspectives* 16/1:6–14.

Index

Abortion policy and services, 33, 154; in Canada, 124–25; in Great Britain, 188–89; in Netherlands, 154–55; in United States, 89–90

Abortion rates, 26, 236–37, 241; age and, 56–57, 59, 238–41; pregnancy rates and, 6–9, 56–61

Adolescents, as target group of contraceptive services, 34, 38–39, 190

Advertising of contraceptive methods, 33, 41–42, 112, 143, 174, 209–10, 223–24

Age: abortion rate and, 56–57, 59, 238–41; contraceptive use and, 14–15, 24, 68–75; planning status of births and, 65–66; reproductive life subgroups, 66–67

AGI country survey, 31–50, 251–60

AIDS: in Great Britain, 207, 211; in Netherlands, 176; in United States, 110–11

American College of Obstetricians and Gynecologists, 94–95

Australia, 2–50 passim, 234–47 passim

Austria, 2–50 passim, 234–47 passim

Belgium, 2–50 passim, 220, 234–47 passim

British Pregnancy Advisory Service, 186

Brook Advisory Centres, Great Britain, 186, 203–04

Canada, 2–50 passim, 217–24, 234–47 passim; abortion policy and services, 124–25; abortion rate, 57–59; advertising of contraceptive methods, 143; assessment, overall, 145–48; contraceptive methods, 121–22; contraceptive use, 67–75; extra billing, 120; family planning services, 121–25; health care system, 118–21; hospital clinics for children, 139; income distribution, 52; information and education, 142–45; intrauterine devices (IUDs), 148; malpractice insurance, 129–30; media treatment of contraception, 143–44; oral contraceptives, 148; parental consent, 127; pharmacies, 138; Planned Parenthood Federation of Canada, 130; planning status of births, 62–66; policies for contraceptive services, 123–24; private physicians, 126–30; public opinion concerning sex, 144–45; responsibility for family planning services, 51; schools clinics, 139; sex education, 142–43; spermicidal suppositories, 121; sterilization, 128–29, 147–48; target groups for family planning, 125–26; universal health insurance, 118–21; university health centers, 138; U.S. abortions for Canadians, 56–57; U.S. compared to, 148–50; youth centers, 138–39. See also Ontario; Quebec

Case-study countries, 2
Catholics, 19
Centres de Santé des Femmes, Quebec, 138
Centres locaux de services communautaires (CLSCs), Quebec, 133–36
Cervical cap, 121, 192, 198–99
Clientele: of family planning clinics, 101–02; of private physicians, 93
Client preferences: for methods of contraception, 108–10, 140–42, 168–71, 206–07; for provider of contraceptive services, 108, 139–40, 167–68, 205–06
Cohabitation, 15
Condoms, 17–21; in Great Britain, 191, 214; in Netherlands, 167; in United States, 88, 107–08
Contraceptive methods, 17–21, 68–72, 104, 121; advertising of, 33, 42, 112, 143, 174, 209–10, 223–24; change in, 168–69; client preferences for, 108–10, 140–42, 167–71, 206–07; contraceptive services and, 117, 147–48, 179–80, 213–16; cost of, 39–40, 89, 93, 101, 108, 127, 134, 136, 154, 163, 165–66, 201; information delivery and, 49–50; media and, 113, 143–44; provider preferences, 46–49, 95–96, 104–05; teaching in school, 33–34; urban/rural variation, 40
Contraceptive services: for adolescents, 34, 38–39; contraceptive methods and, 117, 147–48, 179–80, 213–16; contraceptive use and, 44–49; delivery of, 35–40; of family planning clinics, 102–05, 197–99; of general practitioners, 191–96; for immigrants, 34; information delivery concerning, 41–42; policies for, 87–89, 123–24; of private physicians, 94–96
Contraceptive sponge, 121
Contraceptive use, 13–21, 66–75, 242–43; age and, 14–15, 24, 68–75; in Canada, 67–75, 121–22; contraceptive services and, 44–49; education and, 73–75; fertility and, 21–29; first-time users, 221; governmental policies and, 43–44; in Great Britain, 68–75; income and, 72–73, 214–15; marital status and, 66–67, 68–72; in Netherlands, 67–75, 168–71; in Ontario, 68–75; planning status of births and, 25–29; pregnancy and, 21–29; in

Quebec, 68–75; in United States, 67–75
Cost of contraceptive services, 39–40, 93
Counseling: by family planning clinics, 105–06; by private physicians, 96–97, 127
Country survey questionnaire (AGI), 31–32, 251–60

Data comparability, 16, 63, 67–68
Denmark, 2–50 passim, 234–47 passim
Depo-Provera, 88, 188, 223
Diaphragm, 17

Education: contraceptive use and, 52, 73–75; planning status of births and, 66
England. *See* Great Britain
Extra billing, in Canada, 120

Family physicians. *See* General practitioners
Family planning clinics, 85–86; clientele, 101–02; contraceptive services, 102–05; fees, 100–01; funding, 99–101, 130, 196; in Great Britain, 196–99; immigrants and, 133; low-income population and, 221–22; in Netherlands, 160–64; in Ontario, 130–33; outreach, 102; in Quebec, 133–38; referral by, 131–32; in United States, 98–107, 221–22
Family planning services, 99, 101; barriers to service, 115–17, 146–47, 178–79, 212–13; in Canada, 121–25; domiciliary, 202–03; funding for, 187; governmental policies and, 32–35; in Great Britain, 185–89; legal status of, 32–35; in Netherlands, 153–55; responsibility for, 51; target groups, 125–26; in United States, 85–87
Family practitioners. *See* General practitioners
Federal Republic of Germany, 2–50 passim, 234–47 passim
Fees: extra billing, 120; of family planning clinics, 100–01; of private physicians, 92–93. *See also* Cost of contraceptive services
Fertility, planning status of births and, 61–66; surveys, 15
Fertility rates, 6–9, 11, 54–56, 234–37, 240

Finland, 2–50 passim, 220, 234–47 passim
First-time users, of contraception, 221
Follow-up: family planning clinics, 105; private physicians, 96
Food and Drug Administration, United States, 88
France, 2–50 passim, 220, 234–47 passim
Funding, of family planning services, 99–101, 130, 187, 196

General practitioners, 35–37; in Canada, 120, 126, 129, 145–46; in Great Britain, 191–96; in Netherlands, 156–60; oral contraceptives and, 219–20; in United States, 79, 87, 91–92, 96, 97–98
Germany, West. *See* Federal Republic of Germany
Governmental policies: contraceptive use and, 43–44, 111; family planning services and, 32–35. *See also* Policies for contraceptive services
Great Britain, 2–50 passim, 217–24, 234–47 passim; abortion rates, 56–59, 188–89; adolescents, 190; advertising of contraceptive methods, 209–10; AIDS, 207, 211; assessment, overall, 211–16; British Pregnancy Advisory Service, 186; Brook Advisory Centres, 186, 203–04; Certificate of Contraceptive Technology, 192n4; client preferences, 205–07; condom use, 191, 214; contraceptive services, 197–99; contraceptive use, 68–75; domiciliary family planning services, 202–03; Family Planning Association, 185–86; family planning clinics, 196–99; Family Planning Information Service, 207–08; family planning services, 185–89; Family Practitioner Committees, 183–84; fertility rates, 54–56; General Medical Services Committee, 184; general practitioners, 191–96; *Handbook of Contraceptive Practice*, 195; health care system, 181–85; immigrants, 191, 203; income distribution, 52; information and education, 207–11; intrauterine devices (IUDs), 214–15; low-income population, 222; National Birth Control Association, 185; National Health Service, 182–85; nonprofit facilities,

201–02; oral contraceptives, 213–14; parental consent, 188; pharmacies, 204–05; planning status of births, 62–66; Pregnancy Advisory Service, 186; pregnancy rate, 60–61; private clinics, 201–02; public opinion concerning sex, 210–11; sex education, 208–09; sterilization, 199–201; target groups for family planning, 190–91. *See also* Scotland
Greece, 2–50 passim, 218, 234–47 passim

Handbook of Contraceptive Practice, Great Britain, 195
Health care system: in Canada, 118–21; in Great Britain, 181–85; in Netherlands, 151–53; in United States, 78–90
Health-maintenance organizations, in United States, 83
Hospital clinics: in Canada, 139; in Netherlands, 163–64; in Quebec, 136–38; in United States, 98

Immigrants: family planning clinics and, 133, 162; in Great Britain, 191, 203; in Netherlands, 155–56, 162, 173; as target group of contraceptive services, 34
Income, 31, 33, 38; contraceptive use and, 72–73, 214–15
Information and education: in Canada, 142–45; by family planning clinics, 107; government role, 111; in Great Britain, 207–11; in Netherlands, 171–77; by private physicians, 97, 129; target groups, 112; in United States, 110–13. *See also* Sex education
Information delivery: contraceptive methods and, 49–50; contraceptive services and, 41–42
Insurance. *See* Malpractice insurance; Universal health insurance
Insurance coverage, in United States, 83–85
Intrauterine devices (IUDs), 17–21, 46–47; in Canada, 148; client preferences for, 141–42; in Great Britain, 214–15; in Netherlands, 157, 158–60, 168–71; in United States, 88–89
Ireland, 2–50 passim, 234–47 passim
Italy, 2–50 passim, 218, 220, 234–47 passim
IUD. *See* Intrauterine devices (IUDs)

Low-income population: family planning clinics and, 221–22; in Great Britain, 222; in United States, 52–53, 111, 221–22

Magazines. *See* Media treatment of contraception
Malpractice insurance: in Canada, 129–30; in United States, 82
Marital status, contraceptive use and, 14–15, 66–67, 68–72
Media treatment of contraception: in Canada, 143–44; in Netherlands, 174–76; in United States, 102, 110–11, 113
Medicaid, United States, 80, 81–85, 90, 91, 92–93, 100
Medical policies and procedures, 82; of family planning clinics, 103–04; of private physicians, 94–95
Medicare, United States, 80, 82, 83
Morning-after pill, 88, 188

Netherlands, 2–50 passim, 217–24, 234–47 passim; abortion rates, 56–59, 154–55; advertising of contraceptive methods, 174; AIDS, 176; assessment, overall, 177–78; condoms, 167; contraceptive use, 67–75; family physicians, 156–60; family planning clinics, 160–64; family planning services, 153–55; fertility rates, 54–56; health care system, 151–53; hospital clinics, 163–64; immigrants, 155–56, 162, 173; income distribution, 52; information and education, 171–77; intrauterine devices (IUDs), 157, 158–60, 168–71; media treatment of contraception, 174–76; oral contraceptives, 157, 158–59, 168–71; parental consent, 154; pelvic examination, 162; pharmacies, 166–67; planning status of births, 62–66; pregnancy rate, 60–61; public opinion concerning sex, 176–77; Rutgers Stichting family planning clinics, 160–63; sex education, 171–72; Sickness Fund insurance, 152–53; specialized services, 164–65; spermicides, 167; sterilization, 164–65, 171; Stichting Medisch Centrum voor Geboorteregeling (SMCG), 165; Stimezo-affiliated clinics, 165; target groups for family planning, 155–56; Vereniging Stimezo Nederland, 165

Newpapers. *See* Media treatment of contraception
New Zealand, 2–50 passim, 234–47 passim
Nonuse of contraception, 114–15
Norway, 2–50 passim, 220, 234–47 passim
Nurse-practitioners, 127

Obstetrician-gynecologists, 219; in Canada, 122, 124–25, 128–30; in Great Britain, 186, 188–89; in Netherlands, 156–57; in United States, 79, 86–87, 89, 91–92, 98
Ontario, 76–77; abortion rate, 58–59; contraceptive use, 68–75; family planning clinics, 130–33; fertility rates, 54–56; planning status of births, 63–66; pregnancy rate, 60–61
Oral contraceptives, 17–21, 48, 88, 94, 135, 147, 193, 210; in Canada, 148; client preferences for, 140; family physicians and, 219–20; in Great Britain, 213–14; in Netherlands, 157, 158–59, 168–71; planning status of births and, 29; in United States, 88, 94–95, 104–05, 109, 117
Outreach: of family planning clinics, 102; of practice physicians, 93–94, 127

Parental consent: in Canada, 124, 127; in Great Britain, 188; in Netherlands, 154; in United States, 88, 91
Payment for health care, in United States, 81–83
Pelvic examinations: in Canada, 129, 132, 135; in Great Britain, 198, 204; in Netherlands, 162; in United States, 40, 94, 102, 103
Periodic abstinence, 104
Personnel: of family planning clinics, 102–03; of private physicians, 94
Pharmacies: in Canada, 138; in Great Britain, 204–05; in Netherlands, 166–67; in United States, 107–08
Physicians. *See* Family physicians; General practitioners; Private physicians
Pill. *See* Oral contraceptives
Planned Parenthood Federation of America, 86, 87, 98, 102
Planned Parenthood Federation of Canada, 130

Planning status of births, 9–12, 61–66, 240–43; abortion and, 63–65; age and, 65–66; contraceptive use and, 25–29; education and, 66; fertility and, 61–66; oral contraceptives and, 29; pregnancy rates and, 65; sterilization and, 28–29

Policies for contraceptive services, 30; in Canada, 123–24; in Great Britain, 185, 189; in Netherlands, 154–55; in United States, 87–89

Portugal, 2–50 passim, 234–47 passim

Preference, client's. *See* Client preferences

Pregnancy rates, 10, 11, 16; abortion rates and, 6–9, 56–61; planning status of births and, 65

Pregnancy testing, 189

Private physicians: in Canada, 126–30; in United States, 90–98

Providers of contraceptive services: client preferences for, 108, 139–40; contraceptive methods and, 46–49, 140

Public opinion concerning sex: in Canada, 144–45; in Great Britain, 210–11; in Netherlands, 176–77; in United States, 113

Quebec, 75–76, 224, 234–47 passim; abortion rates, 57–58; *Centres de Santé des Femmes,* 138; *Centres locaux de services communautaires,* 133–36; contraceptive use, 68–75; family planning clinics, 133–38; fertility rates, 54–56; hospital clinics, 136–38; planning status of births, 63–66; pregnancy rates, 60; *Service de regulation des naissances* (SERENA), 135, 139; sterilization, 141

Questionnaire, country survey, 31–32, 251–60

Radio. *See* Media treatment of contraception

Referral: by family physicians, 157; by family planning clinics, 105, 131–32; by private physicians, 96

Reproductive life subgroups, 66–67

Rural residents, 34, 89–90

Rutgers Stichting family planning clinics, Netherlands, 160–63

Schedules: of family planning clinics, 103, 106; of private physicians, 94

School clinics, 139

Scotland, 52

Service de regulation des naissances (SERENA), Quebec, 135, 139

Sex education: in Canada, 142–43; in Great Britain, 208–09; in Netherlands, 171–72; in United States, 111

Sexuality, 110, 113

Sickness Fund Council, Netherlands, 152–53

Socioeconomic status. *See* Education; Income; Low-income population

Spain, 2–50 passim, 234–47 passim

Spermicides: in Canada, 121; in Netherlands, 167; in United States, 88

Spousal consent, 88, 92

Sterilization, 17–21, 33, 40, 48, 67–68, 92, 220; in Canada, 128–29, 147–48; client preferences for, 140–41; data comparability, 67–68; in Great Britain, 199–201; in Netherlands, 164–65, 171; planning status of births and, 28–29; in the United States, 87

Sterilization regret, 141, 171

Stichting Medisch Centrum voor Geboorteregeling (SMCG), Netherlands, 165

Simezo-affiliated clinics, Netherlands, 165

Sweden, 2–50 passim, 220, 234–47 passim

Switzerland, 2–50 passim, 234–47 passim

Target groups for family planning, 33–34; in Canada, 125–26; in Great Britain, 190–91; information and education and, 112; in Netherlands, 155–56; in United States, 90

Television. *See* Media treatment of contraception

Time spent by client: in family planning clinics, 106–07; with private physicians, 97

Time spent with client: family planning clinics, 105, 106; private physicians, 96

Tubal ligation. *See* Sterilization

Unintended pregnancies. *See* Planning status of births

United Kingdom. *See* Great Britain; Scotland

United States, 2–50 passim, 217–24, 234–47 passim; abortion policy and services, 89–90; abortion rates, 57–59;

United States (*continued*)
  advertising of contraceptive methods, 112, 223–24; AIDS, 110–11; American College of Obstetricians and Gynecologists, 94–95; assessment, overall, 114–17; Canada compared to, 148–50; clientele of private physicians, 93; client preferences, 108–10; condom use, 88, 107–108; contraceptive services by private physicians, 94–96; contraceptive use, 67–75; cost of contraceptive services, 93; counseling by private physicians, 96–97; Depo-Provera, 88; doctors' fees, 92–93; family planning clinics, 98–107; family planning services, 85–87; fertility rates, 54–56; role of Food and Drug Administration, 88; health care system, 78–90; health-maintenance organizations, 83; information and education, 110–13; insurance coverage, 83–85; intrauterine devices (IUDs), 88–89; malpractice insurance, 82; media treatment of contraception, 110–11, 113; Medicaid, 80, 81–85, 90, 91, 92–93, 100; Medicare, 80, 82, 83; morning-after pill, 88; parental consent, 88, 91; payment for health care, 81–83; pelvic examinations, 94, 102, 103; pharmacies, 107–08; Planned Parenthood Federation of America, 86, 87, 98, 102; planning status of births, 62–66; policies for contraceptive services, 87–89; poverty status, 52–53; pregnancy rate, 60; private physicians, 90–98; provision of health care, 78–81; public opinion concerning sex, 113; sex education, 111; spermicides, 88; spousal consent, 88, 92; sterilization, 87, 91–92, 141; target groups for family planning, 90; welfare clients, 111

Universal health insurance, in Canada, 118–21
University health centers, in Canada, 138
Unplanned births. *See* Planning status of births
Unwanted births. *See* Planning status of births
Urban/rural variation, in use of contraceptive methods, 40

Vasectomy. *See* Sterilization
Vending machines, 44
Vereniging Stimezo Nederland, Netherlands, 165

Welfare clients, 84, 100, 102, 111. *See also* Medicaid; Medicare
West Germany. *See* Federal Republic of Germany
Withdrawal, 19

Youth centers, in Canada, 138–39